Extensions In Accounting Disclosure

NORTON M. BEDFORD

Series

The aim of this book is to provide a comprehensive conceptual and innovative view of the accounting disclosure problem and to relate this view to specific disclosure issues. Each chapter deals with a specific aspect of the overall goal to help the reader organize and evaluate the book.

Chapter I establishes that the accounting disclosure problem is much broader than merely transmitting existing information to users of accounting reports.

Chapter II demonstrates that both theoretical and practical concepts are available to facilitate an expansion of accounting disclosure, or at least to comprehend the opportunities for such an expansion.

Chapter III organizes at the concept level a generalized structure of the underlying issues involved in communicating accounting disclosures to users.

Chapter IV sets forth specific characteristics of the accounting disclosure problem and examines the scope of each characteristic or aspect of the problem.

)sure

?d.

in Accounting

) Approach

ning, Programming,

estments

ng Principles Board

EXTENSIONS IN ACCOUNTING DISCLOSURE

EXTENSIONS
IN ACCOUNTING
DISCLOSURE

NORTON M. BEDFORD

College of Commerce and Business Administration
University of Illinois

PRENTICE-HALL, INC., ENGLEWOOD CLIFFS, NEW JERSEY

Library of Congress Cataloging in Publication Data

BEDFORD, NORTON M.
    Extensions in accounting disclosure.

    (Contemporary topics in accounting)
    Includes bibliographies.
    1. Disclosure in accounting. 2. Accounting.
I. Title.
HF5657.B35   657   73-971
ISBN 0-13-298083-5
ISBN 0-13-298075-4 (pbk)

PRINTED IN THE UNITED STATES OF AMERICA

10 9 8 7 6 5 4 3 2 1

Prentice-Hall International, Inc., LONDON
Prentice-Hall of Australia, Pty. Ltd., SYDNEY
Prentice-Hall of Canada, Ltd., TORONTO
Prentice-Hall of India Private Limited, NEW DELHI
Prentice-Hall of Japan, Inc., TOKYO

Dedicated
to
MARK

Contents

Foreword

Accounting, broadly conceived as the measurement and communication of economic information relevant to decision makers, has undergone dramatic changes during the past decade. Recent advances in quantitative methods, the behavioral sciences, and information technology are influencing current thinking in financial as well as managerial accounting. Leasing, pension plans, the use of convertible securities and warrants in mergers and acquisitions, inflation, and corporate diversification are but a few of the challenging problems facing the accountant.

These developments and the very pervasiveness of accounting activity make it difficult for teachers, students, public accountants, and financial executives to gain convenient access to current thinking on key topics in the field. Journal articles, while current, must often of necessity give only cursory treatment or present a single point of view. Many of the important developments in the field have not crystalized to a point where they can be easily incorporated into textbooks. Further, because textbooks must necessarily limit the space devoted to any one topic, key topics often do not get the attention they properly deserve.

The Contemporary Topics series attempts to fill this gap by covering significant contemporary developments in accounting through brief, but self-contained, studies. These independent studies provide the reader with up-to-date coverage of key topics. For the practitioner, the series offers a succinct overview of developments in research and practice in areas of special interest to him. The series enables the teacher to design courses with maximum flexibility and to expose his students to authoritative analysis of controversial problems.

ALFRED RAPPAPORT

Preface

There appears to be considerable interest in the expansion of accounting information disclosures. The accounting literature and accounting conferences and meetings for the past several years have appeared to place great emphasis on the need for more complete information disclosures. Conversations with businessmen, economists, investors, and regulatory agencies leave little doubt of their interest in some fundamental thinking on the topic. Students of economic society constantly call attention to the changing and growing complexity of our society and for the need for improved information.

The accounting response to this call for more complete disclosure has been fragmentary. Specific disclosure issues have been examined but no innovative overall examination of the fundamental nature of the problem has been undertaken. The existence of this condition suggests that the need for creative work in accounting may be the most ignored area in the profession. Many tend to view the specific innovations developed and applied by auditors, tax authorities, educators, and management services personnel as creative contributions. Frequently, the term "a work of art" is applied to them. When these specific "works of art" are examined broadly, however, the rapidity with which common patterns of thought are revealed suggests that most are varied applications of the same concept. In fact, an analysis of a random selection of new disclosures suggested by auditors, tax authorities, educators, and management services personnel reveals few original thought patterns. The inference is that much broader creative studies are needed.

Creativity, like all concepts, is a relative notion. It just is not possible to divide things into creative and noncreative categories. Rather one thing is merely more or less creative than another. However, the essential characteristic of creativity is its unusuality. Things are perceived in a new way or things are organized in a new way, or new "things" are perceived, and organized into a body of knowledge. Thus the proposition that more creative work is needed in accounting implies a need for a level of creativity above that conventionally associated with accounting.

Creative works are difficult to evaluate. There is no systematic way to determine which creative proposal is best. Intuitive acceptance by a large segment of society is about the only criterion. Throughout this presentation, constant recourse to this theme will be used to justify propositions. The conclusion and representations proposed are therefore valid only if they are believed intuitively by the reader. While rationalization processes, such as trend extrapolation, consistency among actions, and deductively derived conclusions are also used repeatedly to justify the proposals, one must concede that by another rationalization process a contrary proposal might be supported.

With the foregoing caveat in mind, the following examination of accounting disclosures is presented for consideration. If the resulting propositions are believed then they are worthy of research efforts. If they are not accepted for any rationalization one cares to imagine, they must be assigned a secondary rank in any list of the research needs of accounting.

The objective of this book is to provide a comprehensive conceptual and innovative view of the accounting disclosure problem and to relate this comprehensive view to specific disclosure issues. The hope is that innovative research efforts into new aspects of accounting will be stimulated. Objectives of each chapter, set forth below—each dealing with a specific aspect of the overall book objective—may help the reader to organize and evaluate the book.

> Chapter One—To develop the proposition that the accounting disclosure problem is much broader than merely transmitting existing information to users of accounting reports. Rather it encompasses the scope of application and adequacy of the accounting technology for revealing information as well as the adequacy of

the disclosures made. While the immediate problem may be to induce accountants to disclose fully what they now know about organizations, in the longer view the broader aspects are more important.

Chapter Two—To examine the belief that both theoretical and practical concepts are available to facilitate an expansion of accounting disclosures, or at least to comprehend the opportunities for such an expansion.

Chapter Three—To organize at the concept level a generalized structure of the underlying issues involved in communicating accounting disclosures to users. With a background understanding of the linguistic, psychological, and social aspects of information transmission, accounting disclosure methods may be examined in a more systematic manner.

Chapter Four—To set forth specific characteristics of the accounting disclosure problem and examine the scope of each of the main characteristics or aspects of the problem. An overview relates these aspects of the disclosure issue to social goals and the accounting perception problem. The implication is that the enlarged scope of accounting disclosure may require accountants to view accounting as a broad corporate information system.

Chapter Five—To present an organized framework of the problem of the evidence needed to support accounting disclosures. Means for improving the accounting concept of evidence in order to provide for the disclosure of more relevant information are investigated.

Chapter Six—To examine the feasibility of expanding accounting disclosures so a Comprehensive Public Report might be supported by a set of articulated specific reports directed to different uses. After examining the concept of feasibility, consideration is directed to feasible solutions to disclosure problems using multiple measures, uses, communication media, formats, and classifications.

Chapter Seven—To disclose the scope of study into which theoretical examinations of accounting disclosures might expand. The theoretical justification for an expansion of accounting disclosures is reviewed. Other areas for appropriate theoretical investigation of the accounting disclosure issue are sought.

Chapter Eight—To determine the nature of the expansions in accounting methods that may be used to expand accounting disclosures. Particular emphasis is placed on the rate at which new disclosure methods are being developed.

Chapter Nine—To examine certain developments in current accounting practice in terms of their implications for the future expansion of accounting disclosures.

It is the intent of this book to reveal new research opportunities and to suggest ideas for further study and work on the problem of accounting disclosures. Additional funds, time, and effort will be required to fill in the details of this framework of the accounting disclosure problem.

Urbana, Illinois   NORTON M. BEDFORD

PART ONE

THE UNDERLYING
PHILOSOPHY

CHAPTER ONE

The Nature of
Accounting Disclosures

Accounting may be examined as a process or in terms of the information it discloses. To discuss accounting as a process involves an analysis of the techniques used in the performance of the accounting function. As a process, accounting could be unrelated to the substance produced and could be widely applicable to an unspecified number of situations. On the other hand, as a responsibility for disclosing a designated type of information, accounting is concerned primarily with the substance disclosed and incidentally with the process used.

Actually, it is not possible to separate the process from the disclosures or the disclosures from the process. They are highly interdependent. What is disclosed depends upon the processes available to develop the information, and what needs to be disclosed will influence the techniques included in the accounting process.

This chapter is concerned with the nature of accounting disclosures. It is therefore required that the accounting process first be examined in broad perspective. Subject to the restrictions of the accounting process, the need and means for accounting disclosures to relate to individual, organization, and social problems are next analyzed. This analysis in turn carries implications for expanding accounting measurement and communication techniques. The chapter concludes with a suggested division of research to determine and provide means for continuously adapting accounting disclosures to the needs of society.

This broad view of the nature of accounting disclosures is appropriate, for "in the future, corporations may well be judged, in addition to profit performance, on their influence on general economic growth, on their advances in productivity, the usefulness of their products, stability of employment, and impact upon the community."[1]

An examination of accounting disclosures may be conceived as a study of the information managements *ought* to disclose to the public, or as a study of information that *can* be developed and transmitted to both managers and the public, through the use of the accounting discipline. Practically, both the "ought" and the "can" have to be balanced. Currently, divergent views exist on the issue. Some investors believe management now has information that it ought to disclose to the public. Others imply that management does indeed have the information but ought not disclose it to the public. The operating budget for the forthcoming year is typically cited as representative of information that management has and does not disclose. Other investors and managers insist they lack information because the accounting discipline has not been sufficiently developed and cannot disclose the needed information. Still others contend that the accounting discipline is bounded by an objectivity concept for public disclosure that is quite distinct from efforts to provide managerial information. This last group separates accounting into two disciplines: managerial accounting and public financial accounting.

More theoretical analyses of accounting tend to question any distinction drawn between accounting information and an accounting disclosure. Since no disclosure can be made until the information has been developed, and since information development is a process of disclosing an underlying reality, a broad approach suggests that accounting disclosures span both information development and transmission. In this context, an accounting disclosure is a representation of an underlying reality that may or may not be transmitted to specified groups.

When disclosure is restricted to the transmission of accounting information, accountants become concerned with the proper allocation of accounting information among various groups. In this more restricted sense, the decision as to the proper disclosure to specified groups may well have to be based on a balancing of the different interests of different groups. Disclosures helpful to one group but harmful to another would have to be balanced and judged according to some undefined standard. In view of the complexity of accounting disclosures, it seems desirable to start this study with a broad perspective and consider them as representations of an underlying reality, or a "real world."

[1] Dean E. C. Arbuckle, *Nation's Business,* January 1964.

In the bare essence of things, accounting disclosures are motivational devices used to stimulate actions by certain people, typically referred to as decision makers. But this is more of a statement of a function than a description of the nature of those disclosures or stimuli included in accounting reports and extensively used in modern society. A description is more difficult. It seems appropriate to propose that only by an operational analysis of the accounting process can the nature of accounting disclosures be comprehended. That is, an understanding of the nature of accounting disclosures appears to require an understanding of the accounting process or operations performed in making the disclosures.

OPERATIONAL VIEW OF ACCOUNTING

Procedurally, the accounting process involves the following four steps:

1. *Perception* of the significant activity of the accounting entity or in the environment in which the entity performs. Traditionally, accountants have confined their perception to financial transactions. Implicit in the traditional perception is the belief that financial transactions represent the significant activities.
2. *Symbolizing* the perceived activities in such a fashion that a data base of the activities is available that can then be analyzed to grasp an understanding of the interrelationships of the mass of perceived activities. Conventionally, this symbolization has taken the form of recordings in accounts, journals, and ledgers, using well-established bookkeeping procedures.
3. *Analysis* of the model of activities in order to summarize, organize, and lay bare the interrelationships among activities and to provide a status picture or map of the entity. Traditionally, this analysis process has been viewed as one of developing accounting reports to provide insights into the nature of entity activities.
4. *Communication* (transmission) of the analysis to users of the accounting product to guide decision makers in directing future activities of the entity or in changing their relationship with the entity.

The operational conception of the accounting process views accounting disclosures as maps, pictures, or symbolic representations of entity-related activities. This idea suggests than an examination of accounting disclosures may be undertaken by reviewing (1) the adequacy of the scope of the accounting perception, (2) the efficiency of the symbolization process, (3) the extent of the analytical tools available and the rigor with which they are applied, and (4) the effectiveness of the communication. The implication is that any examination of accounting disclosures should consider whether the picture contains the appropriate features of the entity-related activities, whether the features are portrayed in sufficient detail and with appropriate emphasis, and whether disclosure is made in such a fashion that users understand the functioning of the entity in society.

In more conventional and less precise terms, the nature of accounting disclosures may be examined by noting that accounting is a process for measuring and communicating financial or economic data. While accounting disclosures are typically viewed as financial disclosures, the implication is that they are surrogates of underlying economic activities. The notion prevails that accounting disclosures are disclosures of economic activity measured in terms of money. Mere disclosure of economic activity, however, is an incomplete description of the nature of accounting disclosures, for the accounting measures reveal not only the economic activity but also the business effectiveness with which the activity is performed.

The end result of the accounting-disclosure process is typified by the balance sheet, statement of changes in financial position, and income statement. While the balance sheet discloses the status of an organization at a point in time and the statement of changes in financial position reveals changes therein, the income statement reveals the business effectiveness with which the organization has carried on the economic activity. It does this by disclosing the financial success of matching effort transactions with accomplishment transactions.

There should be no assumption that these three statements are the only communication devices used by accountants to disclose to users the measured economic data. Many other reports are used, especially for internal managerial purposes. Likewise, there should be no assumption that accounting is confined to measuring only those activities that will be reflected in the balance sheet and income statement. Rather, multiple measures are used to develop useful information for multiple purposes. Essentially, accounting is a process for explaining, predicting, and facilitating control of organizational activities. It has no definite boundaries, and a little reflection will reveal that it may be viewed broadly as an information system useful for disclosing relevant information to decision makers. The information developed by the use of the accounting process is the fundamental nature of accounting disclosures. But a full grasp of the nature of accounting disclosures requires that they be examined in terms of their societal aspects as well.

THE SOCIAL PROBLEM

To assert that accounting is an information system that discloses information useful to decision makers in determining means of accomplishing objectives is not a complete statement of the conceptual nature of accounting disclosures because it assumes objectives are known. This asumption must be questioned, because the real problem facing all elements of society today with which accounting disclosures are concerned is to decide which activities a society should undertake or what its objectives should be. It is also a problem for individuals and organizations, as parts of society, as well as for society, in general.[2] To a large corporation, the problem takes the form of determining the proper goals to be pursued (maximum profits for stockholders, stability of work for employees, economic growth, managerial satisfactions, and a host of related issues) and the relative importance of each. To a nation, it exists in the form of such problems as the proper foreign policy and the proper role of government in economic life. To an individual, it exists in the form of the proper balance among all the numerous conscious and subconscious wants, interests, and responsibilities that bear upon him. Because of its scope and ramifications, the problem is studied by a variety of disciplines, each dealing with a small part of it.

THE ACCOUNTING ROLE

Although accounting disclosures have seldom been directly associated with the social problem of desirable goals and values, they are necessarily based on certain assumptions about the objectives of business firms, individuals, and other entities. That is, since accounting is concerned with the development, measurement, and transmission of information, it has had to be concerned with informational needs of the individuals and groups using the information in their pursuit of selected goals and objectives. This relationship of accounting disclosures to needs

2 This is *not* to say that our individual values are inadequate and that we must necessarily create new values. Rather it is to say that the world has become so complex that we do not know what we should do to satisfy our individual wants in the new environment. Stated another way, we have through amazing economic progress so nearly satisfied certain basic wants, such as the desire for food, clothing, and shelter, that we do not now know what we should do to satisfy the complex wants, such as the desire for status, prestige, and self-achievement, that presently bear upon us individually and collectively.

is widely asserted in the statement that "different information is needed for different purposes" and forms a basis for evaluating the quality of accounting disclosures. High-quality disclosures would be of considerable aid to users in attaining desired goals, whereas low-quality disclosures would be of little use. This conclusion, that information needs alone determine the quality of a bit of information, suggests that if business firms, individuals, or other entities adopt new objectives, their informational needs will change and new types of accounting disclosures will have to be provided by the accounting measurement and communication process. When information users do not know the objectives or goals they should pursue, accountants cannot know the information to be measured and communicated to them. Therefore, if accounting is to play more than a passive role in our rapidly changing society and is to take the lead in providing useful information to individuals, groups, and other entities, it is a proper function of accounting to investigate and, when feasible, disclose information on the general problem of the proper goals and objectives of economic entities in society. Only by considering these goals and objectives can accounting disclosures be most useful to decision makers. Assuming an income objective for a university, with only a "no loss" constraint but other objectives, may not result in disclosure of the most useful financial information.

Values, goals, and information

In order to place the accounting-disclosure problem in perspective and to avoid centering on current disclosure problems without an adequate background, it is necessary to recognize that society is changing, and that over the span of a century these changes may influence accounting substantially. Because changes are not well sensed in the short period of five or ten years, even though adjustment of accounting disclosures requires that the changes be recognized, there is a need for an understanding of the foundation stones upon which society and accounting rest. Shifts in the foundations may be observed and a basis for the gradual adjustment of accounting disclosures may be established.

Society now has the concept of established or institutionalized values that indicate in rather general terms the goals and objectives individuals and groups pursue. Society also has the concept of information that, broadly defined, tells individuals and groups what is, has been, or will be, and it has been used to develop rather elaborate means and ways for doing things. Information has served human society rather well, for individuals and groups now do many things, but the values of society are not so well developed that individuals and groups know precisely what they ought to do. Tradition, customs, and authoritative pronouncements and interpretations have been used to set goals and objectives.[3] Society now has no formal way of deciding on a scientific basis whether individuals and group entities ought to spend more or less time on the arts, economic well-being, honesty and integrity, education, religion, communications, and a host of other topics. Nor do specific entities have any "scientific" way of knowing what they should do in a number of situations. The value problem of establishing the proper goals of society and of subentities in society is the most complex problem of all societies. It is a problem with which accounting must be concerned, because if goals are uncertain and accounting information is used to evaluate performance, accounting disclosures may misdirect decision makers toward inappropriate goals if they seek to so conduct themselves that the disclosures portray their actions favorably.

To dismiss the proposition that accounting should be concerned with the goals, on the ground that accounting disclosures are restricted by definition to providing information useful only for known financial or economic goals, is to assume that no ambiguity now exists regarding either external corporate financial reporting or internal management reporting. Yet the question of whether inventories should be valued on a LIFO or a FIFO basis clearly reflects uncertainty as to the goal pursued by the entity. Further, disclosure of financial contributions to pollution control, education, and the community provides specific recognition of entity concern with other values of society. In any event, any broad examination of the accounting-disclosure problem ought to give consideration to the entire spectrum of social and individual values.

SCIENCE OF INSTITUTIONALIZED VALUES

Because of growing questions in society generally about the adequacy of the customary values of contemporary society, there is an immediate need for a scientific method for verifying the social norms and cultural values, now accepted on faith and intuitive judgment, that guide all entities in society. Verification of existing values and goals would be reassuring to business entities if the assumed values and goals were verified as correct. To the extent that assumed values are not in accord with the needs of people, or to the extent that values change from time to time or situation to situation, the verification of existing goals and objectives is a short-run need. Ultimately, scientific methods need to be developed for establishing concepts of what business entities ought to do—or at least for helping them understand what goals or objectives

---

[3] See D. R. Martindale, *The Nature and Types of Sociological Theory* (Boston: Houghton Mifflin, 1960) for a synthetical discussion of tradition, folkways, magic, religion, and other guiding forces in the development of goals and objectives of society.

they are really striving to attain, whether or not there is an "oughtness" to them. To the extent that accounting disclosures are related to this issue, they are concerned with one of the basic issues of the social sciences.

INDIVIDUAL VALUES

Presumably, any verification of the values society ought to have will depend ultimately upon the needs and values of individuals composing society, although the values may be reflected in the activities of organizations as groups of people. It appears that such institutionalized organizational values must exist only as a means to enable individuals as a group to maximize their values. Unfortunately, there is no scientific way of verifying that our current institutionalized value standards are those that do accomplish this goal of maximizing human satisfaction. But if human values are the fundamental element, it follows that the scientific study of social values must involve the study of individual values. This directly ties the study to accounting, for accounting has to be very much concerned with the values and goals of organizations, as instruments for realizing human values.

Traditionally, economic value has been the central part of the substance, as contrasted with the techniques, of accounting. In this context, accounting disclosures deal with a significant part of human values, the economic values, and the relationship of these personal values to organizational values. It is time to examine this restriction on accounting disclosures. It may well be that the widening gulf between technological developments and advances in the social sciences makes it imperative that accounting disclosures be viewed in a broader scope. That is, the uncertainty in society, which could be the result of the impact of advanced technological progress on social values, may require that changing accounting disclosures serve as a catalyst that constantly bridges the gap between the two areas of human activities.

ECONOMIC VALUES AND GOALS

Accountants must keep in mind at all times that economic values alone cannot satisfy all the wants of man. That is, the wants of man may be presented broadly as a hierarchy structure, even though values are actually highly interrelated, somewhat as in Figure 1–1.

There are social science findings that seem to suggest that as the lower-level wants of man, including certain economic wants, are satisfied, man, as the product of his biological and environmental antecedents, tends to be motivated by new stimuli and becomes sensitive to alternative wants higher up in the hierarchy. The assumption follows that man will devise means to satisfy these alternative wants and will

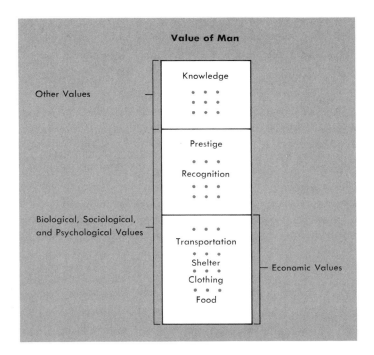

FIGURE 1-1

call for accounting disclosures to aid in this process. The point is that, conceptually, accounting disclosures must change constantly and need not be confined to the economic values of man even though there is no evidence to suggest that, in the foreseeable future, economic entities will not be motivated largely by the human desire for economic values. American society now has many characteristics of a post-industrial society, and any fundamental discussion of accounting disclosures must include consideration of the information needs of such a society.[4] So appropriate accounting disclosures must be examined in terms of the values motivating action in a society. Broadly, actions are related to the values, in that man's wants influence his actions. These actions and related values or wants may be grouped from lower to higher categories, for the purpose of clarifying the concept of different motivating values, as follows:

[4] Daniel Bell contends that the postindustrial society has the following five characteristics: (1) a centralization of theoretical knowledge for innovation; (2) high status for higher-knowledge institutions; (3) important role for human, rather than material, capital; (4) an advanced intellectual technology; (5) a society oriented toward future developments, rather than one concerned only with current problems. See D. Bell, "The Balance of Knowledge and Power," *Technology Review* (Massachusetts Institute of Technology), June 1969.

1. *Animalistic (immediate) want-satisfaction motivation.* Sometimes referred to as impulse buying, emotional reactions, and the like, these actions and related values are typically unplanned and result from man's efforts to satisfy his wants or needs of the present.

2. *Life-long want-satisfaction motivation,* where the objective of man is to maximize over his lifetime his needs and wants. Thus, impulse action, which may result in an undesirable reaction such that life-long wants are reduced because of the response to an immediate want or need, would not be included in this concept of human values.

3. *Civilization want-satisfaction maximization,* which would require that man so conduct himself that over time the satisfaction of wants of all civilization are maximized. This concept of human values, of course, is the basis for a substantial number of our ethical pronouncements, and in this context ethics is related to values.

ACCOUNTING DISCLOSURES AND ORGANIZATIONS

As we previously noted, accounting disclosures have long been concerned with the organizational values, and with the value of income maximization in particular. That is, accounting appears to be more closely associated with organizations than with individuals, and this explains the accounting interest in the nature, function, and operation of an organization. But Barnard's widely quoted definition that an organization is a "system of consciously coordinated activities or forces of two or more persons" suggests that organizations are created by individuals as a group as a means for satisfying individual values.

Given the existence of an organization such as a business entity, it must be that the organization exists only because it is a means whereby a number of individuals find it possible to better satisfy their economic needs. Other organizations, such as a church or a political entity, are established by individuals as means to better satisfy other particular individual needs. The point is that organizational values are derived to a large extent, although far from completely, from individual wants; and therefore, organization values are not in a long-range sense an isolated area of study. For shorter periods of time—say, no more than fifty years—organizational values may dominate human values. It is hoped by all and believed by many, however, that organizational values cannot for too long be studied independent of individual values. The silent struggle between organizational values and individual values seems to be the root of a significant part of the accounting-disclosure problem. Although accounting information may be available within the organization, the desire to maximize organizational values may result in a reluctance to disclose that information to outside individuals, even though such disclosure would enable the individual to better attain his objectives, because it might hinder the ability to attain organization objectives.

RELATIONSHIP BETWEEN INDIVIDUAL AND ORGANIZATION GOALS

In view of the contemporary interest in organization goals and objectives and the process by which individuals temporarily adapt their own goals to those of the organization, a few words of exposition on the relationship between individual and organization goals may be appropriate.

For explanation purposes, assume that an individual is starving, and consider the possibility that this individual would accept an organization objective aimed solely at maximizing his prestige and that of other individuals associated with it. Few of us would subordinate our pressing want and objective of obtaining food to the objective of the organization. Rather, we might attempt to adjust the organization's goals to our goal. Clearly, the wider the gap between individual values and organization objectives, the greater the accounting-disclosure problem. Disclosure of success in attaining organizational objectives may not be considered relevant.

It may be contended, of course, that after the biological needs of man are met, the individual may become more malleable and may adjust to the goals of the organization with which he is associated. Consider, however, the revolt of the slaves of ancient Rome, the French Revolution, the Civil War in the United States, or the "hippies" of contemporary society. For a period of time, individuals may adjust to the goals of the organization, but ultimately the "happy" slave or the "satisfied" worker seems to sense latent personal psychological wants or goals of his own construction and seeks to adjust the goals of the organization. Thus it seems to be appropriate for accounting disclosures to be based on the assumption that, in the long run, the values of individuals will prevail and organization goals will adjust to them. The length of time over which individuals adapt to organization goals before asserting individual goals appears to vary. In some instances, individual goals seem to be asserted quickly, but in others, outmoded organization goals apparently prevail for many years.

The conclusion seems to be that while individual values are of basic concern, any discussion of accounting disclosures must also deal with organizational goals as intermediate items of concern to society.

INTERRELATIONSHIPS AMONG INDIVIDUAL, ORGANIZATIONAL, AND SOCIAL VALUES

It has been contended by some social scientists that many organization goals are derived from the goals of the society of which the organization is a part. Just as an individual adapts to the goals of an organization once the basic individual biologcal needs are met, so the organization, once the basic survival need is met, adjusts to the goals, values, or ethics of the society of which it is a part. According to this conception of an organized systematic framework of the values of a society, individuals first form themselves into organizations in order to meet their biological needs. In order to further performance of this function, organizations are then fitted into an overall, loosely tied together framework known as society. Whether society is constructed before or after a variety of types of organizations exist is not as important as recognizing that society and organizational values come into being to crystallize and articulate certain values of the individual. Note also that society governs organizations, as an observing businessman will quickly assert, except for the remote possibility that one organization might in fact become society in its entirety. This is the basis for the belief that organizational values are adapted to society values, and in turn that individual values are adapted to organizational values.

It is readily determinable, however, that the values of a society change; and although the mysterious force that causes the change is not clear, it manifests itelf in the development of individual values at variance with those prevailing in society. As society adapts to the new individual values, the values of that society change. Thus the completed circle, from individual values to organizational values to social values to individual values, suggests that in the long run it is individual values with which accounting disclosures should have a primary concern. In the immediate and near future, however, divergent organizational objectives and social goals represent another basic problem of accounting disclosures: the possible conflict between disclosing that which best serves the values of society and that which will not hinder the maximum attainment of organization objectives.

ACCOUNTING AND INDIVIDUAL VALUES

The new area that is hereby proposed as appropriate for the advanced study of accounting disclosures is the development of methods for determining more precisely the findings in basic disciplines relating to the personal values of individuals and group values of entities. To accomplish this objective, it will first be necessary to understand the nature of personal values. Measuring the extent to which these values are realized must follow. The inference is that immediate accounting research should be directed to the determination of the current motivations of man. The accounting disciples must know the needs that "income" presumes to satisfy and the needs and values that are not provided for in conventional accounting income disclosures. This is important because of the growing realization that the traditional income concept, or the desire for that type of income as the motivating force that causes economic activity, may not be adequate for the emerging society. No one knows clearly what people want, their real values, and their underlying motivations. This lack of knowledge is now an issue of concern for both professional and discipline survival of accounting. Unless accounting disclosures are relevant to the current needs of individuals and society, accounting may be abandoned as a useless institution. The result of this type of research may well call for a great deal more flexibility in accounting disclosures than has prevailed in the past.

ACCOUNTING AND THE SCIENCE OF VALUES

The process of developing a method for verifying the adequacy of current institutionalized value standards, in order to determine appropriate accounting disclosures, is effectively the science of values. Some long-range social thinkers believe that in the next ten to thirty years there may be a significant increase in the formal study of human values as a science. This should permit an improvement in accounting disclosures to both internal managers and external investors. The role of accounting in such a basis study will apparently be related to the development of reliable and objective evidence needed to establish the nature of certain specific human wants (values) of investors, creditors, managers, employees, and the general public prevailing at different times, and the extent to which these wants are satisfied by various organization activities.[5] Since human values are constantly changing, apparently at an in-

---

[5] Even if accounting is not to exist as a substantial part of the science of values, the new problems existing in the world (such as the question of whether or not to use the bomb) for which no ethical standards have been pronounced means that decisions on such questions will require the further development of relevant, objective information; and the fulfillment of this need may, if the accounting discipline can be adequately developed, fall to the accounting profession. It seems realistic, however, to reject any conception of accounting that holds that in business, where accountancy is most widely used, the manager decides what he wants and the accountant merely informs him what to do in order to gain his objective. Actually, the manager does not know precisely what he really wants, and accounting must be concerned with business objectives as well as with means of attaining the objectives.

creasing rate, accounting disclosures must adjust to a world of constant change. Adjustment to a changing rather than a stable society will be most difficult. It is suggested that the accounting profession can provide for this adjustment in accounting disclosures only by taking the following two actions.

1. It must frequently change its organizational arrangements so that practicing and academic members of the profession view changes as the normal condition and feel comfortable with changes.
2. It must emphasize accounting articles, conferences, and discussions that constantly deal with future developments, and deemphasize discussions of past activities. University curricula must be directed to the accountant of the future, and leaders of the profession must convey the impression that accounting is a dynamic, rather than a static, discipline at the level of both practice and theory.

One may well expect accounting literature to include articles supporting the expansion of the accounting discipline into the area of values to such an extent that the accounting discipline is treated as the applied side of the science of values. Although it may be contended that accounting disclosures are now merely disclosures of the result of a limited view of human values, and that only by encompassing the whole science of values can the boundaries of accounting disclosures be established, the more reasonable position confines accounting disclosures to those values determined to be appropriate by a systematic analysis of particular situations.

SCIENTIFIC ACCOUNTING

The fundamental problem underlying scientific accounting is to determine how to go about verifying specific recommendations or suggestions for accounting disclosures that meet individual or social goals. It is part of the even larger problem of determining how science could ever tell us what we ought to do or what we really want. Several approaches are possible, but a practical accounting study would presumably have to start with what an individual says he wants. These asserted wants would have to be verified by a study of the choices a man makes under various conditions. From such a beginning, the investigation of human needs could turn into a huge anthropological study, well beyond the scope of accounting. If human values were determined, defined, and established, accounting disclosures could aspire to tell an investor, creditor, employee, manager, or other interested party what he ought to do in order to satisfy his wants and could measure the extent to which he attained his goals. Such a concept is, of course, a prudential "ought" and should not be confused with the notion of a moral "ought" commonly attached to the concept of ethics.[6]

Regardless of the scope of the area in which accounting theory and research operate, if accounting assumes a role in the area of determining objectives of organized groups, whether or not they are based on the science of values, the nature of scientific accounting could be described as a process for:

1. Enunciating goals and objectives for organized entities that are compatible with individual and society values
2. Determining the information needs of decision makers to attain the goals and objectives
3. Measuring socioeconomic activity in such a way as to develop the required information
4. Communicating the measurement results to the information users

INFORMATIONAL NEEDS AND CONTEMPORARY ACCOUNTING DISCLOSURES

The concept of information is somewhat ambiguous and the role of information in society is just beginning to be understood. Information, a stimulus that evokes action, differs from other stimuli in that it appeals primarily to man's sense of "reasoning." It stimulates action by indicating to a decision maker those things he should do to attain his values. At a minimum, information plays the role of reducing any uncertainty regarding the proper action for a decision maker to take. That is, while it frequently plays a significant role in the process of revealing goals pursued, information is also conceived as an aid to decision makers in removing doubt about how to attain a specified goal. In the first role, information

---

[6] The connecting line between prudential "oughts" and moral "oughts" may be the element of time. Moral "oughts" are those ethical standards made for the sake of future generations as well as current generations, whereas prudential "oughts" are confined to the current generation. Thus, moral "oughts" include prudential "oughts," even though the latter may be modified in the light of the needs of future generations. When we turn to the needs of future generations, we are investigating something most involved, for we can never know for certain what future man will want. It might, of course, be possible to develop a theory of the development of growth of man's wants over time, and from this theory study scientifically the moral "oughts" for society. But such a theory could not be well defended at the present time. For this reason, it seems appropriate to restrict accounting research activity, in the area of deciding what society should do, to the boundaries of prudential "oughts." This restriction on the scope of accounting research leaves to the anthropologists the gigantic, complex issue of moral "ethics," if such are to be within the scope of science.

is related to the needs and desires that man should have. In the second role, it is related to the specified goals. In both roles, it aims to reduce any uncertainty in the minds of a decision maker as to what he should do. The greater the uncertainty of a decision maker, the greater the amount of information that can be given him. When he is almost certain or has even decided what to do, little information can be provided. This means that an increase in uncertainty will increase the opportunity to provide a greater amount of information. It also means that the type and amount of accounting disclosures needed in society will depend upon the degree of uncertainty under which decision makers are operating.

In the main, accounting disclosures have traditionally been confined to those meeting the informational needs for attaining specified goals. But these are now inadequate, because objectives are changing. Until the precise nature of all these changes in values and goals are fully understood, it may be that the most important practical problem of accounting information is the development of a general understanding of, and a means for revealing, the limitations of the accounting disclosures now provided. Gradually, the limitations could be eliminated by expanding accounting disclosures.

The dilemma may be explained as follows. If the aim of business managements were to maximize cash on hand at the end of a year, then it would be possible to determine the informational needs of managements to meet this objective. No human-value considerations would be involved. But no business has this as its objective. Rather, businesses attempt to maximize income, return on investment, prestige, or power, and there exists no uniform definition of these concepts or the proper trade-off among them. Illustrative of this definitional deficiency is the assertation by Churchman that periodic accounting income cannot be defined so that it will qualify as the proper value measurement to guide entity operations, for the following reasons: [7]

1. The entity life over which income is to be calculated is not precisely defined. This precludes the proper accrual and deferral of certain expenses and revenues in one period of time.

2. Opportunity costs, as might result from alternative uses of capital and lost sales, are not included as expenses. For some concepts of income, they should be disclosed.

3. Since a proper allocation of overhead within an organization requires precise knowledge of the way the overhead is used, the proper allocation cannot be made, because there is no precise knowledge of the effectiveness of overhead in various parts of the organization.

[7] C. West Churchman, *Prediction and Optimal Decision* (Englewood Cliffs, N.J.: Prentice-Hall, 1961), p. 51.

4. Since costs act as one of the motivators of human action, cost accounting designed to measure values should depend on psychological considerations, but it rarely does.

This implies that traditional accounting disclosures may not be adequate reflections of the value or goal attainments of industrial firms.[8]

MEASUREMENT METHODS AND ACCOUNTING

The nature of accounting disclosures is revealed in part by an examination of the measurement and analytical tools used to develop accounting information, because the ability of accountants to develop meaningful information depends heavily on their kit of tools. Traditional tools have served accounting well in the past, for accounting disclosures have long provided the most useful information to management for operating a business entity. Since 1940, new analytical tools have been developed to provide management and decision makers with useful information. These new tools have been gathered together under diverse new disciplines, such as administrative science, management science, operations research, and organization theory—competitors of traditional accounting in the sense that the information they provide may be more useful to management than traditional accounting information—which are typically interdisciplinary arrangements of traditional basic disciplines. They are made up of parts of such basic disciplines as economics, sociology, psychology, mathematics, statistics, political science, neurology, servomechanism engineering, anthropology, and advanced computer design. Whether or not they are included as part of accounting measurement and analytical tools will have a bearing on the nature of accounting disclosures to managements and others interested in organization activities.

THE NATURE OF MEASUREMENT IN ACCOUNTING

Accounting disclosures cannot be made unless activities can be measured, so any comprehension of the nature of accounting disclosures

[8] There seems to be an international interest in improving accounting. In June 1962, the Chinese Communist government sponsored a national conference in Peking, attended by 400 officials in banking, government, armed forces, and businesses, which discussed the important role played by accounting in the cause of building socialism and decided that present accounting was far below needs.

requires familiarity with the accounting-measurement problem.[9] The primary objective of accounting measurements is to disclose the amount by which specific characteristics of an object or situation have changed. That is, accounting may seek to disclose how much more income, prestige, or power a company has between two points in time. Ideally, accounting-measurement mechanics should aim to disclose this as a continuous change; but more often, accounting measures the amount of changes in things from one point in time to another. In this sense, the accounting process of measurement, like all measurements, involves measuring something once and then measuring it again. Change would refer to the amount of the differences in the two measurements. To perform such a measurement, three things are required:

1. There must exist some characteristic of an object or situation that is to be measured.
2. There must be available an instrument or means, such as transactions or markets, to make the measurement.
3. A trained observer must be present to make use of and observe the instrument or means.

Now, the result of a characteristic, an instrument, and an observer in a unified operation is a measurement. When the same things are measured more than once, different measurements may be obtained. These measurements may vary because the object's characteristic has changed, the instrument has been inaccurate, or the observer has made a mistake. Therefore, if we are to make any judgment regarding the extent to which the object or thing has changed, it is necessary to examine the object's characteristic, the instrument, and the observer, as well as the measurement. To do this, it would be appropriate to select:

1. The object's characteristic according to the criterion of relevance for the problem under consideration (income, prestige, power)
2. The instrument according to the criterion of applicability to the observation to be made (set of rules as to how to measure)
3. The observer according to the criterion of competence, or capacity to use the instrument correctly (the trained observer)

Assuming the three elements are appropriate, the change in two separate measurements over time would provide an accounting measure

---

9 The Committee on Foundations of Accounting Measurement defines an accounting measurement as "an assignment of numerals to an entity's past, present, or future economic phenomena, on the basis of observation and according to rules." *Accounting Review Supplement,* 1971, p. 4.

of change of activity. Unfortunately, specifications of characteristics, instruments, and competence may be set forth in varying degrees of detail. As a consequence, varying levels of preciseness and confidence may prevail in various measurements. This inability to measure precisely and unequivocally is a matter of concern to both accountants and the users receiving accounting disclosures. There seems to have developed no acceptable means for specifying in an accounting disclosure the degree of confidence one might attach to various measures. There tends to exist, unfortunately, the assumption that all accounting measurements are exactly right. This is unfortunate, because they never can be and also because the assumption restricts the opportunities for expanding accounting disclosures. A mass public-education program by the organized profession may be needed to explain the nature of measurements with the intent of opening new doors for accounting disclosures. But this must be a future development. Traditionally, accounting measurements have been the result of a change in economic status before and after a transaction. It may now be possible to change the concept of accounting disclosures somewhat by expanding the application of accounting measurements.

THE NEED TO EXPAND ACCOUNTING MEASUREMENTS

Although the need for an expansion of accounting disclosures is covered in the next chapter, it is appropriate in this introductory chapter to refer to the need to expand accounting measurements in order to comprehend the nature of accounting disclosures. That is, realization of a broader measurement function for accounting means that the accounting profession needs to be fully aware of the emerging analytical tools, particularly those that appear to fall within the scope of the discipline of accounting. The case supporting the proposal that the accounting discipline should absorb many of the new measurement and analytical methods rests on the following three needs:

1. The new methods represent a threat to the status of the present scope of the accounting measurements used in all business concerns, and accounting needs to meet this threat.
2. Changing economic events and conditions are everywhere in evidence, and accounting needs to adjust and advance just to keep up with the times.
3. Many features of the new methods fit well into the traditional accounting discipline and for completeness need to be included as part of it.

Acceptance of certain of the new quantitative tools as part of the accounting discipline would tend to cause accountants to view the management function as essentially a decision-making function. Decisions on what to do in the future would be viewed as the result of planning, and decisions on how to carry out what is planned would be viewed as control. From this point of view, accounting disclosures would be viewed as information useful to management and others in making planning and control decisions.

New accounting measurement tools

The new analytical tools, from which the accounting discipline has the opportunity to select, represent techniques to replace a certain amount of the intuition of the past. They are interdisciplinary in nature and change as the entire idea develops. Lists of them frequently include such interesting titles as these:

1. Inventory theory
2. Linear programming
3. Dynamic programming
4. Cybernetics
5. Queuing theory
6. Sequencing theory
7. Routing theory
8. Line balancing
9. Replacement and maintenance theory
10. Information theory
11. Network theory
12. Search theory
13. Game theory
14. Gambling behavior
15. Symbolic logic
16. Factor analysis
17. Probability theory
18. Monte Carlo method
19. System simulation
20. Stochastic processes

Without our going into a discussion of any of these, it seems reasonable to propose that a new scope and a new technology are available to advance accounting disclosures, if the profession so desires.

COMMUNICATION METHODS

The term *accounting disclosures* implies a laying bare of something for someone to see. Thus, the income statement is a disclosure, a revealing, of the effectiveness and nature of certain enterprise activities. Implicit in this process is the assumption that the reader of the disclosure comprehends it; and so an effective accounting disclosure must also include an effective communication process. For this reason, the study of the nature of accounting disclosures must include an examination of the communication methods used in the disclosure process.

A broad examination of the communication methods used in accounting disclosures may be approached by noting that accounting includes the process of conveying or transmitting the information to the right person at the right time. This fact ties accounting to the area of human communication theory and information systems for entities. It means that accounting-communication methods need not be confined to the routine, regular reports that traditionally follow some type of a business organization chart. Also involved in the area of accounting-communication methods are various psychologically based methods for transmitting information and understanding its varied impact on different individuals and groups. An understanding of these psychological aspects of accounting-communication methods is essential for a comprehension of the nature of accounting disclosures.

ACCOUNTING RESEARCH

In concluding this introductory chapter, it seems appropriate to outline a possible research program to deal with the problems faced in any attempt to improve accounting disclosures.

If the preceding overview of the nature of accounting disclosures is valid, fundamental research in accounting should be directed not only to an understanding and measurement of values, but also to ways of transmitting this type of information to others. Such a wide scope for accounting research suggests that two broad research roles be recognized, as follows:

1. *Concept research,* wherein research in accounting is conducted by university researchers or others having contact with the basic disciplines of human knowledge. This research would be directed to such issues as:
   a. The scope of the discipline
   b. The measurement of human values
   c. The organization of accounting thought
2. *Professional research,* wherein research is concerned with the articulation of the fundamental research developments in terms of the current practice, and in the establishment of standards for accounting practice from the basic research developments.

IMPLICATIONS

Acceptance of the view outlined in this chapter of the nature of accounting disclosures will open many doors to accountants. First, it probably means that when the body of accounting knowledge is fully developed the scientific accountant may improve a significant part of the executive function in business by providing it with pertinent accounting information. Second, the systematic study of accounting disclosures will open a field for research of immense scope. Third, it will confer on the accounting profession higher social responsibilities, and with them, greater prestige and status in society. These responsibilities and rewards are to be available to some profession in the near future, and it seems reasonable to suggest that they might accrue to accountants.

REFERENCES

BARNARD, CHESTER I., *The Functions of the Executive*. Cambridge, Mass.: Harvard University Press, 1958.

BRAY, SEWELL, *The Accounting Mission*. Melbourne, Australia: Melbourne University Press, 1951.

CHERRY, COLIN, *On Human Communications*, 2nd ed. Cambridge, Mass.: M.I.T. Press, 1966.

CHURCHMAN, C. WEST, *Prediction and Optimal Decision*. Englewood Cliffs, N.J.: Prentice-Hall, 1961.

GALBRAITH, JOHN K., *The Affluent Society*. Boston: Houghton Mifflin, 1958.

————, *The New Industrial State*. Boston: Houghton Mifflin, 1967.

HERRICK, C. J., *The Evolution of Human Nature*. Austin: University of Texas Press, 1956.

IJIRI, Y., *Foundations of Accounting Measurement*. Englewood Cliffs, N.J.: Prentice-Hall, 1967.

MASON, EDWARD S., ed., *The Corporation in Modern Society*. Cambridge, Mass.: Harvard University Press, 1959.

MATTESSICH, RICHARD, *Accounting and Analytical Methods*. Homewood, Ill.: Richard D. Irwin, 1964.

RUESCH, J., "Synopsis of the Theory of Human Communication," *Psychiatry*, XVI (1953).

SHUCHMAN, ABE, *Scientific Decision Making in Business*. New York: Holt, Rinehart & Winston, 1963.

THURSTONE, L. L., *The Measurement of Values*. Chicago: University of Chicago Press, 1959.

WARD, A. DUDLEY, *Goals of Economic Life*. New York: Harper & Row, 1953.

CHAPTER TWO

Concepts Underlying
the Expansion of
Accounting Disclosures

In order for a concept to be defined precisely, the operations involved in implementing it must be specified. Further, changing the operations may result in changes in the meaning of the concept. This fact suggests that varying the operations involved in making accounting disclosures is a means for expanding them. Expansion may result in such theoretical alternative views of accounting disclosures as (1) disclosures appropriate under various decision-situation models, (2) multiple disclosures to accommodate alternative decision situations, and (3) disclosures indicated as appropriate by the use of the scientific method of investigation. In terms of future operational expansion of accounting disclosures, the following opportunities are available:

1. Disclosure of social as well as private costs
2. Disclosure of human resources
3. Disclosure of budgets and equipment status
4. Disclosure of management effectiveness

To provide for these concept-expansion opportunities, there is a need to develop some type of an accounting monitoring system to make accountants sensitive to desired changes.

Conceptually, expansion of accounting-disclosure concepts may be limited, unless means are proposed to encourage the expansion of the structure of accounting knowledge. To deal with this possibility, Chapter 2 concludes with an outline of three alternative structures of the scope of accounting thought: (1) an income structure, (2) a wealth structure, and (3) a socioeconomic structure.

It is proper that accountants continuously examine means for adjusting the basic concepts underlying accounting disclosures, for "we must produce a great age, or see the collapse of the upward striving of our race." [1]

Consider the following proposition: So rapid and so fundamental are to be the changes in society in the future that accounting disclosures will have to be expanded in scope and in quality just to maintain their relative role in society. Then impose upon that proposition the rising expectations of the accounting profession, and face the realization that one of the most fundamental problems of the profession may be to provide for the orderly but rapid expansion of accounting disclosures.

There are several ways to approach this problem, including both model building and the use of the scientific method, but the best starting point appears to involve an examination of the nature of accounting disclosures. It was stated in Chapter 1 that an understanding of the nature of accounting disclosures requires an understanding of the accounting operations performed in making them. Precise meaning must now be attached to this operational point of view, toward the objective of perceiving opportunities for improving accounting disclosures in the future.

OPERATIONAL CONCEPT OF DISCLOSURES

Operationalism is, of course, a philosophical point of view, emphasized by P. W. Bridgman and subsequently examined in various psychology publications.[2] In effect, it holds that the precise meaning of a concept can be understood only by learning the operations involved in measuring or describing it. It implies that the only way to describe accounting disclosures is to describe the operations involved in making them. Actually, operationalism is best thought of as a process for developing a precise meaning for a concept. Prior to its use, an examination of the nature of a concept is aided by noting its constitutive meaning. Thus, an understanding of the nature of accounting disclosures is best grasped by first noting their general constitutive meaning, and then, by describing the operations involved in making such disclosures, developing a precise description of their nature.

1 Alfred N. Whitehead, in the preface to Wallace B. Donham, *Business Adrift* (New York: McGraw-Hall, 1931).
2 See P. W. Bridgman, *The Logic of Modern Physics* (New York: Macmillan, 1927).

The advantage of a precise operational conception of the nature of accounting disclosures is that it enables one to expand the concept by merely changing the operations involved in making such disclosures. An analogical illustration may clarify the role of an operational definition as a supplement to a constitutive definition. For that purpose, consider the accounting valuation of inventories. Constitutively, the valuation is described as the value of the merchandise inventory. The constitutive notion of "value" provides a general meaning, but only when one describes operationally how the valuation was made does one obtain a precise understanding of what is meant. If inventories were valued on a first-in, first-out basis there would result quite a different notion of an accounting inventory valuation than if the last-in, first-out method were used. The fact is that only by understanding the operations involved in measuring it can the accounting notion of an inventory valuation be precisely defined. The inference is that by changing an operation, a concept can be changed; and the opportunity to change an accounting-disclosure operation represents an opportunity to expand or contract the scope of the disclosure concept.

BACKGROUND
FOR EXAMINING DISCLOSURE EXPANSION

The foregoing discussion surely provides sufficient justification to undertake an examination of the nature of accounting disclosures and their expansion. Physically, accounting disclosures may take many forms, ranging from numerical statements to graphic displays presented either orally or visually, in temporary or permanent mode. But underlying them all is the implication that they represent a transmission of information. Although it might be more accurate to contend that they represent a *potential* transmission of information, accounting disclosures, in general and in a constitutive sense, are pieces of information. But information may have various operational meanings. In fact, the term is so broad that even constitutively, it may be defined in a variety of ways. Fortunately, from the operational point of view, the notion seems to underlie them all that information aids organizational decision makers in either (1) setting goals, or (2) maximizing the attainment of goals.

Accounting disclosures, being a subset of the set of all information, appear to emphasize that portion of knowledge, data, or news that aids decision makers in their efforts to attain goals, and thus they tend to be restricted to the latter of the two categories of information. Since information necessarily varies with the goal pursued, it follows that different disclosures of accounting information are needed for different goals.[3] To the extent that goals are unknown, accounting information cannot be defined in a constitutive sense. To the extent that goals are ambiguous, accounting disclosures must be ambiguous, for if "the trumpet be uncertain," the uncertainty as to the way information is to be used will result in an accounting effort to provide information generally useful for a variety of possible goals but specifically appropriate for no one. In times of rapid change, goals are not well structured, and this condition makes it difficult to develop one definite and everlasting structure of accounting disclosures. But difficulty is not an acceptable excuse, and the fact is that at any point in time, a definite, precise statement of the goals of accounting-information users is needed.

In the context of the preceding discussion, it appears that an effort to expand accounting disclosures is an effort to expand the concept of accounting information. This expansion may take place by either (1) expanding the quantity of information communicated to users, or (2) increasing the quality of the information transmitted to users. Given the implication in the preceding chapter that there exists a need for the expansion of accounting disclosures, it seems appropriate to begin an examination of the nature of the possible expansion and ways of inducing it by a theoretical introduction.

MODELS AS ACCOUNTING THEORY

According to one conception of the best way to develop the accounting discipline, it is the function of accounting theory to go beyond the current practices of the profession and to explore possible new developments, so that when the need or opportunity arises for practice to expand, theory will have been there before and will provide insights to practice in the move. Such a notion views accounting theory as a collection of abstract models, each based on a different set of assumed goals, environmental constraints, and operating opportunities. Each theoretical model is an explanation of what accounting disclosures should be if the assumed conditions were found by observation to be the actual conditions. As conditions change, different models would be used to explain or justify different accounting disclosures. In this sense, theory as a composite of the various models is an explanation of the accounting disclosure that should prevail under various sets of assumed conditions and goals.

---

[3] A. C. Littleton's classic *Structure of Accounting Theory* (American Accounting Association, 1953) is based on the assumption that the goal of income is the sole goal of business organizations.

The justification for this conception of accounting theory is that our society is changing rapidly. With this rapid change, accounting practice faces new situations for which no precedents exist. About the only recourse for guidance is some model of accounting theory. This need for practice to turn to theory for guidance may be explained in the following manner.

Because of the constantly changing nature of both persons and environment, precise environmental constraints, operating opportunities, and goals must necessarily change. These conditions could also change as measurement methods are improved; but more often, the conditions will change as the underlying technological and social processes change. For example, the impact of an environmental change on accounting disclosures is illustrated by the fact that depreciation did not come into existence until capital goods were produced. A more current illustration is the fact of lease-purchase acquisitions, which represent a new condition that did not have to be disclosed until contracts for such acquisitions were developed. The point is that there are thousands of forces, ranging from political changes through technological developments to changes in personal values of individuals, that tend to change the substance of accounting information. Accounting disclosures must adjust rapidly to these changes if they are to be constantly relevant to the information needs of users.

Accounting-disclosure changes do not occur easily, for doubt always exists as to the best way to provide the disclosure required by the social changes. Without the time to investigate and determine the proper change, accounting must develop a host of theoretical models of proper disclosure in advance and in anticipation of changes, so that practice can quickly adjust. The point is that where goals are not known, where measurement methods are constantly being improved, or where economic processes are continuously changing, a set of abstract models is about the best conception of a theory of accounting disclosure. Such a view of disclosure theory would be compatible with the proposition that accounting theory goes before practice, showing practice how to deal with new situations as they arise. Under this conception of accounting-disclosure theory, various levels of plausible accounting models would exist. Some would vary from current accounting practice by little, while others, more speculative, would go far beyond current practice. In this conception of things, the scope of accounting theory and the number of structures of accounting-information systems would have no boundaries. Presumably, there would have to be some classification of such accounting-model structures so that practical men could appreciate their theoretical constructions and possible applications. But this is a separate study, that of appropriate models for particular situations, and is beyond the scope of this book.

Multiple theory structures reconsidered

Although the existence of a multitude of accounting models, each used in practice at different times to comply with the needs of information users, would provide for a ready expansion of accounting disclosures, it would place an almost insurmountable task on theoretical-model builders. Actually, such a situation may never arise, for the notion of theory outlined in the preceding paragraph may assume a much more rapid change in conditions and goals than in fact is taking place. This idea also assumes that all the facts to be included as accounting information can be known and included in the model in advance. And finally, it assumes that the reasoning process within each model, which explains what practice should be under each situation, is valid. Despite these reservations, this conception of accounting theory has the advantage of being so broad that it treats theory somewhat as an abstract art that opens up the creativity and intuition of the artist in conceiving possible new facts and goals to support new accounting-disclosure models.

SCIENTIFIC METHOD AS ACCOUNTING THEORY

To be contrasted with the view of accounting-disclosure theory as a series of models or theoretical structures, each based on different sets of assumed facts, is the conception of theory as a process of scientific investigation. According to this method for determining appropriate accounting disclosures, there are four processes involved in the systematic development of a structure of accounting information:

1. Fact-finding, or the sensing of changes in society
2. Induction, or the generalizing of the findings into an overall framework
3. Deduction, or the deriving of the information needs to meet the changed conditions
4. Verification, or the validating of the fact that the suggested disclosures meet the needs of information users

The use of this "scientific method" for developing accounting theory requires the accounting researcher to be, first of all, a sensitive trained observer who immediately becomes aware of changes in goals and social conditions. By inductively gathering together these changes into an interrelated structure, the accounting researcher may propose a preliminary hypothetical statement of appropriate accounting disclosures. A deductive process may be used to fill in gaps in such inductively derived hypotheses. Finally, the researcher must verify the hypothesis by observing results, in terms of user satisfaction with the new information, before submitting it to accounting practice for use.

There are a number of limitations to the use of the scientific method in developing and expanding accounting disclosures. The main problem is the determination of the facts about changes. Technically, a fact cannot exist without a theory of what a fact is, and the concept of a fact differs according to the point of view of the observer, because a "point of view" is the result of a set of beliefs built into the observer. This means that one of the greatest needs for the scientific development of an expansion of accounting disclosures is an articulation of the "built-in" assumptions underlying the accounting resereacher who observes changes in society.

Problems in using the scientific method

The observation difficulty is only the first problem in using the scientific method to determine appropriate accounting disclosures. Nevertheless, if the built-in assumptions of the accounting researcher were known and accepted, it would be possible to conduct research at the fact-finding level and tie the facts together with overall explanations that would be explanatory hypotheses. The inductive process by which observed facts are translated into such an overall hypothesis to explain the facts involves:

1. The formation of a number of possible overall explanations (hypotheses) of the facts
2. The judgmental selection of one of the hypotheses as the most meaningful

This is a highly subjective process, for an almost unlimited number of hypotheses could be developed. About the best that can be done is to select a few of the hypotheses and attempt to verify one to a degree that some confidence in it develops. Normally, this confidence is built up by using the hypothesis for predicting a result. Should several predicted results actually occur consistently, confidence would be created that the hypothesis is valid.

The inductive determination of the overall nature of the observed changes, difficult as it would be to establish in a reasonable period of time, might be used to derive appropriate accounting disclosures. An extension of the inductively developed overall view could be undertaken by reasoning deductively to other generalizations from the inductively derived generalization. The use of a formal axiomatic deductive process for accounting-theory development has only recently been proposed.[4]

---

[4] See R. Mattessich, *Accounting and Analytical Methods* (Homewood, Ill.: Richard D. Irwin, 1964), for an explanation of the use of the axiomatic deductive process in accounting-theory construction.

For the present, the use of the scientific method for expanding accounting disclosures would appear to rest on an intuitive deductive process, and this is not a particularly logical process. But if the axiomatic method were used, the rigorously derived generalizations could be used to indicate what will occur if the suggested accounting disclosure were made, assuming the inductively derived generalizations were considered accurate.

As a final step in the scientific method, it would be necessary to verify that the expanded or changed accounting disclosures did indeed meet the need of users in the changed society. Since users will have access to other sources of information, verification that accounting disclosures are precisely appropriate would be difficult.

Adaptation of the scientific method

Despite the reservations concerning the use of the scientific method as a means of providing for the expansion of accounting disclosures, it may be that it can be adapted to the accounting field and used to contribute to a solution of the problem of accounting disclosures. That is, because the application or use of the scientific method varies from discipline to discipline, it may be possible to adapt it and use it to suggest accounting disclosures by the following two steps:

1. Accepting the proposition that accounting is concerned with human actions, systematic observations could be made of human actions. The data derived from the various observations could be explained, as hypotheses, in terms of the human motives, needs, wants, and values causing the actions. Studies of this type have been and are being conducted by researchers in psychology, anthropology, and the entire social-science area. Some accounting research should start with the findings of these basic disciplines. Other research, aimed at developing hypotheses, might require cooperative interdisciplinary studies. Given hypotheses of the needs, wants, and values of individuals, supported by further empirical research to justify treating the hypotheses as theories, accounting research would be directed to empirical studies of the type of information needed by individuals to best satisfy the wants suggested by the theories. That is, observations would be made of the extent to which different types of information enable an individual to satisfy the wants suggested by the theories of human wants and values. From these observations, hypotheses could be developed regarding information needs. After testing, the hypotheses could be verified as a theory of appropriate information disclosures. To the extent that the resulting information could be expressed quantitatively, it may be considered a theory of accounting disclosures. Such a process for developing accounting-disclosure theory carries opportunities for other research. Paramount among such opportunities is re-

search in measurement and analytical methods. That is, accounting research could be directed to developing new measurement and communication techniques for supplying information to decision makers.

2. After the conclusions regarding the most appropriate information have been initially established, deductive analyses could be used to indicate appropriate accounting disclosures for a variety of specific purposes and the most effective way of communicating or transmitting that information to users. These substructures or models of accounting disclosures would be based on the asumption that it is possible to provide information so that results of actions can be predicted. If actual results should vary from predicted results, and assuming that the deductive process contains no errors, reason would exist for questioning the applicability of the inductively derived structure of accounting disclosures to the needs of the proposed users.

CURRENT EXPANSIONS
OF ACCOUNTING DISCLOSURES

Even though the scope of accounting theory may seem to be limited only by the scope of the scientific method, it must be recalled that the necessary adaptation of the scientific method to the accounting discipline may require a considerable amount of effort and time. The fact is that most accounting researchers are not now equipped to use the scientific method in dealing with the basic problems of accounting disclosures. Furthermore, it may be that the human-behavior aspects of accounting disclosures are so involved that the adaptation of the scientific method to the accounting problems may require an entirely different type of researchers than those now dedicated to the accounting profession.

Without minimizing the need for turning to the scientific method and the adaptation of it to accounting as the long-run means for expanding accounting disclosures, we must also recognize that any discussion of the expansion of accounting disclosures would not be complete without an examination of expansions that may be considered now, well before the scientific method can be used for that purpose. The point is that there are now a number of conceptual developments suggesting that certain expansions in accounting disclosures are needed at the present time. Broadly, these expansions arise from (1) improvements in measurement methods, (2) changes in the environment of organizational entities, and (3) advances in the operating methods of organizations.

Before examining each of these expansions, a word of caution must be inserted: Without scientific verification, one cannot be entirely confident that proposed expansions are proper. Nor are efforts to make basic changes in ways of doing things smooth and uninterrupted. To illustrate, it took 150 years after Pope Gregory corrected the Julian calendar before Great Britain adopted it. But Great Britain's acceptance opened the door, and the universal way for men to date time expanded rapidly from 1732 to 1795. However, the transition was not complete, for in 1795, France revived the Egyptian calendar as The Calendar of Reason, and for twelve years, the universal use of the Gregorian calendar was delayed. Now, a calendar change is a much more basic change than is a change in accounting disclosures. It involved omitting the period September 3 through September 13, 1732, and changing New Year's Day from March 25 to January 1 in the case of Great Britain. Nonetheless, any proposed expansion of accounting disclosures must also anticipate a critical acceptance. It has been said that "for every progressive step proposed, a thousand voices will arise to defend the past." Thus, change is difficult even though the increasing awareness of the rate of change in society tends to make change easier now than in the past. Nevertheless, without the use and public acceptance of the scientific method, proposals for expanding accounting disclosures will not find immediate acceptance. With this qualification in mind, and deferring until later chapters the discussions of expansion in measurement methods, it seems appropriate to consider the following conceptual proposals for expanding accounting disclosures.

PROPOSED EXPANSIONS
OF ACCOUNTING DISCLOSURES

Disclosure of social costs

The social environment in which business organizations operate is changing, and these changes suggest expansion in accounting disclosures. Broadly, there seems to be a growing awareness that our society is an overall system and that business is merely part of that society. Possibly owing to improved communication methods in the form of higher education, television coverage of various aspects of life, and improved reporting of news, more and more people tend to view society as a whole unit and to examine each subpart of that society, such as the institution of business, in terms of its contribution to the entire social system. Many business firms, aware of this holistic view entertained by members of society, have assumed social responsibilities, as well as income responsibilities to shareholders. But public accounting disclosures have not been expanded to include audited reports on the social contributions of business, or any organization, to society. The failure of accounting disclosures to keep the public informed of the social-responsibility activities of business firms may have weakened public support for the institution of business in society. The sensitivity of business firms to the need to disclose information on these additional business responsibilities is revealed in various annual reports, where the "President's Letter" section frequently refers to many noneconomic activities of the company. There may be some question as to the portion of this emerging public-disclosure requirement that should be included as accounting disclosures, but undoubtedly there are certain parts that clearly fall within accounting.

Specifically, the disclosure of the "public" costs as well as the "private" costs of business activities is an accounting responsibility. To the extent that the public believes a company's activities pollute the environment at no private cost to the company, there is a social cost attached to that company's operations that is not now revealed by accounting disclosures, either publicly or internally. These social costs can be measured to some degree, and attention could be directed to the nonmeasured social costs by itemizing them and assigning a nominal cost to them, such as the traditional one-dollar valuation of goodwill. Among these social costs might be the pollution of the air, water, and land caused by company operations, the destruction of public properties such as the use of "free" highways for private transportation, and the use of state-educated employees for private work. The point is that only by accounting disclosure of these social costs, side by side with the disclosure of the company's social benefits, can the public decide whether the business institution is a contribution to society.

Inferences can be drawn that the proposal for expanding accounting disclosures to include social costs and social revenue or benefits is unrealistic, because the impact on specific business enterprises would be disastrous. In such a situation, the introduction of such expanded accounting disclosures may have to be introduced over a period of time. But introduced they must be, for failure to include them as accounting disclosures may in the long run be disastrous to accounting, in that its role in society may be reduced; to the business institution, in that society may tend to reject it as it now exists in the free enterprise system; or to both accounting and business.

Disclosure of human resources

In addition to the inclusion of "social" costs, it may be that accounting disclosures could be expanded to include in some way various nonvalued or undervalued resources. Among these resources are the highly trained, efficient human resources of the company. These disclosures need to be made because in a period of rapid technological change, educated and well-trained employees become more and more the important resources of a company. This type of disclosure may involve nonfinancial disclosures, such as a classification of employees by age, education, health, and morale. It may include a disclosure of customers by size, by loyalty, and other characteristics. But whatever the nature, full accounting disclosures of all company resources to owners, creditors, employees, and the general public are needed to facilitate the smooth operation of society.

Disclosure of human resources is a most involved undertaking and carries various social and economic consequences. For example, disclosure of the financial value of employees as a company asset would create not only accounting measurement problems but also managerial problems of preventing loss of employees because of the financial loss that would then be recorded. If management were successful in preventing employees from leaving the company, a social loss might result from the consequent loss of mobility of labor. Similarly, problems arise if managers were to become more interested in maintaining existing customers and creditors rather than obtaining new ones. Thus the nonfinancial disclosure of human resources seems to be the more appropriate disclosure method.

Disclosure of budgets and equipment status

As to the expansion of accounting disclosures required by virtue of advances in operating methods of business and other organizations, the rapid growth of budgeting suggests that public disclosure of the annual budget at the beginning of the year following, by a public disclosure of actual operations compared with the budget, might be appropriate. Although business firms may contend that such a disclosure would reveal information to competitors, and CPA firms may rightly contend that such information cannot be objectively measured, the fact is that some company officers now do disclose, early in the year, expected earnings per share for the calendar year. The point is that such disclosures are now being made to some degree in an unsystematic and somewhat unreliable manner, and in the interest of public confidence in business, these disclosures might best become accounting disclosures.

Other expansions of accounting disclosures of changes in operating methods of a company would include annual comparison of technological equipment used over a period of time; probably a five-year trend would be sufficient. Also, all significant changes in personnel, products, organizational adjustments, and the like could be disclosed. Since these are now frequently announced in newspaper reports in a sporadic manner, a comprehensive disclosure of them at the end of a year would be more significant to persons interested in the operations of the company.

Management audit

The need for some type of an objective disclosure of management effectiveness represents another opportunity for expanding accounting disclosures. As the management process becomes more standardized and less of an art, the opportunity for a disclosure of the extent to which management actions conformed to standard management practices becomes possible. Some measure of managerial performance may have to be developed, for there is so much art in management that none now exists, but the demand for such a disclosure is clearly evident.

MONITORING SYSTEM

Undoubtedly, there are many other disclosures that will have to be made in the future. The foregoing list is more illustrative than comprehensive. The unsystematic way in which accounting disclosure needs are now sensed calls attention to the need for accounting researchers to develop the scientific method and apply it to the problem of expanding accounting disclosures.

Broadly, the expansion of accounting disclosures is necessary at the present time because the values, norms, beliefs, and attitude of individuals in society are changing, and one can never be certain what will be demanded from the institution of business by society from one period of time to the next. A rather complete accounting disclosure seems to be the best approach. Some guidance to appropriate disclosure is afforded by a study of technological changes under way and those anticipated, for technological changes appear to be the basic source of social changes, in that they change the way things are done. But in the main, the appropriate expansion or adjustment of accounting disclosures to social changes will have to rest upon some type of a "monitoring" system set up by accountants to provide an awareness of changes in process.

Actually, the "monitoring" system for accountants might have to be established by the organized profession. Its function would be to sense and make accountants generally aware of changes in process. The determination of the appropriate accounting disclosures needed to adjust to these changes may or may not be beyond the scope of such a monitoring system. The fully developed accounting "monitoring" system would have to be sensitive to all types of changes in society and would be operated by highly trained observers of all types of developments in the world—observers with an ability to relate these developments to accounting-disclosure needs. In addition, the accounting profession would have to have confidence in their monitoring system and be willing to adjust their practice to its findings.

SCOPE OF ACCOUNTING

The expansion of accounting disclosures is also limited in terms of the nature of the social needs on which accounting assumes a responsibility to provide information. For example, it is seldom suggested that accounting assumes responsibility for providing information to meet the human desire for good health. But it is well established that accounting disclosures should provide information that will assist individuals to meet their desire for income. In between these two extremes, there are a number of rather recent developments in accounting practice that have not been included in most overall structures of accounting theory, such as national-income accounting, operations research, and systems-engineering developments. These include both new measurement methods, to be discussed in Chapter 7, and a new type of entity, the nation, with which accounting could be concerned.

Actually, when one proposes the foregoing concepts as a basis for the expansion of accounting disclosures, one is in part proposing an expansion of the structure of knowledge known as accounting, for the method to be used to make the disclosure may require a different structure for both theory and practice. Concerning the nature of the structure that will emerge as accounting disclosures are expanded, one can now only speculate. But it is now possible to view the organized body of knowledge known as accounting thought into the three conceptual structures outlined below. There should, however, be no effort to restrict the number of structures that might be developed to meet specific needs of specific users. But for society at large, the following three structures might now represent boundaries for the development of accounting disclosures:

1. The Income Structure
2. The Wealth Structure
3. The Socioeconomic Structure

Before we examine these three information structures in terms of their interrelationships and areas of distinction, it must be noted that other suggestions have been made regarding the appropriate scope of accounting theory and the type of structures of accounting information that should be developed to provide an appropriate base for suitable accounting disclosures.[5]

5 Carl Devine has called to our attention four areas in which research in accounting could be undertaken ("Research Methodology and Accounting Theory Formation," *Accounting Review,* July 1960), as follows:

ACCOUNTING-DISCLOSURE STRUCTURES

It has been suggested that the structure of accounting should extend into the fields of psychology, sociology, ecology, anthropology, political science, and biology, in order to provide realistic bases for accounting disclosures. This proposal is based on the assumption that human wants and desires are the basic guides to individual and organizational actions, and that the environment, broadly conceived, has a decided impact on these wants and desires. Those who support this broad structure for accounting also propose that it be developed by mathematical and logical methods. Giving due consideration to proposals such as the foregoing one, but recognizing the desirability of limiting the number of structures to those with which society at large is somewhat familiar, only the three structures listed above have been developed. The fact-finding process, the intuitive development of generalized hypotheses, the inductive support for the hypotheses leading to their acceptance, the deductive process used to reach the conclusions included in the three structures, and the verification process used to substantiate them are not well developed. There is, however, considerable authoritative and intuitive support for the proposition that the basic titles of the

---

1. *Logical Structure and Deductive Systems,* wherein the research would be directed to tie accounting together by means of a logical apparatus so it would represent a deductive or axiomatic system.
2. *Measurement and Induction,* wherein the scientific method is used to develop hypotheses (the concept of a trained observer) and then verify or disprove the hypotheses.
3. *Behavior Relation,* wherein the research is directed to the study of behavioral patterns. This may involve the use of psychological studies prepared by others. The issue is to determine how people behave.
4. *Welfare and Normative Responsibilities,* wherein the research is in the area of ethics and how people should behave.

Ray Chambers has outlined for us the conditions for the scientific study of accounting ("The Conditions of Research in Accounting," *Journal of Accountancy,* December 1960). From his suggestions, the following conditions for accounting research are proposed:

1. Stipulate the limits of the field of accounting.
   a. Behavioral science may be used.
   b. Applied mathematics may be used.
   c. Communication theory may be studied.
   Corollary: Do not limit the field to that which is done in practice.
2. Recognize the varied sources of ways of developing the basic assumptions of accounting, and take cognizance of the ever-present possibility that postulates of greater utility may sometime be developed.
3. There should be no limits to the types of accounting processes, events, and activities to be observed.
   Corollary: Encourage imagination in attempts to formulate concepts.
4. Recognize a hierarchical structure of accounting ideas to establish meaningful relationships among accounting concepts.

three structures proposed are widely recognized in society. The income structure has been outlined by Littleton.[6] Tentative, skeletonized wealth and socioeconomic structures are presented in Table 2–1 in comparative form.

TABLE 2–1

Structures of Accounting Theory

Wealth Structure	Socioeconomic Structure
I. Implied limits of the field of accounting:	I. Implied limits of the field of accounting:
A. The objective of the accounting function shall be limited to the measurement and communication of economic data.	A. The objective of the accounting function shall be limited to the measurement and communication of data revealing socioeconomic activities that use economic resources.
B. The underlying tools (disciplines) that may be used in performing the function shall be restricted to economics, descriptive statistics, and the bookkeeping mechanism.	B. The underlying disciplines (tools) that may be used in performing the function shall include the behavioral sciences, probability and statistics, mathematics, and information theory, as well as both the bookkeeping mechanism and the electronic computer.
C. The purpose of the accounting function shall be limited to descriptive or explanatory theory and information to explain what is, has been, or might be economic activity.	C. The purpose of the accounting function shall be confined to information and descriptive and normative theory that explains what is, has been, or might be, and possibly what should be, appropriate social activities.
II. Nature of basic assumptions upon which the theoretical aspects of the field rest:	II. Nature of basic assumptions upon which the theoretical aspects of the field rest:
A. The motivation assumption is that the desire for wealth causes the activities with which accounting is concerned. While it takes various forms, this motivation assumption is reflected in at least two distinct desires: 1. The desire for income (short- and long-term) 2. The desire to avoid loss	A. The motivation assumption is that the desire for certain socioeconomic objectives causes the activities with which accounting is concerned. The motivation is reflected in such desires as: 1. A desire for income (short- and long-term) 2. A desire for prestige 3. A desire for power 4. A desire for multiple goals 5. A desire for a "good" society that will survive

6 Littleton, *Structure of Accounting Theory.*

Wealth Structure	*Socioeconomic Structure*
B. The measurement assumptions are those assumptions made to facilitate the measurement process. Those assumptions commonly recognized are: 1. That entities exist and are the units whose activities are measured 2. That changes in the economic value of resources reflect the activities of an entity 3. That an adjusted money unit is an acceptable unit of measurement 4. That the reliability of the measurement is advanced by objectivity reflected in market prices and consistency of the type of market price used	B. The measurement assumptions are those assumptions made to facilitate the measurement process, such as: 1. That any organizational entity may be conceived (nation, business, person) and may be the unit whose activities are measured 2. That activities within and among organizations occur and are measurable as they accrue or flow 3. That any homogeneous measuring unit may be used to quantify accounting data; in fact, that multiple-measurement language could conceivably be used 4. That the reliability of the measurement is advanced by including probability measures of variations from the measurement
C. The communication assumptions made to facilitate the communication process include the following: 1. That numerical data are an effective means for communicating information 2. That information representing adequate disclosure may be conveyed by means of a balance sheet, income statement, and supporting footnotes 3. That information must be communicated consistently, both as to time periods and as to the communication medium, even if the measurement is tentative	C. The communication assumptions made to facilitate the communication process include the following: 1. That multiple-measurement languages may be needed to communicate information 2. That multiple reports should be used to communicate information, including cash-flow statements, encumbrance reports, activity statements, balance sheets, and a variety of others 3. That disclosure of entity activity must be provided as needed from data classified to allow retrieving for multiple purposes, and that both consistent reporting—as to time and as to statement forms—and special reporting are needed
III. The activities, events, and methods included within the field of accounting: A. The accounting methods used to measure and communicate information include:	III. The activities, events and methods within the field of accounting: A. The accounting methods used to measure and communicate information include:

T A B L E 2 – 1 *(cont.)*

Wealth Structure	*Socioeconomic Structure*
1. Double-entry recording 2. Statement analysis 3. A variety of methods in financial accounting, income tax accounting, auditing, fiduciary accounting, cost accounting, and budgeting	1. Double-entry recording and other information-collection and -storage processes 2. Statistical and mathematical analysis 3. A variety of methods in financial accounting, income tax accounting, auditing, fiduciary accounting, management accounting, management advisory services, national-income accounting, and others
B. The accounting entities are: 1. The business unit 2. Governmental units 3. Individuals 4. Others	B. The accounting entities are: 1. Business units 2. Governmental units 3. Nation or region 4. Individuals 5. Others
C. The accounting activities are: 1. Cash transactions, past and planned 2. Deferred cash transactions (accounts receivable and payable) 3. Cash-equivalent flow transactions such as depreciation	C. The accounting activities are: 1. Socioeconomic transactions or flows 2. Activities of significance to managers and others, which need to be measured and communicated
D. The environment of accounting is represented by: 1. A social system highly motivated by wealth objectives 2. A variety of research and authoritative pronouncements and philosophical studies 3. A variety of political states	D. The environment of accounting includes: 1. Any social system 2. The use of the research-scientific method of inquiry 3. An international applicability

Further development of the socioeconomic structure may, in an ultimate sense, require the use of symbolic logic and a rigorous deductive process, but the current immediate need is for a clarification of the meaning of the socioeconomic concept.

These structures reflect the change that will result in the accounting body of knowledge, depending upon the extent to which accounting disclosures are expanded. In the next chapter, an effort will be made to suggest improvements in accounting communication methods and thus in accounting disclosures. The results of the analysis of this chapter and the next are combined in Chapter 4 to provide an overall view of the scope of accounting disclosures.

REFERENCES

BRIGHT, JAMES R., ed., *Technological Forecasting for Industry and Government*. Englewood Cliffs, N.J.: Prentice-Hall, 1968.

CHAMBERS, RAYMOND J., *Accounting, Evaluation and Economic Behavior*. Englewood Cliffs, N.J.: Prentice-Hall, 1966.

COOMBS, C. H., *A Theory of Data*. New York: John Wiley, 1964.

GARNER, W., *Uncertainty and Structure as Psychological Concepts*. New York: John Wiley, 1962.

HARVEY, O. J., ed., *Motivation and Social Interaction, Cognitive Determinants*. New York: Ronald Press, 1963.

IJIRI, Y., *The Foundations of Accounting Measurement*. Englewood Cliffs, N.J.: Prentice-Hall, 1967.

KEMENY, JOHN G., *A Philsopher Looks at Science*. Princeton, N.J.: Van Nostrand, 1959.

LITTLETON, A. C., *Structure of Accounting Theory*. Urbana, Ill.: American Accounting Association, 1953.

SCHRODER, H. M., DRIVER, M. J., and STREUFERT, S., *Human Information Processing*. New York: Holt, Rinehart & Winston, 1967.

CHAPTER THREE

The Communication
Aspects

The effectiveness of accounting disclosures depends as much on the means by which the disclosures are transmitted to users as on their substance. Transmission of information is particularly involved because it depends upon symbolic representation of things, and representations never reveal all characteristics of an activity. Furthermore, these symbols may be transmitted through different media that may influence the interpretation of the symbol. Transmission of accounting disclosures is also influenced by the varying comprehension capacity of receivers. Such capacity is significantly influenced by the value needs of the recipient, his sense of certainty or uncertainty as to appropriate acts, and other interferences (noise) in the reception process. This chapter concludes that definite guidelines are needed to improve accounting disclosures. Basically, accounting disclosures must be concerned with communication, for "a man is not an isolate being in a void; he is essentially integrated into society. The various aspects of man's behavior—his means of livelihood, his language and all forms of self-expression, his system of economics and law, his religious ritual, all of which involve him in acts of communication—are not discrete and independent but are inherently related. . . ." [1]

[1] Colin Cherry, *On Human Communication* (Cambridge, Mass.: The M.I.T. Press, 1966), Chap. 1.

It is difficult to separate consideration of what is to be communicated from that of the communication process. This difficulty has led to the development of a theory of communication that spans both the substance and the process of communication. Nevertheless, this chapter is concerned primarily with the "mind-to-mind" transmission of a piece of information. More precisely, the communication aspects of accounting disclosures refer to the processes by which the accountant transmits his observations on socioeconomic activities to users of that information.

THE PROBLEM OF SYMBOLS

Accounting disclosures rely heavily on symbols, which represent things and actions in the socioeconomic world, and whose use is based on the assumption that the message sender (accountant) and the message receiver (decision maker) have a common understanding of the meaning of the symbols.[2] For example, the symbol "Depreciation Expense—$3,000" may, to an accountant, represent an allocated portion of the original cost of the assets being depreciated. If the decision maker thinks the symbol indicates the decline in value of the assets, the communication would not be effective, and the image in the mind of the accountant as to what has happened would not be transmitted to the decision maker. The illustration points to the fact that the assumption of a common understanding of the meaning of symbols is not universally valid, and that one of the current and continuing responsibilities of accountants concerned with the communication aspects of accounting disclosures is the reiterative assertion of the meaning of the symbols used. To the extent that accountants disagree on the meaning of a symbol, there is a need for authoritative pronouncements of the "generally accepted" meaning of the symbols used. For special types of reports, or in any reports where the message receiver may be in doubt as to the meaning of a symbol, a glossary of terms (symbols) used should accompany the accounting-disclosure medium.[3]

[2] For a discussion of a general theory of signs (semiotics), which has as a goal an explanation of all forms and manifestations of signs, see Charles Morris, *Significa-tion and Significance* (Cambridge, Mass.: M.I.T. Press, 1964).

[3] Illustrative of this glossary is Sun Oil Company's 1969 pamphlet, *Understanding Sun's Accounting Terms,* which is introduced with the statement, "Many shareholders of corporations do not fully understand financial terms used in annual reports, according to a survey conducted by Opinion Research Corporation of Princeton, N.J.

"ORC explains the situation this way: Traditionally, U.S. companies have leaned over backwards to report their activities fully and accurately. In doing this, the tendency has been to use technical terms which have precise meanings for financial analysts and others in the field of finance. The trouble is that these terms often are so technical that they have little meaning for shareholders."

One of the subtle problems of the assumption that symbols have common meanings to message senders and message receivers is that the symbols assume different meanings in different situations. Illustrative of this condition is the use of the symbol "loss" to refer to the "disappearance of service resources without providing revenue" at one time, and as the "excess of expense over revenue" at another time. Not only does the meaning of a symbol change, but also, the meaning of an understood symbol takes on subtly different connotations in different situations; and therefore, the significance of the accounting disclosure changes in subtle ways. For example, the meaning of "interest expense" differs with the interest rate. That is, "interest expense" has a different connotation when the rate is 8 percent than when it is 4 percent, because the separate rates may cover different risk elements. Since the interest charge includes payments for such things as waiting, productivity of resources, inflation, and other risks, a high interest rate may reflect a greater proportion for inflation than a low rate does. Also, the meaning of the interest charge varies with time and geographic area, so its risk element might vary even if the rate were the same at different times and in different places. Illustrative of variations in the interest rate and in the precise meaning of "interest charges" are Tables 3–1, 3–2, and 3–3.

TABLE 3–1

Risk Differences:
Interest Rates in the U.S. in mid-1969

Bank interest earning assets	Rate
Mortages	7.43%
Other loans	8.50%
U.S. government obligations	6.64%
Other securities	7.27%
Weighted average	7.66%

TABLE 3–2

Geographic Area Differences:
Average Interest Rate in Selected Countries

Country	Mid-1969 %
Switzerland	4.60
France	6.24
Germany	6.02
Great Britain	7.89
Spain	4.76
USA	6.21

TABLE 3-3

Time Differences: Interest Rates in the U.S.

Banking Sector	1960 %	1962 %	1967 %	1969 %
Loan rate	5.00	4.86	6.00	7.66
Deposit rate	1.38	1.56	3.36	3.60

Source: An International Survey of Interest Rates (Zurich: The Union Bank of Switzerland, 1970).

A more concrete example of a change in the meaning of a symbol is a change in the method of computing annual depreciation without changing the symbol. Depreciation computed under the "declining-balance" method is a different thing from depreciation computed by the "straight-line" method, and the changed meaning of the symbol "Depreciation Expense" must be noted somehow in the accounting disclosure.

APB Opinion 20 on *Accounting Changes* deals implicitly, but not explicitly and not comprehensively, with some of the problems of changing symbol meanings. More immediate attention to the problem may be needed.

The extent of the confusion in accounting disclosures owing to fluctuating meanings of accounting symbols may be much greater than is commonly assumed. Recognition of this condition tends to result in a call for an increase in the number of symbols used, to assure precise communications in accounting disclosures, but making precise terms available does not ensure their use. These limitations to the basic assumption that symbols have a specific meaning understood by both message senders and message receivers indicate a need for continuous education on accounting terminology.

COMMUNICATION MEDIA

Subject to the foregoing restriction, the communication aspects of accounting disclosure may be examined in terms of the process of transmitting to users certain observations or inferences noted by accountants. The media by which this communication is effected may vary widely, including pictures, television, oral words, physical gestures, written words and numbers, graphs, charts, and models. The traditional accounting disclosures have been confined to written words and numbers but, as we will note later, this restriction may have to be abandoned in the future.

As a starting point for this analysis of the communication aspects of accounting disclosures, the views of an accounting practitioner will relate the discussion both to current thinking and to expansion opportunities in the future. Speaking of the universe of accounting reports, C. E. Graese offers the following observations:

> A report of whatever form—financial, management, internal, external— is in the nature of something universal. It selects the essential data from the myriads of information that surround the particular entity or subject matter of interest, interprets the data, and presents a meaningful story for the concerned reader. From the comprehensive "universe" of the environment studied, the essence is extracted for analysis and for action . . . the variety of reports that can be issued internally can be as overwhelming as the environment mirrored in them is complex . . . but beneath the universe of reports there are some basic rules that apply to all, although in varying ways and at various times. Several examples will suffice to illustrate their value and simplicity:
>
> 1. Make results identifiable with responsible executives.
> 2. Compare results with expected performance at the activity level achieved.
> 3. Present results on an exception basis that emphasizes significantly good or bad performance.
> 4. Use standards for accumulating and transferring costs.
> 5. Segregate controllable from noncontrollable expenses.
> 6. Prepare statements that are easy to read—leaving plenty of white space; omitting cents; using understandable terminology; etc.
> 7. Integrate individual statements in a pattern that clearly follows the organization chart so that figures can be "exploded"; express results so that key figures can be easily traceable when carried over to the next "higher" statement.
> 8. Highlight results and do not try to present all the answers.
> 9. Stagger release of statements where necessary to allow for ease in assimilation of contents.
> 10. Issue statements on a timely basis.
>
> Nothing is more useless than a report submitted to one executive containing figures that are the responsibility of another. Nothing is more absurd than a report that is incomprehensible to the intended reader. These are some of the simple ideas expressed in these rules and in many others that could be promulgated. All that is necessary is the recognition that behind the universe of reports that flow past us interminably stand the several crucial events and circumstances they describe, and the reader who seeks enlightenment.[4]

---

[4] C. E. Graese, "The Universe of Reports," *Management Controls*, March 1970. pp. 42–43.

Underlying the basic rules applicable to all types of reports are the following communication tasks:

1. Attracting the attention of the user
2. Relating the information to his needs
3. Maintaining his interest in the report
4. Stimulating action

Performance of these tasks is no simple process, for each user differs in some way to some degree from other users. An accounting disclosure that is an effective transmission to one user may be ineffective to another. The fact is that the content of a message to a message receiver depends, in part, on what the recipient is seeking. What a message reader is seeking depends upon his total past experience, how he views his role in the organization and in society, and his fundamental needs. All these are reflected in the values—immediate, intermediate, and ultimate—held by the message receiver.[5] This idea suggests another view of individual and organizational values might well precede the discussion of the message-transmission process, and the next few pages are directed to that end, seeking to establish a philosophical base for examining the communication aspects of accounting.

CAPACITY OF MESSAGE RECEIVERS

An attempt to understand the receptive capacity of a message receiver, and thus understand how he will "read" a message, has to be—until we learn more about human behavior—little more than a broad introduction to the problem. The greatest opportunity for an approach to the problem appears to lie in the perception and cognition areas of psychology.

It seems appropriate to start this examination of the way a decision maker has been conditioned to "read" an accounting disclosure by noting that all deliberate, planned human conduct, personal and collective, seems to be controlled by human perceptions of the value or worth of ends pursued. Such perceptions manifest themselves in the form of human

[5] Santayana expresses the concept by stating, "Data are but signals; and they are signals *a priori*, because intelligence is an expression of adaptation in the past and of capacity for further adaptation. In view of this, a dictum is a challenge; and animal intelligence does not cry, 'There it is' but 'What is that?'" George Santayana, *Physical Order and Moral Liberty: Previously Unpublished Essays* (Nashville, Tenn.: Vanderbilt University Press, 1969), p. 93.

wants. The greater the intensity of the want, the more vigorous seems to be the human action response to an accounting disclosure indicating appropriate action to satisfy the want. Therefore, the nature of the values or needs held by information users must be known if accounting is to disclose the most useful information on socioeconomic activity.

It seems to be fairly well recognized that psychologists explain human behavior in terms of such concepts as homeostasis, needs strains, and tensions, whereas economists relate human behavior to objects as if the objects have an intrinsic or common, if varying, value. Because of the different views, the exchange value of the resource may or may not represent an accurate measure of its means for satisfying the psychological wants of any one particular decision maker. For example, certain churches have indicated an interest not only in the income earned on their investments but also on the contribution to society made by the companies in which their funds are invested. To these churches, an accounting disclosure of economic gain is an inadequate measure of the extent to which their wants or values have been satisfied.

Underlying both the psychological and the economic view of "value" is the limitation that only human perception of needs, resources, and activities represents the substance of accounting. There exists no "real" world with discrete, universally observable "events" with which accounting deals. All "transactions" and other recorded activities are human constructs developed to aid the development of civilization. Thus, like any information technology, accounting involves the sensing, coding, transforming, transmitting, and translating of information.[6] In its "sensing" or "perception" role, of both what the accountant perceives in the world of activities and what the decision maker perceives in the accounting disclosure, accounting must have in mind some notion of value. Broadly, this means that accounting must be concerned with three value questions, as follows:

1. Are values inherited as part of the basic nature of people? That is, are there such things as basic human wants?
2. Are values created by people and environment? That is, what is the impact of other people and an environment on individual human values?
3. What is the hierarchy of values?[7] Which values or goals are more important under which circumstances? For example, what values are included or covered in the income concept?

6 Thomas L. Whisler, *Information Technology and Organization Change* (Belmont, Calif.: Wadsworth, 1970), p. 11. Henry Margenau, in *The Nature of Physical Reality* (New York: McGraw-Hill, 1950), p. 13, has even stated that "it is the methodology of science that defines physical reality."

7 For an insight into the hierarchy of human needs, see Abraham H. Maslow, *Motivation and Personality* (New York: Harper & Row, 1954).

Answers to these questions are complex. "Common sense" notions about human nature all too often prove unreliable. Certain social science studies suggest that over time the motives of top management change toward professional pride, then to a desire for prestige, and on to the desire for power and universal approval. To the extent that decision makers' values differ, not only is there a difference in what the accountant should communicate; there may also be necessary a change in the process by which the transmission is effected. For example, if the income statement is used to transmit information to a decision maker interested in income, presumably a "prestige statement" in some unknown form should be used to transmit information to a decision maker interested in prestige. This facet of the communication aspects of accounting disclosures tends to be ignored in the accounting literature. In fact, the information technology for the production of information seems to have attracted the interest of man over the ages to the neglect of the information technology for the distribution of the information. Ranging from the signal drums of Africa, to the smoke signals of the Indians, to the abacus of the Orient, to the bookeeping mechanism of the Italian merchants, and on to the electronic computer of modern America, the information technology has varied and seemingly has improved over the ages. But the psychological aspects of information distribution or transmission have not been developed in a systematic manner. They should be.

PSYCHOLOGICAL ASPECTS
OF ACCOUNTING DISCLOSURES

To emphasize the point that the nature of the value needs of a decision maker requires different transmission processes, consider the analogical proposition that just as different physical products (eggs, fresh vegetables, automobiles, steel) are distributed by different processes, so should different information products be distributed differently.

Not only does the nature of the information to be transmitted influence the type of transmission process; also, the type of decision maker to whom the information is transmitted influences that process. Frequently, these two factors are interrelated at any one point in time, in the sense that the type of information needed varies with the type of decision maker involved. For example, the accounting-disclosure implications involved in transmitting information on income, prestige, and power are that distinct classes of decision makers are motivated by different stimuli, as follows:

1. *Income* disclosure may suggest that the business was perceived to be operated for the benefit of the owners.
2. *Prestige* disclosure may imply that the organization was perceived to be operated for the benefit of all participants—employees, customers, owners, and others.
3. *Power* disclosure may imply that the organization is perceived to be operated for the benefit of the top executives of the company.

As to which values should be accepted for developing company-wide communication structures for accounting disclosures, there appears to be no firmly based support for any one set of values upon which accountants could rely. There are at least five psychological concepts of human behavior involved, and various combinations of them indicate the complexity of the task of developing the one communication structure of accounting reports. These five concepts may be stated as follows:

1. Human behavior is the result of a stimulus of some type and a response to the stimulus.
2. Human behavior may be explained as a homeostasis phenomenon, with man seeking a balance among multiple changing wants.
3. Human behavior is the result of basic emotional and physical needs.
4. Human behavior is determined by groups and organizations.
5. Human behavior may be explained by an involved psychological theory of behavior.

Illustrative of the failure of professional discussions to consider adequately the psychological aspects of accounting disclosures is the recent controversy over segmented disclosure of the activities of certain conglomerate companies. Other than unsupported assertions that readers cannot comprehend detailed disclosures, there are no rigorous analyses of how different bases for identifying segments might motivate different behavior.

This failure to include consideration of the psychological aspects of accounting disclosures does not mean that the profession is not concerned with the behavioral aspect of disclosures. The materiality concept is based on the behavioral response to a measure, since something is material only if it would cause a reader to act differently if it were disclosed differently. The inference must be that failure to consider explicitly the behavioral aspects leaves the communication portion of accounting disclosures on a somewhat unstable foundation.

Despite the unstable foundation of the endeavor to determine how

a message receiver will "read," or what he will perceive in, an accounting disclosure, the hope is that support will be given the proposition now gaining academic recognition, that the communication of accounting disclosures must be based on the assumption that values are the bases of human and organization activity and that there is a relationship between information and the articulation and transmission of symbols about values.

This proposition implies that accounting should maintain a close relationship with the general concept of information. A brief examination of the concept of information from the vantage point of accounting disclosures will provide further insights into the accounting-disclosure problem. Recognizing that different readers "read" different things in accounting statements suggests the notion that accounting statements are basically data bases from which statement readers retrieve the information they consider important. That is, readers appear to use accounting reports as though they are data bases and retrieve different information from them at different times. For example, a reader wanting information on the ability of a company to pay its short-term debts may extract current assets and current liabilities from the complete balance sheet, compute the current ratio from the retrieved data, and thus obtain an indication of the information wanted. A little reflection suggests that financial ratios are all based on selected data retrieved from accounting statements. In this context, financial statements are indeed data bases.

Recognizing that public accounting statements are essentially data bases from which different users extract different information for different purposes puts accounting statements in a different light. They are not direct-communication devices. Rather, they are good or bad depending upon the extent to which users can retrieve from them the information they want.

When accounting statements are viewed as data bases from which information users retrieve selectively and individually appropriate information, they represent a second type of data base. The first type of data base may be referred to as the accountant's data base (ledger information, and so on), which is collected and maintained by the accountant. This is the source of the second type of data base, which may be designated as the user's data base.

The implications of the notion that public accounting statements are data bases are extensive. They are no longer communications directly to users, but appropriate data bases from which various types of information can be retrieved by different users. As data bases, they are closely associated with the concept of information.

INFORMATION, UNCERTAINTY, AND DECISIONS

Information is a product that has the capacity to reduce the uncertainty in the mind of a decision maker as to the appropriate action to take or value to accept. The more uncertainty is reduced by a message, the greater the amount of information supplied. As a corollary to this, the greater the uncertainty, the greater the opportunity to provide information by an accounting disclosure. In this context, the study of information involves a study of the different types of uncertainty a decision maker faces in attempting to satisfy his wants or attain his goals. Broadly, uncertainty is a subjective phenomenon that influences the confidence with which a decision is made. If a person believes the probability of an event occurring is very low, he has little confidence in a prediction that it will occur. On the other hand, if he believes that the probability is high, he will predict it with greater confidence. Since accounting disclosures, as information, reduce decision-making uncertainty, an understanding of the nature and types of uncertainty in the minds of decision makers should facilitate the development and communication of relevant accounting disclosures. Broadly, there are three reasons why uncertainty will always exist, as follows:

1. *Uncertainty because of incomplete investigation.* The decision maker can devote only a limited part of his resources to the process of gathering and compiling information. That is, even if a decision maker were willing and could collect all the information necessary to compute the profit of a proposed venture with certainty, it might not pay him to do so because of time constraints or because the cost of gathering the information might exceed the profit he could obtain. Thus, he would be better off to make a decision without being completely informed and without having reduced his uncertainty to zero. The fact that this type of uncertainty may exist makes it extremely difficult to know just how extensive accounting disclosures should be, because when one starts to gather information in advance of its use, one may know neither its cost nor its benefits. For purposes of identification, this type of uncertainty is referred to as *frictional uncertainty*.

2. *Uncertainty because of the inability to predict future conditions.* The second factor that prevents decision makers from obtaining complete information is the fact that the future is to some degree unknowable. Individuals have limited ability to predict the future, and, to the extent that there are mental and physical limits to the development of information about the future, prediction is necessary. There are conditions, of course, that make information about the present seem useful for the future. Among these are (a) the belief that current trends will continue, (b) the belief that events

that will cause deviations from current trends can be sensed with an adequate monitoring system, (c) the belief that conditions are such that activities will be the same in all future environments, and (d) the belief that results will be realized before future changes materialize. Although accounting disclosures should attempt to support or reject these beliefs, there will always remain the type of uncertainty identified as *prediction uncertainty.*

3. **Uncertainty because of imperfect communication systems.** Most decision makers do not gather their own information. They assign the task to accountants, among others. As a result, the willingness of a decision maker to accept the accuracy of an accounting disclosure and let it, in a psychological sense, reduce his uncertainty depends on his impression of those who have transmitted the information and the nature of their measurements. In this respect, note that uncertainty may continue to exist because of the use of a single-valued communication symbol when multiple values are necessary. When measurements are only probable, communications are improved if they are so revealed in the accounting disclosure. Finally, as noted previously, inefficient verbal communication symbols (words) may cause uncertainty to continue; for instance, what, precisely, do "good," "satisfactory," and similar notions mean? Accounting disclosures seek to minimize it, but this type of *communications uncertainty* will always exist.

Subject to the three foregoing limitations to uncertainty-reduction efforts, the task of accounting disclosures is to reduce a decision maker's doubt or uncertainty as to which act to perform. Accordingly, two information concepts must be noted for future reference, as follows:

1. The amount of information
2. The value of information

As to the amount of information, it has been established previously that the greater the uncertainty of a decision maker, the greater the average amount of information that could be provided by telling him what to do. The following two propositions indicate the relevance of this condition to the communication aspects of accounting disclosures:

1. The greater the decision-making uncertainty, the greater the opportunity for the message sender (accountant) to transmit more information.
2. The greater the uncertainty of the decision maker, the better his "reading" of messages (accounting disclosures). This is based on the assumption that the greater the decision maker's need for information, the greater is his sensitivity to and interest in information in accounting disclosures.

As to the value of information, the implication is that it is not so much the amount of information, which merely reduces decision-making uncertainty, as it is the value of the information, which provides for decision-maker want satisfaction, that increases the decision-maker's capacity to "read" accounting disclosures.

"NOISE" IN ACCOUNTING DISCLOSURES

The foregoing propositions provide broad guidance in transmitting accounting disclosures, but there is more to the communication process than this. The accountant still faces the problem of avoiding outside interferences with his communication process. When an opportunity exists to provide a large amount of information, it is important that the accounting message get through. Using the term "noise" to refer to all the distractions that might interfere with the reception in the mind of the decision maker of appropriate parts of the accounting message or data base, accounting disclosures must be so designed that the information loss due to noise in the communication is minimized. Illustrative of the noise that interferes with the effectiveness of accounting disclosures are the following:

1. Misunderstanding of the meaning of symbols
2. Tendency for the message receiver to let his mind wander and thus not sense the meaning of the message
3. Physical destruction or loss of the message
4. Tendency for external distractions, such as misinformation from other sources, to distort the message receiver's acceptance of the accounting disclosure
5. Different background of message sender and message receiver, so that different inferences and predictions are made from the same accounting disclosures
6. Frustrated mental condition of the decision maker, arising from the following five causes of conflict in an organization:
    a. Abuse of exercise of power
    b. Exploitation of people
    c. Development of subcultures, ethnic and otherwise
    d. Disappointment of losers
    e. Inequality of opportunity

Other illustrations of noise in the accounting-disclosure process undoubtedly exist and probably should be specified when a specific accounting-disclosure system is to be developed. Whatever their nature, the accounting-communication problem is to reduce or eliminate the noises associated with accounting disclosures.

Noise can be reduced by inserting redundancy into accounting disclosures. On the assumption that disclosing the same bit of information more than once in the same message will increase the probability that the message will be retrieved by the information user, redundancy is indeed an effective way to fight noise in messages. There are several ways to introduce redundancy into accounting disclosures:

1. Adding a "highlights" section to the disclosure
2. Supplementing the numerical report with a graph, bar chart, or other pictorial representation of the information
3. Including summarizations and subtotals frequently in the accounting-disclosure statement
4. Including verbal comment, such as parts of the president's report in the annual report of companies, on various aspects of an accounting-disclosure statement.

INFORMATION QUALITY: A TRANSMISSION DEVICE

The proposition that the communication of accounting information is improved by improving the quality of the information seems to be the implicit assumption of most accounting research. The implication is that improvement in quality alone will improve communications. As previously noted, however, an improvement in the quality of accounting information assumes a knowledge about the uncertainty condition of decision makers that may not be available to the accountant. Particularly is this so in the case of those accounting disclosures directed to the general public. About the best that can be done is to return to the problem of value in general, and assume the quality and hence communication of accounting information can be improved by knowing the general nature of value—a most involved notion. John Dewey has pointed out that views on the nature of value in general range from the belief that values are but emotional epithets or ejaculations, to the contention that a priori, necessary, standardized, rational values are the principles upon which art, science, and morals depend for their validity.[8] Ambiguity of linguistic expressions purporting to designate distinctive value-facts also contribute to the confusion surrounding the notion of value. For example, the word *value* is used as a verb and as a noun. If things have value, or the property of value, apart from connection with any activity, *value* is a noun. If things have value because they are the object of a certain kind of activity, *value* is a verb.

---

[8] John Dewey, *Theory of Valuation* (Chicago: University of Chicago Press, 1939), pp. 4–66.

Current theories of value imply that value means "to enjoy" in the sense of receiving pleasure or gratification from something, or "to enjoy" in the active sense of concurring in an activity and its outcome. Also, there are variations in the status of value expression. Thus, one finds that (1) *value* means something "good for," or useful, or (2) *value* means something "good in itself," or that (3) "pleasant" and "gratifying" are the first-rank value expressions.

Other views of value include Laswell's identification of the eight basic values: power (participation in the making of decisions), wealth (access to goods and services), well-being (bodily and psychic integrity), enlightenment (finding and spreading of knowledge), skill (acquiring and using of dexterities), respect (social-class position), affection (friendship and sex), and rectitude (morality).[9] Charles W. Morris, in a more expansive mood, suggested thirteen varieties of values.[10] Out of the mist surrounding the term *value* emerges the dim outline of a basic motivating force directly causing both individual and organizational activities. The nature of this force is so obscure that it provides little direction for improving the communication of accounting disclosures by improving their quality. A more realistic approach would be to designate the audience for whom the disclosure is intended and develop communication devices suitable for transmitting accounting information for that audience. Clearly the notion of a general-purpose accounting disclosure to all people for all situations for all times poses an impossible communication problem and might have to be abandoned. Even when it is viewed as a data base from which different users extract different information, the notion that one public accounting disclosure can serve everyone is suspect. Different data bases are needed for different types of purposes.

COMMUNICATION GUIDELINES

The haziness of the concept of perceived value is the main reason that attention must be directed to the communication aspects of accounting disclosures. The vagueness of the concept of perceived value, coupled with the difficulty of ever measuring the general value of something, practically precludes any effort to improve the quality of accounting information to the level where quality alone would assure effective communication of the accounting information. Since it is not possible to

[9] Harold D. Laswell, *Power and Personality* (New York: Viking, 1966), p. 17.
[10] Charles W. Morris, *Varieties of Human Value* (Chicago: University of Chicago Press, 1956), p. 1.

make decision makers so sensitive to accounting disclosures that they will "read" the disclosures accurately and completely, one must turn to the development of an organized system for improving the transmission of accounting information.

The American Accounting Association's *Statement of Basic Accounting Theory* suggested five guidelines for the communication of accounting information, dealing with the following topics:

1. Appropriateness to expected use
2. Disclosure of significant relationships
3. Inclusion of environmental information
4. Uniformity of practice within and among entities
5. Consistency of practices through time [11]

Various other proposals have been set forth in recent years. The inference is that the traditional view, that the quality of information could be improved to the point where quality alone would assure effective transmission of accounting data, seems to be giving way to more direct communication means. Resort to developments in motivation is rather common as it is recognized that accounting disclosures are basically stimuli that influence directly or indirectly, as information available in data bases, the actions of decision makers. The study of the communication aspects of accounting disclosures must turn to psychological studies.

The realization that accounting disclosures are motivational devices and should be presented according to psychological studies is based in part on the assumption that accountants know better than the decision makers the information needed. It implies that the decision makers should be motivated by accounting disclosures to take proper action. Because of unresolved ethical aspects of such a view of disclosures, it seems reasonable to suggest that wide research and study of this aspect of accounting disclosures be given less emphasis until more is known as to what is a "good" or "proper" data base or information for decision makers.

Abandonment of the psychological base for the communication aspects of accounting disclosure, as user data bases, leaves only the possibility of personalized multidisclosures as a means for improving communications. The underlying assumption of personalized multidisclosures is that one accounting data bank can be stored in the memory of a large computer, or in some type of easily accessible library or ledger, from

---

[11] *A Statement of Basic Accounting Theory* (Evanston, Ill.: American Accounting Association, 1966), p. 14.

which individual decision makers can extract needed information quickly without recourse to accounting statements. This development is typically referred to as an information storage and retrieval system.

As management information systems expand and grow in size, it seems reasonable to assume that technological means will become available whereby all interested decision makers (investors, employees, customers, suppliers, and the like) will have access to computer screen displays and can call for information as needed. In this context, the communication aspects of accounting disclosures are closely tied to developments in home television, telephones, computers, and display units. In such a system, the psychological aspects of accounting disclosures as user data bases may tend to become less important as motivational devices. But the psychological aspects of human communication in transferring an image in the mind of a message sender to the mind of the message receiver will always be with accounting. Under a computer-based communication system, the greater responsibility for the clarity of the individual accounting disclosure may rest with the message receiver rather than with the message-sending accountant.

The implication of the foregoing analysis of the communication aspects of accounting disclosures is that a great increase in accounting data will have to be collected, stored, and made available on a continuous basis for transmission. An examination of the scope of such data is the subject matter of the next chapter.

REFERENCES

ARANGUREN, J. L., *Human Communication*. London: Weidenfeld and Nicholson, 1967.

CHERRY, COLIN, *On Human Communication*. Cambridge, Mass.: M.I.T. Press, 1966.

CHURCHMAN, C. WEST, *Prediction and Optimal Decision*. Englewood Cliffs, N.J.: Prentice-Hall, 1961.

JOLLEY, J. L., *Data Study*. New York: McGraw-Hill, 1968.

MARGENAU, HENRY, *The Nature of Physical Reality*. New York: McGraw-Hill, 1950.

MASLOW, ABRAHAM H., *Motivation and Personality*. New York: Harper & Row, 1954.

MORRIS, CHARLES, *Signification and Significance*. Cambridge, Mass.: M.I.T. Press, 1964.

WHISLER, THOMAS L., *Information Technology and Organization Change*. Belmont, Calif.: Wadsworth, 1970.

PART TWO

THE CONCEPTUAL ISSUES

CHAPTER FOUR

The Scope of
Accounting Disclosures

Chapter 2 supported the proposition that accounting disclosures will have to be expanded if the accounting profession is to maintain its relative role in society. In this chapter, specific aspects of the general philosophy of expansion are examined. It is recognized that accounting disclosures can be expanded by increasing the types of users reading accounting reports as data bases; enlarging the quantity of the disclosures to permit uses of accounting for additional purposes; expanding the type of data and thus including new types of data in accounting statements; improving and increasing the measurement tools used to develop more precise accounting data; developing data more relevant to decision makers' needs, thus increasing the quality of the data in accounting reports; and creating new accounting data-transmission devices and methods.

When efforts are undertaken to examine the appropriate scope of the various features of accounting disclosures, it is imperative that means be developed for sensing the essence of the problems. The development of appropriate sensing of disclosure needs requires the ability to perceive well. This involves a familiarity with the nature of perception and its relation to accounting data. Viewing accounting as a corporate information system is an effective way to remove unrecognized barriers to the expansion of accounting disclosures. The chapter points to the broad problems involved.

Justification for this broad framework for examining the scope of accounting disclosures rests on the belief that ". . . what is most needed today are new realizations about man's place in the universe, a new sense of life, a new pride in the importance of being human, a new anticipation of the enlarged potentialities of mind, a new joyousness in the possibility for essential human unity, and a new determination to keep this planet from becoming uninhabitable." [1]

Sporadic in time of occurrence but consistent in direction, the scope of accounting disclosures has been expanding in the United States since 1900. Initially unaware of the importance of disclosure to shareholders and the public, and subsequently concerned that disclosures might aid competitors, managers initiated disclosure practices slowly. But investor demand for information, coupled with public doubts that nondisclosure implied questionable company activities, encouraged expansion of its scope. Slowly disclosure practices expanded in scope and in quality, and the advent of the 1933 and 1934 securities acts resulted in a quantum advance. Attestation by certified public accountants increased and the general reliability of disclosures became commonplace; subsequently, the American Institute of Certified Public Accountants took various actions to improve their quality by supporting principles of disclosures. Currently, all segments of society appear to be insisting on an expansion in the scope of accounting disclosures and to many it appears that another quantum expansion is in the offing. As a consequence, a broad overview of the problem is appropriate, and a detailed examination of the various aspects of accounting disclosures may be fruitful.

Any endeavor to describe and prescribe the scope of accounting disclosures must necessarily be limited by a selection of the characteristics to be covered. In terms of relevance to the current needs of the profession, the following characteristics seem to be worthy of discussion:

1. The users to be supplied information
2. The uses to which the disclosures are directed
3. The type of information to be provided
4. The measurement techniques to be used
5. The quality of the information disclosed
6. The disclosure devices used

SCOPE OF USERS

Traditionally, the users of accounting disclosures have been described as investors, creditors, management, and the general public. Although it has been generally recognized that there are various levels of

---

[1] Norman Cousins, "Environment and the Quality of Life," *Saturday Review,* March 7, 1970, p. 47.

management, with the result that a variety of management reports are generated, the assumption has been that investors as a class and creditors as a class are slightly separate but each a homogeneous group of individuals. Yet financial analysts tell us that some investors are interested in security, while others are risk takers; that some are interested in liquidity, while others seek growth; and that some are very much ill-informed, while others are highly sophisticated. Creditors, too, range from those with short-term interests, where cash position is important, to those with long-range commitments. The implication is that accounting disclosures need to be directed more specifically to the various types of users.

The active general-public users, including labor unions, students, economists, management scientists, governments, environmentalists, and others interested in various aspects of business activity, have been the most rapidly growing group in recent years. In large part, this unusual growth reflects the belief that the role of the large corporation in society is growing in importance. The information needs of this broad diverse group of users cannot be ignored if the free-enterprise system is to continue its development. If such information needs are not supplied, government—responding to public political pressure—may have to assume responsibility for greater control. In fact, the lag by the profession in providing appropriate disclosures to small investors in the pre-1930 period may have contributed in part to government requirements for disclosure, as enforced by the Securities and Exchange Commission, and to the emergence of the profession of financial analysts who interpret the accounting disclosures to users. The implication is that accountants and managers may have to recognize the general public users of accounting disclosures and realize the inadequacy of the traditional view that public accounting disclosures are directed to existing shareholders.

SCOPE OF USES

The typical layman's assumption regarding the function and use of accounting disclosures is that they help shareholders decide if and when to buy and sell specific shares of stock. Furthermore, the view prevails that the accounting disclosure is confined to the annual report. Some laymen, unfamiliar with corporate annual reports, assume that the primary use of accounting disclosures is for income tax assessment purposes. Also, there prevails the views that accounting disclosures merely reveal how well off an accounting entity is economically and how well it performed economically over a period of time. In this latter context, there is no assumption that accounting disclosures are decision-oriented at all. They are considered a mere display of "facts" that are to be used to meet a psychological desire or need to know a firm's progress and status.

Without disparagement of these views, it seems more realistic to view accounting disclosures as means for coordinating, planning, and controlling entity actions by outside agencies, management, or persons associated with the entity in any capacity from employee to shareholder. The growing use of capital budgeting suggests that the use of accounting disclosures for management planning purposes has grown rapidly in recent years, although the use of accounting disclosures for control have also expanded extensively. The uses for internal (management) control seem to have advanced more completely than those for external (government and shareholders) control, which are still somewhat unsophisticated. Emerging as a potential use of accounting disclosures is the direction and control of actions in such areas as unemployment and national well-being.

The entire issue of the social responsibilities of business portends sudden and unusual disclosure demands on accounting. Suggestive of this growing demand is the statement in the 1968 annual report of Union Carbide that "Union Carbide is deeply concerned with the social, economic, and political forces that shape the environment in which it operates. . . ." Whether or not business is called upon to formally and publicly disclose its efforts and successes in the social-responsibility area, the insistent question, "To whom is the large corporation responsible?" may be expected to inspire business firms to seek outside certification and disclosure of their social contributions. Professional accountants must anticipate that business will turn to accounting for such disclosures. Related disclosures may also be needed: For example, the notion has also been proposed that aggregation of accounting disclosures of several companies can be used for coordinating national economic activity.

Internally, accounting disclosures have been used extensively as corrective control devices, to correct activities that vary from predetermined plans. More recently, there has been the tendency to use accounting disclosures as preventive control devices, to motivate appropriate actions before variances occur. Illustrative of this development is the accounting disclosure of budgetary allowances in such detail that recipients of such disclosures are specifically informed regarding desired actions.

The apparent conclusion from the foregoing recitation of uses of accounting disclosures is that uses are being expanded. A number of accountants believe further expansion of uses is appropriate.

SCOPE OF ACCOUNTING-INFORMATION TYPES

When one thinks of types of accounting information, the first thought that comes to mind is that the scope is confined to the monetary type of information. The problem with this view is that, given sufficient measurement leeway, such a restriction on accounting information types is not particularly meaningful. Because our society is so much an exchange society, almost any activity can be assigned a monetary amount. As a current example, there is now discussion in accounting literature regarding means for placing a monetary value on the social resources used by a company.

The notion that accounting disclosures should be restricted to transaction-type information, the second conventional characteristic of accounting data, requires a definition of a transaction before this is a meaningful restriction. According to a certain line of thinking, depreciation is not a transaction; yet it is a normal accounting disclosure. Accruals in general are contrary to the conventional view of transactions, and accruals are a growing part of accounting disclosures. In general, the definitional task is so involved that the transaction concept is an inadequate means for placing a restriction on the scope of accounting information.

If accounting disclosures are not to be confined to certain monetary measures and may exceed the bounds of the typical transaction concept, the scope of the types of information to be included in accounting disclosures remains open-ended at the present time. The standards of relevance, quantifiability, freedom from bias, and verifiability have been proposed as the appropriate constraining criteria.

Given a broad view of the scope of the types of information that may be included in accounting disclosures, it seems desirable to propose that accounting disclosures be expanded to include external data, as well as internal data, relevant to firm activities. The following scope of the type of external information has been proposed:

> In the area of external information, the accountant might well begin to collect data on general economic conditions, developments in the industries, actions of competitors, and actions of government bodies. In general, there seem to be four types of external data which the accountant could collect and process. First, data on general economic conditions prevailing in the country. This could include data on national economic activities as reflected in various indices of production, gross national product, or price levels. It should include information on interest rates, prevailing loan practices of banks, and general costs of financing a business entity. It should also cover general labour conditions, unemployment rates, educational levels, types of personnel available, and the country's available resources—for example, total forest and mineral resources, the forthcoming year's farm output, and general resources to be available for use in the near future by all of society.
> Second, data on all types of government activities should be collected to reveal matters such as political developments, particularly as reflected in various sampling polls. In fact, the accountant might assume responsibility for evaluating the validity or accuracy of various polls. Included in

this type of external data would be statistics and reports of a quantitative nature on foreign affairs, trade agreements, and political and economic developments in other countries, together with some indication of proposed government action. Data on government regulatory actions, legislatures, and administrative rulings and court decisions influencing future activities of the firm should also be included.

The third type of external information would concern industry developments. It would include data on technological developments having a potential impact on the firm's production and distribution techniques, data on the relative role of the industry in the total economy and changes in it, cost ratios in general prevailing in the industry, and similar statistics to indicate how well the individual firm is performing relative to the total industry in which it operates. Also included would be reports on matters such as the general efforts of the industry to combat the inroads of another industry.

The fourth type of external data would be on the actions of competitors and others in the basic competitive environment within which the firm operates. This would include data on actions taken by competitors, such as personnel hiring policies, salary scales, sales and advertising policies, number of customers. It would include data from surveys of customers indicating their reactions to company products, policies, and general methods of operation.[2]

The external data are necessary in order to understand the meaning of the internal data. For example, an increase in annual income as measured by internal data takes on different degrees of significance if external data indicate general economic conditions are good or bad, or that the federal government is or is not subsidizing activities in which the company is engaged.

In substance, a review of the types of information to be included as accounting disclosures suggests that while accounting is not now a comprehensive business information system for the firm, it could become one. As a comprehensive computer-based business information system, accounting would encompass:

1. Routine electronic data-processing systems for lower-level operations
2. Management information systems, to provide appropriate information to management
3. Corporate public-information systems, to provide for public disclosure of corporate activities of all types

The types of information to be included in such a comprehensive information system might tend to exceed the well-established scope of quantifiability as a boundary to accounting information. There are

2 Norton M. Bedford, "Expanding Opportunities in Accounting Practice," *The Accountants' Journal* (New Zealand), May 1970, pp. 362–63.

both technical and efficiency, as well as professional attitudinal, reasons indicating that any expansion of accounting information to include nonquantitative data is probably undesirable. The inference is that accounting-type information of a quantitative nature would have to be coordinated with the nonquantitative information that would be provided by other groups. That is, accounting should be considered as a distinct type of quantitative information in the total business information system.

SCOPE OF MEASUREMENT TECHNIQUES

Once we have restricted accounting disclosures to quantitative data, the issue immediately arises as to the scope of the measurement technology to be used in developing accounting disclosures. Traditionally, the accounting methodology has been largely confined to arithmetic. Undoubtedly, arithmetic will remain a basic measurement technique, but there is reason to believe that the scope of the discipline should be expanded to include probability measures, algebraic analysis, various management-science techniques, and numerical analysis, as well as computer simulation. There is no empirical evidence that users will be satisfied with a formula that provides a single-valued average for depreciation, for uncollectible estimates, for pension-fund liability, for loss reserves, and for many other valuations when they become aware that probability measures can be added to the accounting disclosure. Nor does it seem reasonable to assume that simple extrapolation of a break-even chart will be used for forecasting purposes when various management-science models can provide more reliable projections. The rapidity with which a computer can test alternative proposals for action on a simulated model of the firm suggests that this measurement technique will be used to supplement many procedures. If one accepts the technological imperative that what can be done will be done, an expansion in the scope of accounting-measurement techniques may be expected as accountants endeavor to provide the desired information.

The expansion in scope of accounting-measurement techniques to provide the needed disclosures will apparently have its origin in education, where the limitations of a single-valued arithmetic measure have become evident to students familiar with probability. It has become quite apparent to students and others that monthly depreciation expense, for example, is a probability and should be so measured, for the inevitable error of a single valuation may otherwise come as something of a later surprise in the form of an unusual gain or loss. Many executives now on a bonus plan that is tied to the income measurement are learning that extraordinary charges owing to incorrect depreciation in the past can significantly distort their annual bonuses. Although these executives seldom call for a reallocation of past bonuses from former to current executives by a retroactive adjustment of depreciation charges, they could have been advised of the possibility of loss, by probability measures of annual depreciation. With the computer, large-scale information processing has become feasible, and the tendency prevails for students and researchers to attempt to include as accounting disclosures additional information supplementary to that now provided by accounting measures.

Broadly speaking, there seems no reason to restrict the scope of accounting disclosures to any measurement techniques. There may, of course, be certain communication problems that would preclude the disclosure of information so developed. But this would be a quality restriction, to be discussed in the next section.

SCOPE OF QUALITY OF INFORMATION DISCLOSED

Materiality is one of the most difficult of all practical accounting-disclosure problems. Typically, a material disclosure is defined as one that would influence the actions of its recipient. An immaterial bit of news would be accounting information that would not motivate action by a user, regardless of the way it was disclosed. But such a conception of materiality is not an operational guideline, for how can one know all the decision situations that various users might encounter? Efforts to make the concept operational are frequently confusing. For example, paragraph 21 of Opinion No. 9 by the Accounting Principles Board states, "In determining materiality, items of similar nature should be considered in the aggregate. Dissimilar items should be considered individually; however, if they are few in number, they should be considered in the aggregate." Aside from the lack of any explanation as to why the rule will improve the operational content of the materiality concept, one wonders whether the number of items, rather than their amount, is really a suitable guideline for aggregation, and in what respect items must be similar to permit aggregation. In view of the confusion surrounding the term, a broader approach to the overall problem of effective disclosure may be appropriate.

Essentially, materiality is related to the quality of accounting information, and this means its reliability. The more reliable the information, *ceteris paribus,* the higher its quality. Illustrative of the different quality of accounting disclosures would be unaudited financial statements as contrasted with audited statements. *Quality* also refers to the way information is disclosed.

In general, for public accounting reports, the implicit assumption has been that alternative accounting principles may be permitted because they would not motivate an alternative decision or action and would not represent different quality information. Currently, however, there exists a rather strong belief that this implicit assumption does tend to reduce the overall quality of accounting disclosures. The need then arises for a standard for the quality of accounting disclosures. Should the endeavor be to provide disclosures of such high quality, at a higher cost, that no user of the disclosure could be misled, or should a 10, 20, or 50 percent misinterpretation by users of accounting disclosures be acceptable? Whatever the past quality of accounting disclosures has been—and the favorable reputation of a CPA certification indicates it has been of rather high quality—the growing complexity and resulting precision needed in society suggests that constant improvement in disclosures is required just to maintain the same level of information quality. Illustrative of the growing efforts to improve the accuracy and reliability of public accounting disclosures are the *Statements of Auditing Procedure* by the Committee on Auditing Procedures of the AICPA. Theoretical work is needed to support the statements. Control devices are needed to enforce compliance with them.

Quality also refers to the relevance of the disclosure to user needs, but this presumes a knowledge of the needs of specific users. The SEC materiality requirement is relevant to this aspect of the quality of public accounting disclosures. As set forth in *Regulation S-X*, this requirement is as follows:

> The term "material," when used to qualify a requirement for the furnishing of information as to any subject, limits the information required to those matters as to which an average prudent investor ought reasonably to be informed before purchasing the security registered.[3]

For internal management purposes, the quality of accounting disclosures is judged in terms of the positive contribution of accounting disclosures to decision making. While quality for public reporting is improved by reducing the possibility of misleading a user, quality for internal purposes is directly correlated with its effectiveness in aiding the "right" decision. There are several reasons for the positive objective of improving decision making in the internal area, as contrasted with the minimization of the negative information in public disclosures. The

[3] U.S. Securities and Exchange Commission, *Regulation S-X*, Paragraph 1.02.

main result of the two attitudes is that accountants place greater emphasis on relevance and less on objectivity for managerial reporting than they do for public reporting. Objectivity dominates public disclosure.

Overall, there appears to be limited information to provide a definitive proper scope for the quality of accounting information. In terms of accuracy and consistency, over time and among different companies, there seems to be general agreement that lower-quality information should be eliminated from the scope of accounting information. In terms of materiality and verifiability, the objective of relevance sometimes requires that lower standards of objectivity be applied. Thus, attempts to disclose the value of human resources may require that highly relevant, though somewhat subjective rather than objective, measures be used.

SCOPE OF DISCLOSURE DEVICES

Changes in methods for disclosing accounting information are slow in being realized. Even though there have been elaborate studies showing the usefulness of graphs, charts, pictorials, and the use of multimedia for disclosure, disclosure by means of numerical reports predominates. There is a growing inclination to use an executive information room where slides, computer terminals, and other display methods can provide information at the time it is needed for internal management decisions, but this is an exception to the basic pattern.

In general, there appears to be a slight tendency for the conventional disclosure device of numerical reports to be used less by all types of users. Other types of disclosures, such as extracted or abbreviated reports drawn from the basic reports, are gaining in favor. In this context, the conventional types of reports tend more and more to represent something of a data base for a variety of other analyses and reports.

In a prescriptive sense, the communication aspects of accounting disclosures appear to be in need of considerable improvement. Yet the area does not have great appeal for researchers. The limited evidence available may be sufficient to indicate that the scope of accounting disclosure methods should be expanded. It is interesting to note that a number of companies now publish their annual reports in newspapers. Also, the chart room and the computerized information-display room are used for internal purposes. But the study of such topics as the role of color in disclosure devices, the impact of different words for disclosure, and the entire psychology of transmitting information seems to be lacking in the area of accounting-disclosure devices.

By way of a summary of the various features of accounting-disclosure issues, the matrix display in Table 4–1 may be useful.

TABLE 4–1

Scope of Disclosures

Disclosure Characteristic	Current Situation	Current Trends	Future Possibilities
1. Users	Shareholders, creditors, managers, and general public	Interest groups of shareholders, creditors, managers, and general public	Greatly expanded; general public groups
2. Uses	To evaluate economic progress, enable tax assessments, and aid investment decisions	To plan company activities, motivate control activities, and improve investment decisions	To provide for inter-company coordination, meet specific user information needs, and develop public confidence in firm activities
3. Types of Information	Transaction-based monetary valuations of internal activities of the firm	Accruals and motivational valuations of internal activities	Internal and external data to reveal both internal activities and the environmental setting of the internal activities of a socioeconomic nature
4. Measurement Techniques	Arithmetic and the bookkeeping system	Expanding into computer-based storage, probability measures, and limited mathematical analyses	Further expansion into the total management-science area
5. Quality of Disclosures	Excellent in terms of past needs, although the reliability of different items varies	Attempts to narrow the use of alternative principles and define the materiality concept	Improved relevance for specific decisions without reducing reliability of accounting disclosures
6. Disclosure Devices	Numerical reports such as balance sheet, income statement, and various managerial-structured reports	Charts, information rooms, and computer printouts as supplements to structured numerical reports	Multimedia disclosures based on the psychology of human communications

OVERVIEW OF ACCOUNTING DISCLOSURES

The preceding discussion has been concentrated on the scope of specific disclosure issues. It is necessary also to view the scope of accounting disclosures from a social point of view. In terms of society, the basic nature of the problem of the scope of accounting disclosures is the problem of the goals of society and the cost of attaining these goals. As of now, no factual information is available to refute such well-publicized criticisms as the dramatic but unsubstantiated assertion that a large proportion of the goods and services produced by our economic system comprises trivial gadgets and fashions. Nor is information available to support optimistic assertions that business is leading American society into a level of civilization greater than any ever before known to man. Apparently, American society has very little information to answer the questions Americans want answered. As a result, not only are the goals of the American economic system being questioned, but also the cost of attaining the selected goals appears to many to be well beyond the value of the goals realized. Information is needed to support or refute these assertions. It is not now available, since appropriate measures have never been calculated. As a result, we do not know such things as the amount of noise produced by our civilization—by the airplane, automobile, furnace, trains, machinery, radio, and television—as well as all the other social costs of that civilization, many of them unmeasured and unrecognized. It is contended that forces in our society have polluted the air, water, and soil; destroyed man's privacy; stifled his creative urges; reduced his capacity to enjoy life; and generally emphasized his machine-like capacity to the neglect of his humane senses. To many, it seems apparent that American civilization has problems. To others, American civilization has great opportunities that are not being realized.

Accounting is closely related to these social problems and opportunities and to an extent may be partly responsible for them. That is, performing a quantitative information function, accountants have measured and disclosed the private costs of the consumer-selected choices and have ignored or discounted certain overall elements of social costs and benefits. As a result, accounting must bear some responsibility both for opportunities not realized and for any loss of dignity of human life that is due to overall misdirected economic activity or to the overcrowding, pollution, transportation failures, crime, and inadequate housing and education that may have resulted. It is becoming increasingly apparent that with changes in society, the conventional accounting disclosures cover a smaller proportion of those activities that affect the quality of human life.

This is not to say that accounting has been an ineffective institution for society. To the contrary, any objective review of the socioeconomic development of the United States to which accounting has contributed so much must be favorable. People in the United States appear to have more of their wants satisfied than did their fathers and grandfathers. But each society at each period of time has its own kind of values, and historically, as one set of values is realized by a society, it moves on to new values. It is the current shift to new social values that may make conventional accounting disclosures appear to some to be out of place with the social disclosures needed to guide society. The implication is that accounting disclosures must change constantly, for ours is an evolving, renovating society that has avoided stagnation for two hundred years because professions and individuals have adjusted to new values. An appropriate adjustment in the scope of accounting disclosures may now be the need of the land.

The fact seems to be that the Industrial Revolution gave to man a productive capacity that, due to a lack of information for decision-making purposes, he seems unable to handle well. A significant increase in the quality of information might enable him to deal with the complexity introduced by the use of the Industrial Revolution machinery. Since accounting is a major decision-making information system for socioeconomic society, the inference is that the scope of accounting disclosures, from a societal point of view, must be expanded. Using the computer as an extension of the human brain, decision makers may be expected to start calling for a great improvement in the quality of accounting information.

Sensitivity to this need to expand the scope of accounting disclosures has resulted in a number of proposals for change. Mattessich, for example, suggests replacement of the conventional view of the scope of accounting with a broader conception, for the following reasons:

A. There is a need to relate recent achievements of managerial science and economics to accounting because:
   1. Accounting concepts and methods are being applied to a variety of micro- and macro-organizations.
   2. Recent technological, mathematical, and scientific developments are going to have an even greater impact on accounting, and accountants need to be aware of this "danger" in order to meet it with an evolutionary rather than a revolutionary solution.
   3. The present state of accounting is heavily criticized because:
      a. Accounting income is not an objective value for evaluating managerial performance.
      b. Accounting theory is authoritarian and not of a scientific-hypothetical character.
      c. Accounting teaching emphasizes procedures and does not relate new scientific achievements to accounting knowledge.

B. There is a need for a new approach in teaching accounting because:
   1. Accounting will "fall behind" other academic disciplines unless it brings in the new information brought about by research, discovery, and invention.

       a. Accounting should deal with such topics as the idea of "measurement."

       b. Basic scientific questions underlying accounting should be studied.

  2. Recent reports on business education indicate a need for more of an analytical approach to all subjects. This calls for an inclusion in accounting of:

       a. Sophisticated mathematical and statistical tools.

       b. More quantitative-analytical thinking.

       c. A synchronization with organization theory through a knowledge of modern logic, philosophy of science, measurement theory, behavior science, and system simulation, which will tear accounting loose from old views.

C. There is a need for a general theory of accounting because:

  1. There is a promise of efficiency and economy in the use of the scientific method, which includes:

       a. The observation of particular cases.

       b. Their description and measurement.

       c. The extraction of their common features.

       d. The formulation of the generalized case.

       e. The application of the generalized conception to new but related events.

  2. There exist a number of accounting systems which need to be tied together.

  3. There is a need to reexamine the traditional language of accounting.

  4. There is a need to drop the "multipurpose" accounting report in favor of a number of "monopurpose" reports which need to be tied together more fully.

D. There is a need for an analytic-behavior interpretation of accounting because:

  1. Accounting as a discipline has been criticized because it is descriptive and classificatory, has no analytic content, and employs no empirical hypothesis.

  2. There is an increased interest in the formalization of decision-making processes.

  3. There is a need for criteria for determining when a given accounting model (system) is optimal or even satisfactory.

E. There is a need to improve accounting practice because every system of measurement, serving not purely theoretical investigations but purposes of everyday life, constitutes a compromise of three conflicting aspects: Accuracy, Economy, Versatility. Accounting practice is deficient in each area because:

  1. Not only is the degree of accuracy of many accounting measures very low, but frequently accountants are operating in a vacuum of reliability which does not provide any error measurement at all.

2. Accuracy has been sacrificed for economy in the past and electronic data processing reduces the relative importance of economy.
3. Monopurpose accounting systems will reduce the versatility of many accounting measurements.

In addition, varied goals and goal clarification call for more relevant and practical decision-making accounting measurements.[4]

One response to such calls for an expansion of the scope of accounting disclosures is the emergence of social accounting. Social accounting is a somewhat new method of accounting that goes beyond the conventional data-recording process and attempts to measure the way people perceive, interpret, and react. It is based on the assumption that changes in perception and interpretation, as well as changes in the conditions themselves, can be quantified systematically by uniform "social indicators."

Recognizing that the scope of accounting should probably be expanded merely opens the door for expansion. When one turns to the question of what additional concepts accountants should include in their discipline, one is really entertaining the issue of what accountants ought to perceive in the real world as significant and relevant information to decision makers. The development of an effective perception process, as a result, becomes a requirement for the expansion of the scope of accounting disclosures.

THE ISSUE OF THE QUALITY OF LIFE

The fundamental problem facing the accounting profession is to perceive those activities that contribute to a higher quality of life. To the extent that economic activities tend to improve the quality of life, it appears that the accounting perception process is reasonably adequate. But there is now continuous discussion on the quality of life as it is reflected in human well-being. Concern for the ecological balance of the world, crime, health, and similar issues calls into question the accounting assumption that an economic perception is an adequate reflection of the quality of life. There seems to be a need for some type of a measure of human progress, as well as, or possibly overriding, the measures of economic progress. Currently, a number of indexes have been developed that purport to indicate changes in the quality of life. For example, the First National Bank of Minneapolis has proposed to measure ten com-

---

[4] R. Mattessich, *Accounting and Analytical Methods* (Homewood, Ill.: Richard D. Irwin, 1964), Chapter 1.

ponents that taken together would indicate the quality of life in the Minneapolis–St. Paul area. The components include such items as job opportunities, housing, and conditions of health.

Most of the indexes professing to measure the quality of life tend to measure instead several economic aspects of life, such as jobs, automobiles, television sets, and home ownership. Few include a measure of the value of leisure or such other intangible, noneconomic human needs as status, new knowledge, and the arts. Thus, even a perception that accounting should expand in scope to include measures of improvements in the quality of life is an imprecise perception. Also, quality of life is such a broad concept that any index or measure of it that would include both economic and noneconomic factors would be questioned by different groups. Only by a significant improvement in the accountant's capacity to perceive significant events can measures of changes in the quality of life be meaningful. Yet such seems to be the long-run goal society is now tending to assign to accountants.

MEANING OF ACCOUNTING PERCEPTION

If one accepts the existence of a possible need for accountants to study perceptual processes, it becomes necessary to establish a common meaning for the term. Clearly, perception has something to do with awareness. This is intuitive, since it makes sense that one perceives an object by being aware of its existence. But perception is more than just a mere feeling, for it also involves attaching a meaning, an understanding, a recognition, to the objects and conditions of which one becomes aware. The inference is that perception is an explicit recognition and understanding. For example, walking down a street in a large city talking to a friend, you may be subconsciously aware that large buildings are on both sides, but this is not perception, because you may not have explicitly recognized them. You are aware of the existence of the skyscrapers, in the sense that you know they are there; nevertheless, your awareness does not mean you have perceived them. Something more formal than awareness is necessary.

For accounting purposes, the following definition of perception may be appropriate: Perception is the process of recognizing and understanding the implications of goal-oriented stimuli. Consistent with this functional definition, the ultimate goals of developing accounting-perception criteria or ability are to provide for the recognition of every stimulus that is important to users, and to assign a meaning to the symbolic representation of the stimulus that is in direct correspondence to the underlying meanings present in or intended by the source emitting the stimulus.

The significance of such an accounting objective for the scope of accounting disclosures is this: The ability to recognize every stimulus that is important implies that the accountant perceiver must be sensitive to both user needs and his environmental surroundings. The ability also implies that the perceiver must be able to discern which stimuli are relevant and which are irrelevant to the high quality of life objective.

To recapitulate, perception is the process of recognizing user-oriented stimuli and attaching significance to them. The goal of an accountant perceiver should be to recognize all relevant stimuli and to interpret them accurately for different users.

The reaction of an accountant perceiver in attaching a meaning to what he perceives is also important. The fact is that the accountant may not record the meaning he attaches to the stimulus he has recognized. Although the behavior a perception elicits is fundamentally related to the perception itself, it is possible that the actual action taken may be totally distinct from the process of perception. For example, a person may recognize a threatening stimulus, realize it is threatening, and yet not respond to this threat. Such may be the situation when the perceiver "freezes." In any event, any normative study of perceptions should recognize that the actual action may vary from the normative responses that the perceptions should elicit.

General theories of accounting perception

Although there have developed a number of theories on perception, one can be encouraged by a number of observations that appear to be common to all of them. According to Bartley, eight generalizations are possible from these common observations.[5] Five of these appear to be relevant to accounting perceptions:

1. *Self-closedness and circularity.* This generalization is that an accounting perception includes many different elements that we almost subconsciously aggregate into one observation. For example, the many activities involved in the purchase of an asset are telescoped into one transaction. It is well supported that perceptual aggregates, regardless of their complexity, appear as definitely defined units.

2. *Interrelatedness, compounding, includingness.* This generalization is that the elements that compose the accounting aggregate of perception are interrelated and interdependent, as would be the case in the ordering, receiving,

[5] S. H. Bartley, *Principles of Perception* (New York: Harper & Row, 1969).

inspecting, and accepting of a purchased asset. The common observation of researchers is that the aggregate is made up of elements whose existences and actions affect one another in predictable ways. In fact, the generalization holds that perceived aggregates themselves can be joined or interrelated.

3. *Space and time building.* This generalization extends the theory from the "here" and "now" of the operation of self-closing aggregates to the space and time dimensions from which the aggregates are assembled. This generalization holds that any one accounting perception is related to past exposures to stimulus elements, past trials, and past learnings. Illustrative of this is the perception and accrual of estimated uncollectibles at the time a sale is made.

4. *Flexibility.* This generalization notes that perceptions are often subject to distortion, even though the human brain tends to provide order and stability by filling in the continuities between discrete events. Flexibility, however, exists along with this order and stability. For example, the accounting accrual of depreciation tends to provide order and stability by filling in the continuity between the acquisition and disposition dates of an asset, although there is, within limits, some flexibility afforded by permitting alternative depreciation methods. Limits are recognized by all psychological theories of perception that keep any continuity-created deformation within certain bounds. The transactionalists have shown, however, that these bounds within which flexible deformation can occur are very broad.

5. *Establishment and persistence of constant relationships.* This generalization states that perception involves the ability to perceive invariant relationships amid a flux of stimulations. That is, to perceive a chair from a distorted angle, or a sale from a sales slip, cash, or invoice, is to be aware of certain constant relationships among the parts of the thing observed. This perceptual constancy is a stabilizing principle that counterbalances the flexibility principle. Effective accounting perceptions depend heavily on this principle.

It is to be hoped that accountants will learn how to use such perception principles more effectively in the future and use them to enlarge the scope of accounting disclosures.

THE CORPORATE INFORMATION SYSTEM

Consideration of both specific characteristics of accounting disclosures and the overriding social and psychological aspects involved suggests a need for a substantial expansion in the scope of accounting disclosures at both the theory and practice levels. Social scientists are sensitive to this expansion need. Maslow asserted some time ago, "I am impressed again with the necessity, however difficult the job may be, of working out some kind of moral or ethical accounting scheme. . . ." [6] Later, he states, "I'm going to dictate sometime soon my thoughts on how stupid our present accounting systems are, because they leave out practically all the important personal, psychological, political, educational intangibles." [7] So great is the expansion needed that it has been suggested that accounting should be considered as the total organization information system. The statement assumes the existence of a computer-based information system, and the rapid development in the human capacity to use computers indicates that the assumption is not unreasonable.

As the corporate information system, accounting would be vastly expanded. Accounting disclosures would increase in number. Actually, accounting disclosures might take one of two forms:

1. A retrieval process in which the capacity to retrieve from a large integrated corporate data base would be the only limit to the scope of accounting disclosures. In this role, accounting disclosures would be limited only by the ability of the accountant to retrieve appropriate information and by the scope of the data base supporting the information system. Over time it seems that this would enable the scope of accounting disclosures to be broadened to the capacity of the computer used.

2. A hierarchical-directed reporting system in which the needs of specific users are supplied by specific-purpose accounting disclosures. This assumes a formal reporting system and is based on the fact that repetitive operating information is needed at regular time intervals.

Both the retrieval process, wherein disclosures are personal, individually retrieved information, and the specialized, directed reporting system, wherein the total information-disclosure system is a coordinated reporting system to meet alternative needs, are well beyond the current capacity of the accounting profession to implement. But they represent the ultimate end of the current trend of accounting-disclosure developments, and so they provide a guide or standard for evaluating specific proposals for expanding accounting disclosures. The most compelling implication is that for improvements in accounting disclosures, the general-purpose disclosure device will have to be expanded to provide different information for different purposes, or else resort to a series

[6] Abraham H. Maslow, *Eupsychian Management* (Homewood, Ill.: Richard D. Irwin, 1965), p. 59.

[7] *Ibid.*, p. 80.

of supplementary special disclosures for different users and uses. Implementation of these disclosure standards will require a data base substantially larger than the ledgers now supporting accounting disclosures.

THE CORPORATE DATA BASE

The size of the corporate data base is a very practical limitation to any conception of the proper scope of the accounting-disclosure system. Also, the data base is now generally decentralized throughout most companies and, of course, certain data useful only for special areas should be kept decentralized. But the duplication of data useful for several types of disclosures, often classified under different names, is costly and inefficient, and much of it probably should be centralized into one integrated data base, where it can be organized, expanded, and systematically disclosed by well-qualified accountants. In any event, any proposal for a significant expansion of the scope of accounting disclosures is not particularly meaningful until a suitable data base can be developed. In this respect, some of the work on management information systems and data theory might well be used to organize a computerized corporate data base.

Conceptually, both means and needs for an expansion of accounting disclosures are available. The feasibility of such an expansion has yet to be tested. Overall, it appears that the conceptual framework for expansion will serve as little more than a guide for specific trial-and-error approaches to a bit-by-bit expansion of accounting disclosures.

REFERENCES

BRAY, F. SEWELL, *The Accounting Mission.* Melbourne, Australia: Melbourne University Press, 1951.

CHAMBERS, R. J., "The Conditions of Research in Accounting," *Journal of Accountancy,* December 1960.

DEVINE, C. T., "Research Methodology and Accounting Theory Formation," *Accounting Review,* July 1960.

FIEBLEMAN, JAMES, "A Set of Postulates and a Definition for Science," *Philosophy of Science,* Vol. 15 (January 1948).

GRINKER, ROY R., SR., *Toward a Unified Theory of Human Behavior,* 2nd ed. New York, Basic Books, 1967.

KIRCHER, PAUL, "Theory and Research in Management Accounting," *Accounting Review,* January 1961, pp. 43–49.

LAZARFELD, P., ed., *Mathematical Thinking in the Social Sciences.* Beverly Hills, Calif.: Glencoe Press, 1954.

LITTLETON, A. C., *Structure of Accounting Theory*, Chapter 8. Urbana, Ill.: American Accounting Association, 1953.

NORTHROP, F. S. C., *Logic of the Sciences and the Humanities,* Chapters 1–6, 14, 21, 22, 24. New York: Macmillan, 1947.

WARD, A. DUDLEY, *Goals of Economic Life,* Chapters 2, 3, 10, 11, 12. New York: Harper & Row, 1953.

CHAPTER FIVE

The Standard of
Evidence

Standards or levels of evidence supporting accounting disclosures need to be publicly announced, because of the tendency to assume that accounting disclosures are 100 percent accurate, adequate, and appropriate. The traditional standard of "objective evidence" is imprecise and tends to preclude the inclusion of certain relevant information in accounting disclosures. The term "freedom from bias" reflects the intent of "objective evidence" and provides a means for indicating the level to which subjective observations are included in accounting disclosures. Upon analysis, it appears that users want objective evidence or information free from bias on the existence, time of occurrence, description of items involved, values assigned, and independency of the activity. This can be provided by developing new operational rules, to replace the traditional ones used to ensure objectivity in the form of such methods as acquisition costing, documentary evidence, and consistency.

Broadly, the standards or levels of evidence to be specified should indicate the type of evidence used to assure (1) freedom from bias, (2) relevance of the disclosure to user needs, and (3) "full disclosure" by management of the information it has. The need for the standard of evidence exists because "every experience is as such perfectly private to the percipient. No one can share his sensations with anybody else. Where then is the common or objective element? If it is some point or aspect of what is experienced that is common, why do we deny objectivity to some experiences and allow it to others? It is no answer to say that the act of experiencing, the mental part, is private and the object or thing common, because that does not solve the difficulty of delusions and dreams. Besides, it amounts only to saying that objects are objective, a proposition that sounds like a tautology, but it is not even true." [1]

The accounting endeavor to disclose significant information includes a "confirmation" process, to assure the accountant that his perception is correct and to assure the information user that the reported observation is accurate and unbiased. Conceptually, this confirmation process would involve taking a second or third look to confirm the perception or to validate the reported observation. Just as the traveler needs reassurance from road signs that he is on the right road, the accountant and information user seek reassurance that the information provided is relevant to their needs and is accurate. But 100 percent reassurance of accounting disclosures is never possible, because of the complexity of the endeavor; and the issue logically arises as to the proper standard or level of reassuring evidence required before observations or perceptions can qualify as accounting information. For example, the degree of evidence that can be provided of the realizable value of a fixed asset is frequently considered to be so low that realizable value should not be used as an accounting disclosure.

In the legal profession, rules of evidence exist that distinguish acceptable from unacceptable information in the courts, but no well-developed set of criteria of evidence exists to permit an evaluation of the admissability of data on the many alternative possible perceptions and observations that may be made by accountants. Evidence, of course, is to be distinguished from principles in that lack of evidence represents a constraint on the implementation of principles. Thus, while in principle a physical count should be made of inventories, evidence that the count was accurately made might be in the form of statistical sampling results, a recounting process, a rule-of-thumb verification, physical observation, or other criteria applicable in the circumstances.

There is a need for well-defined standards of evidence to support accounting disclosures. That is, if evidence is considered proof, there is a need to indicate the degree of proof supporting the implication that an accounting disclosure is accurate, adequate, and appropriate. In this sense, evidence is a means for indicating the degree of confidence in the accuracy and relevance one might attach to accounting disclosures. It is time for accountants to establish and announce to the public at large the standards of evidence supporting accounting disclosures. At the present

[1] A. D. Ritchie, *Scientific Method* (London: Routledge and Kegan Paul, Ltd., 1923).

time, the general public apparently believes decisions are based on accounting data's having a high degree of accuracy and relevance. Business decision makers are more aware of the tenuous nature of the relevance and accuracy of the data available for their decision problems, but they manage to operate with it. What many businessmen appear not to be aware of, however, is the extent of the error in much of the data they use. As a consequence, the accounting profession faces a problem, because both the degree of relevance and accuracy of accounting information is unknown and unspecified, and this bothers its users.

The simple fact is that accountants, unlike the natural scientists, have not paid sufficient attention to the accuracy of their measurements and their observations of activities. The nature of the accounting problem of accuracy is best revealed by reference to Figure 5–1.

A careful interpretation of the diagram suggests that the conceptual accounting task of perceiving or being aware of the relevant activities in the real world is an awesome undertaking. Add to this the difficulty of observing accurately the phenomena perceived, and the great difficulty of the accounting task of collecting, analyzing, and disclosing information on significant past and expected activities becomes apparent. To view the accounting task as anything less than the total task, however, is to reduce it to the point where it may some day be confined to a set of procedural rules and turned away from a meaningful professional activity. Leaving until later the equally fundamental task of measuring so as to fully disclose the activities observed, note that effective disclosure of significant activities requires some type of a

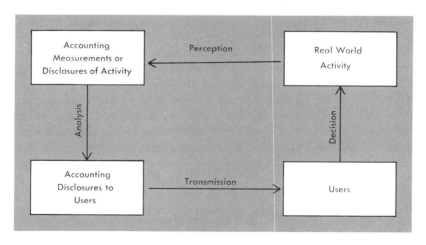

FIGURE 5–1

uniform signal or evidence if all accountants are to observe the selected activities commonly. Otherwise, the tendency for different perceptions to prevail will preclude meaningful disclosure.

The problem of evidence to support accounting disclosures is closely related to the task of determining which or whose perceptions of activities shall be used. There are many supporters of various perceptions, ranging from a sensing of current market values to an awareness of human-asset values, and the decision as to which perceptions to use will be influenced significantly by the extent to which they are perceived or believed to be supported by evidence that the perception will be commonly viewed. The final selection of observations to be disclosed may, of course, be the result of a trade-off between relevance and the so-called objective evidence of the information. But this conventional trade-off may not be needed, for there is reason to believe that traditional views of objective evidence may be expanded while maintaining the same level of reliability as the conventional evidence. Other types of evidence may provide the same degree of reliability or confirmation and also permit the disclosure of more relevant information. These other types of evidence need to be set forth, examined, and discussed until some type of a consensus emerges as to their acceptability. Before this can be done, however, one must examine in more detail the questions, "What is evidence?" and "Why is evidence needed at all?"

It has been noted that effective disclosure of accounting information requires that it be accepted as valid and appropriate by receivers of the accounting communication. Users must believe that the disclosures are reliable, and reliability seems to depend upon the notion that evidence exists to indicate that the disclosure is free from bias, in both the measurement and the observation process, and appropriate for the use intended. The term "objective evidence" is typically used to designate the quality of freedom from bias; the term "full disclosure" refers to the requirement that management not withhold information from other interested parties; and the term "materiality" implies concern for relevance to user needs. Thus, from the point of view of an outside recipient of an accounting disclosure, there is a need for three types of evidence. For each, there is a need for a standard or level of the evidence used. The three questions on evidence are these:

1. What is the *evidence* that constitutes "objective evidence"?
2. What is the *evidence* that the disclosure is relevant ("material") to the user's needs?
3. What is the *evidence* that management has "fully disclosed"?

OBJECTIVE EVIDENCE

As a characteristic of accounting disclosures, the objective-evidence requirement can be used to place rather stringent constraints on any expansion of such disclosures. Justification for a restricted interpretation of this constraint rests on the need to curb the human tendency to present personal views, or, in the case of a conflict of interest between the user and the reporting firm, to motivate users to act in the firm's interest rather than their own. In extreme form, the constraint is designed to prevent purposefully inaccurate disclosures. The insertion of the objective-evidence constraint, as a means for overcoming both subconscious bias and purposeful bias in accounting disclosure, cannot be questioned. The well-recognized frailty of the human being makes it or its equivalent an imperative.

The foregoing justification for the objective-evidence constraint suggests that objective evidence is the means to an end rather than an end in itself. What is sought as an end appears to be disclosures that are accurate and appropriate. Although one may debate the issue as to whether or not accurate information is always appropriate by suggesting that a certain type of biased or inaccurate information may motivate appropriate action more effectively than accurate information, such an assertion assumes certain user responses that may not always be valid and that have not been set forth as final findings by psychological studies.[2] Given the unpredictability of users' responses to the stimuli of specific biased accounting disclosures, the criterion of accuracy seems to be a desirable characteristic of accounting disclosures. But "accuracy" assumes a common perception of facts by trained accounting observers. If a common perception of facts is the fundamental issue, it implies that alternative means to obtain objective evidence might well be investigated as possible solutions to the basic problem of accurate disclosure. Possibly an expansion of the objective-evidence concept will provide the needed solution that will permit expanded accounting disclosures. This would provide the continuity with change so much desired by practicing accountants.

Traditionally, the term "objective evidence" has been used in different ways in the accounting literature. It has carried the implication that a paper document or a formula exists that can be seen physically, and there also exists a hazy notion that the action denoted by the document or formula can be verified by subsequent documents,

---

[2] For further discussion of this issue, see Thomas H. Fitzgerald, "Why Motivation Theory Doesn't Work," *Harvard Business Review*, July–August 1971, pp. 37–44.

physical actions, or objects, or the results of the formula. In fact, recourse to statistical sampling and reliance on the system of internal control does not require that the document be physically seen. In this context, objective evidence includes the objectivity of the sampling methods to some specified level of confidence and the judgmental decision of the observer that the system of control is effective to an unspecified level of confidence. Because of the unspecified level of confidence attached to it, the concept that the system of internal control constitutes evidence that objective evidence exists needs to be examined in more detail. Nevertheless, subject to the validity of the sampling procedure and internal-control system at the operational level, the concept of objective evidence has dominated public accounting disclosures.

The notion that an exchange between an independent buyer and an independent seller represents objective evidence of the value involved, as well as the existence of the activity, indicates that objective evidence is sought on more than one characteristic of the activities to be disclosed. Conceptually, it appears that objective evidence is sought on at least the following characteristics of an activity:

1. The existence of the activity
2. The time of occurrence
3. The description or classification used
4. The value of the elements involved
5. The independence of the parties interacting

Before examining the type of objective evidence appropriate for each characteristic, an examination of the term itself is appropriate.

Definition of objective evidence

If one turns to a dictionary, one finds that the more appropriate definitions of the words "objective" and "evidence" read somewhat as follows:

> *Objective*—belonging to nature or the sensible world.
> —publicly or intersubjectively observable or verifiable, especially by scientific methods.
> —independent of what is personal or private in our apprehension and feelings.
> —of such nature that rational minds agree in holding it real or true or valid.
> *Evidence*—something that furnishes or tends to furnish proof.

Although specialized accounting terminology is necessarily more precise than these explanations, the dictionary definitions do provide a basis for entertaining a broader view of objective evidence.

In certain scientific fields where the emphasis is on operational meaning, the term "objective evidence" refers to the fact that if equally competent researchers perform the same experiment, they will obtain the same result. Hempel, for example, states:

> An operational definition of a term is conceived as a rule to the effect that the term is to apply to a particular case if the performance of specified operations in that case yields a certain characteristic result. For example, the term "harder than" might be operationally defined by the rule that a piece of mineral, X, is to be called harder than another piece of mineral, Y, if the operation of drawing a sharp point of X across the surface of Y results in a scratch mark on the latter. Similarly, the different numerical values of a quantity such as length are thought of as operationally definable by reference to the outcomes of specified measuring operations. To safeguard the objectivity of science, all operations invoked in this kind of definition are required to be intersubjective in the sense that different observers must be able to perform "the same operation" with reasonable agreement in their results.[3]

Thus, objectivity refers to the characteristic of being intersubjectively observable by independent observers, all of whom report a common observation of an action. Applying the definition to accounting, the inference would be that an activity is objective or is supported by objective evidence if independent accountants observe the activity and record the same information.

The need for the term "evidence" arises because the accountant cannot directly observe all the internal and external activities related to the firm. He must use some type of surrogate. In fact, he assumes that the surrogate available to him has a one-to-one relationship to the actual activity. Thus he may assume that the sales invoice is an adequate surrogate of the actual sales activity that he did not observe. In effect, "evidence" is thus supplemental to "objectivity" because both the evidence, in the form of a surrogate, and the actual activity may be objective. This insight, that objective evidence refers to evidence that is objective as well as evidence that the activity is objective, reveals that evidence to the effect that the market value of an asset is a certain amount may be evidence of an activity that is not objective and would not meet the test of objective evidence.

In a simpler sense, of course, one could ignore the objectivity

3 Carl G. Hempel, "A Logical Appraisal of Operationalism," *The Scientific Monthly,* October 1954, p. 215.

aspect of an activity by assuming that in economic affairs all observations are common and that subjectivity is not present. If observations of activities are indeed common to all observers, "objective evidence" apparently refers to the objectivity of the evidence that an observation was made. But a discussion of the objectivity of the evidence is not the real issue, although some tend to be confused between the objectivity of an activity and the objectivity of the evidence. A simple illustration may help emphasize the difference: Evidence in the form of a piece of paper indicating that the market value of an asset is a specified amount could be a highly objective thing, but the objectivity of the actual fact that the market value is the specified amount could still be in question. Different accountants might observe different values. When one objects to this by saying that evidence is proof and that different observations may merely mean that many pieces of paper are needed to prove that the actual event is as stated, one is really struggling to obtain a surrogate (the results of the several pieces of paper) that is indeed a one-to-one mapping with the actual event. From this, it becomes apparent that paper documents are surrogates of the underlying activity, and as such they are supplementary to the objectivity of the actual activity.

There is, of course, the possibility that conceptually the surrogate may be valid but that operationally it may contain errors. An example would be the possibility that a sales invoice is accepted conceptually as a suitable surrogate of the actual sales activity but that an error could exist in the sales invoice. Such clerical errors could distort the one-to-one relationship between the surrogate and the actual activity, but this problem of mechanical accuracy is incidental to the basic problem of developing means for observing activities.

As a final point on the undesirability of the view that "objective evidence" refers to the objectivity of the evidence, note that various pieces of such objective evidence could each indicate different views of the nature of the activity. In such a situation, various items could all qualify as objectives in themselves but be so much at variance with each other that the underlying activity would clearly be nonobjective. It seems to be the objectivity of the underlying activity with which accountants are concerned, for, in social affairs where economic values are concerned, equally capable independent accountants may observe different values in identical activities. For example, the determination of the value of an exchange of machine A for machine B would undoubtedly differ among accountants. For this reason, it is believed that the preferred definition is the one in which objectivity refers to intersubjectivity (common to multiple observers) and evidence refers to the surrogate (accepted proof) of the activity.

Turning to the intersubjectivity of accounting observations, one wonders what a common observation really is. Is it merely a sensing through our eyes, ears, and other senses of an activity, or does it also involve an inference regarding the nature of the activity based on a partial sensing of the activity? Margenau explains the issue in the following terms:

> Let us make sure that we understand the difference between the seen tree and the physical object, tree. The visual, tactile, kinesthetic impressions composing the former are supplemented by two kinds of qualities when knowledge of the objective tree results. The first kind has reference to sensations, though not actually present sensations. The immediately given involves nothing but a few spatial aspects of the tree at any moment: One side of the surface is seen, parts of the surface are touched, the trunk is found to be solid, and so forth. Various aspects can be combined in integrative fashion; we may look at different places and combine in one synthetic impression the different bits of awareness. Whether we say that we have at this stage already passed beyond the evidence of what is immediate is of no importance; to affirm it would indeed be an artificial limitation of the realm of sense data. The transaction, as has been noted, is a gradual one. But we do not stop here. We draw on memory and attribute to the tree an interior which is not now seen, an interior which is brown and hard when seen and felt, though not now exposed to view and touch. We assume that it has roots which could be made visible by digging, cambium that would bleed if its bark were injured. All these properties might be called integrative, since they result from an addition of a multitude of remembered perceptions.[4]

Assuming that Margenau's analysis is correct and that an observation of any activity is a complex process involving both the immediate perception and the educational framework by which the initial perception is integrated into an observation, it appears that objectivity can be attached to an accounting observation only if accountants have a similar professional educational experience as background and a similar immediate view of the activity. Practically, this could never occur, so variations among accounting observations of value must be expected, unless precise operational rules are set forth. These operational rules could specify the types of evidence to be accepted as confirming the existence or objectivity of the perception. Different types of evidence would be appropriate or relevant to different types of phenomena, and the determination of the proper type of evidence for different types of phenomena is a universal problem. In a discussion of Rule 1 of the Rules of Evidence set forth in the 1965 annotation of uniform laws on

---

[4] H. Margenau, *The Nature of Physical Reality* (New York: McGraw-Hill, 1950), p. 59. For an operational definition of "observation" see R. L. Ackoff, *Choice, Communication, and Conflict* (Philadelphia: University of Pennsylvania, 1967).

miscellaneous acts, the National Conference of Commissioners on Uniform State Laws noted:

> The only test of relevancy is logic. With this simple statement we must be content. Nothing could be gained in a code of rules by making it a thesis on the subject of logic. The courts will have to continue to decide what inferences might reasonably be drawn from knowledge or from perception in or outside of the courtroom on the basis of common sense. No attempt is made in these rules to catalog, even generally, what evidence is relevant to what issues.[5]

This return to common sense does not solve the problem, however, for common sense is not a precise concept. It may tell us that different accountants could very well decide that different valuations of an exchange were appropriate. But there is a range within which independent accountants would value the exchange, because of their special competence.[6] This suggests multiple validation as a means for assuring freedom from bias in the accounting-observation function.

But there are limitations even on multiple validation of the objectivity of an observation, in the sense that one asserts there is a certain probability that a given observation falls within a specified range of the appropriate common observation, if such could be known. This is so because every observation has its constitutive meaning or substance as well as its operational meaning. Both are essential. An operational definition alone, being merely the application of a set of measurement rules, tends to overlook the human emotional interest in the substance of the observation. A constitutive definition alone, that merely tells what a phenomenon is, tends to degrade into vagueness, impreciseness, and confusing notions of the objectivity of an activity.

Aside from the constitutive requirement for an accounting disclosure, a statistical-probability distribution of multiple independent observations creates attitudinal problems for users. Morgenstern calls attention to this problem in the following terms:

> Although the natural sciences—sometimes called the "exact" sciences —have been concerned with the accuracy of measurements and observations from their earliest beginnings, a great crisis was nevertheless suffered by them when it became clear that absolute precision and certainty of

---

[5] *Uniform Law Annotated,* Vol. 9A (Brooklyn, N.Y.: Edward Thompson Co., 1965), pp. 594–95.

[6] It has been estimated that independent real estate appraisers vary little more than 10 percent in independent valuations of smaller residential property, although their range is much greater for large pieces of property.

important kinds of observations were impossible to achieve in principle. The situation in the social sciences may not be simpler . . .[7]

Methods of obtaining objectivity

It has been noted that only by setting forth the specific rules to be applied can the concept of objectivity be defined in an operational sense. Operational rules or methods traditionally used to provide objectivity include the following:

1. Acquisition (historical) costing
2. Documentary evidence
3. The consistency doctrine
4. The attest function

Acquisition costing. Accountants familiar with accounting practices in the period prior to the post-1929 depression are well aware of the degree of bias that can be purposefully inserted into financial reports unless the accounting disclosures are restricted to objective observations. From that awareness, they may have overreacted and reached the conclusion that only exchange transactions provide sufficient freedom from bias to warrant inclusion as accounting information.

As to the objectivity provided by acquisition costing, note that it aims only to provide objectivity as to the value of the items exchanged. Also, it is a restricted view, in that it is determined ultimately by one buyer and one seller who alone determine the price, although both are heavily influenced by the opinions or observations of other buyers and sellers in the market. Furthermore, when the fringe aspects of the exchange between the buyer and seller (commissions, transfer taxes, transportation, installation, and so on) can be handled alternatively as part of acquisition cost, the term loses some of its constitutive objectivity. Equating acquisition cost with the present value of the cash outlay required to have the item at the time needed is no solution, for it inserts various subjective elements into the observation of the value of the items involved in the exchange activity.

In fact, the main operational-objectivity feature of acquisition costing is derived from its consistency over periods of time. Once determined, acquisition-cost valuation does not change. This unchanging feature precludes subsequent insertions of subjectivity, a restriction that may not be possible with other valuation methods. Only in this context

[7] O. Morgenstern, *On the Accuracy of Economic Observations,* 2nd ed. (Princeton, N.J.: Princeton University Press, 1963), p. vii.

is it unequivocally appropriate to contend that acquisition costing has greater freedom from bias than other valuation methods, but this is no insignificant contribution to the overall standard of freedom from bias in an objectivity sense.

It is sometimes contended that acquisition cost is biased in the sense that it implies certain valuations are appropriate for a user when other valuations are more relevant. This refers, of course, to the relevance of the disclosure rather than to its freedom from personal bias.

On balance, it appears that the method of acquisition costing does not contribute as much to the reliability of accounting disclosures as would appear at first glance.

Documentary evidence. The use of documentary evidence as a means of improving objectivity in accounting disclosures cannot be examined fully until the concept of evidence has been reviewed. But in the sense that it refers to the requirement that some type of business document attesting to an activity must be available, this concept functions to exclude many varied types of observations that are made about any activity. To the extent that some subjective views are thus eliminated from consideration, it appears that the business-documents requirement should narrow the scope of possible bias in accounting disclosures.

Unfortunately, no list or even description of the multitude of business papers that represent business documents has been accepted by the accounting profession. For internal disclosures, procedures for reporting may be specified in such detail that specific documents are designated as the source of information on activities. In this operational sense, business documents would limit subjectivity somewhat.

But there are so many activities with which accounting is concerned for which suitable business documents are not objectively available (accruals, uncollectibles, depreciation schedules, and the like) that the objectivity provided by the business-documents rule as a method is far from comprehensive in scope of activities. In general, however, business documents do provide information on various characteristics of an activity.

The consistency doctrine. The use of consistency as a means for assuring objectivity is based, in a broad sense of the term, on the operational view of objectivity. This is so because consistency assumes that one method will be used repetitively for similar activities. Thus, the use of FIFO year after year precludes a great number of opportunities to insert bias into a disclosure.

Consistency does not require that the initial observation be free from bias. Rather, it aims to reduce the significance of that bias by maintaining the rule used to obtain the observation or measurement of activity. In this context, "consistency" refers to consistent use of the same rule for similar observations. The objectivity obtained from the use of the consistency doctrine is a relative rather than an absolute removal of bias. To secure unbiased information under this doctrine, the user must look at several disclosures typically over time. Trend would be the unbiased significant factor. Assume, for example, that the initial observation of an activity is exaggerated in some way. In accordance with the consistency doctrine, subsequent observations will be exaggerated in the same way, but the variation in the identically measured observations would indicate the relative difference between them in an unbiased disclosure. Objectivity as a relative concept is probably the highest degree of unbiased disclosures that will ever be possible in many situations.

The main disadvantage of the use of the consistency doctrine as a method for assuring objectivity is the limited scope in which it can be applied. Its use is restricted to situations where repetitive activities of a similar nature occur, and normally it can be applied only to the characteristics of value and description of an activity.

Various attempts have been made to extend the consistency doctrine so that it could be used to cover different types of activities in different industries and thus disclosures of different companies might be meaningfully compared. This would be possible if the instances of bias in disclosure were all similar. Differences in disclosures would then be free from bias. But this is not now practical.

The attest function. The role of the attest function, whether from internal or external sources, is to provide an outside review of proposed disclosures and is aimed precisely at the target of assuring objectivity. As a method, it operates in both preventive and corrective modes. Knowledge that disclosures must be attested to by an outside party motivates efforts to provide initially accurate disclosure, and the attestation process itself may reveal errors in disclosures that should be corrected.

While the nature of the attestation varies from situation to situation, attestation standards used by CPA auditors illustrate the scope of the attestation process. The 1954 statement of the AICPA will suffice to illustrate the concept involved. The statement contained the following four standards for public financial reporting to which the CPA certification is to be attached (parenthetic comments added).

1. The report [attestation] shall state whether the financial statements are presented in accordance with generally accepted principles of accounting [the rules agreed upon by the CPA accounting profession].

2. The report [attestation] shall state whether such principles have been consistently observed in the current period in relation to the preceding period. [*Consistency* refers to the comparability of data between the periods.]

3. Informative disclosures in the financial statements are to be regarded as reasonably accurate unless otherwise stated in the report [attestation]. [This standard indicates that a material inaccuracy must be disclosed.]

4. The report [attestation] shall contain either an expression of opinion regarding the financial statements, taken as a whole, or an assertion to the effect that an opinion cannot be expressed When an overall opinion cannot be expressed, the reasons therefor should be stated. In all cases where an auditor's [attestor's] name is associated with financial statements, the report [attestation] should contain a clear-cut indication of the character of the auditor's examination, if any, and the degree of responsibility he is taking.[8]

In more recent years, the courts of the land have tended to insist, by the liability suits they have supported against CPA firms, that the attestation not permit disclosures that mislead investors and creditors.

In general, the attest function is probably the most effective operational method available for curbing intentional bias in accounting disclosures. Given the general nature of man, it is an essential function in all modern societies. To a degree, it also contributes to a solution to the problem of subconscious bias, in that it requires a second observation of activities. Furthermore, its role in this latter area is gradually expanding, but as yet it is not a means for assuring that accounting disclosures are the best possible disclosures.

EXPANDED VIEW OF OBJECTIVE EVIDENCE

Despite the operational rules used to implement the standard of objective evidence, the resulting disclosures have not satisfied users of accounting information. As noted previously, it is now apparent that users want accounting information supported by evidence that disclosures are (1) free from bias, (2) fully disclosed by management, and (3) relevant to user needs. In a sense, three types of evidence are needed to replace the former evidence that an activity was objectively observed. Realistically, they represent types of objectivity desired. The operational rules to implement them are not well developed, but certain rules seem to be emerging.

[8] American Institute of Certified Public Accountants, *Generally Accepted Auditing Standards* (New York, 1954), p. 14.

Freedom from bias

Undoubtedly, several of the traditional rules or methods used to ensure objectivity in accounting measurements will continue to be used. One other operational rule that may be added is statistical validation.

The statistical-validation method of minimizing bias in accounting disclosures approaches the issue in part as an aspect of the full-disclosure doctrine and in part as a means of eliminating the bias in any average. To illustrate, if depreciation is based on an expected life ranging from 4 to 16 years with an average of 10 years, annual depreciation based on a 10-year life could be biased so much for a particular asset that a user might be misled. By a probability display of expected depreciation, full disclosure of observations is made and the possibility of extreme bias is reduced.

In its more advanced form, statistical validation might require that every accounting disclosure include a carefully determined probability of error of measurement or observation. This would eliminate the implicit bias in the implied precise accuracy of a single-valued disclosure.

Evidence of full disclosure

The notion of disclosure actually embraces two related concepts. First, it may refer to the extent that the accounting record reveals, reflects, or discloses the actual activities taking place. In this context, disclosure refers to the observational capacity of the accountant and the effectiveness of his measuring methods. Full disclosure in this context would occur when the accounting record fully disclosed the relevant activities. It refers to the scope of the accounting function, for full disclosure would mean different things if the scope of accounting were broadened or narrowed.

In the second sense, disclosure refers to the information that is reported to a user. The study of this type of disclosure approaches the problem in terms of user needs and the extent to which the accounting information that management discloses meets these needs. Full disclosure in this context implies that the user is given as much information to meet his needs as management has available for distribution.

The two concepts are distinct, for the first deals with the broad field of representation. It involves consideration of the human perception process and with methods for accurately symbolizing what is perceived. Concern for outside-user needs would be a secondary consideration, for the view would prevail that if the problems of observation and symbolization could be solved, the applied problem of disclosing the needs of a user could then be dealt with more effectively.

Given the wide scope of the disclosure notion, it becomes apparent that the accounting use of the term refers to some level of disclosure —a level well below "full" disclosure. Practically, the full-disclosure doctrine has not been well defined. The notion prevails that management should provide sufficient accounting disclosures to enable a prudent investor to perform well in economic competition. This view articulates possibly as well as any the accounting conception of full disclosure. For internal management purposes, such a rule would require more complete internal disclosures, because competitors would also be well-informed, and in order to compete more information is needed by management than is required by shareholders.

It is difficult to list items of evidence that would indicate that full disclosure was being made, but it is possible to list evidence suggesting a low level of full disclosure. Thus, the level of compliance with full public disclosure would be low under conditions such as the following:

1. Members of company management or company employees make unusual gains by trading in company stock.
2. The general public becomes aware from nonaccounting sources that the company is increasing social costs.
3. Financial analysts obtain extensive nonaccounting data in analyzing the investment desirability of the common stock of the company.
4. Shareholders, creditors, and employees are unable to determine profitable and unprofitable activities of a company.
5. Unexpected unfavorable occurrences are frequent.
6. Competitors disclose more fully than the reporting company.
7. Management, employees, shareholders, creditors, and the general public are unable to explain the function or contribution of the entity in society.
8. Rumors and suspicious attitudes about company activities prevail in the minds of the general public.

The disclosure doctrine started as little more than a broad admonition to "disclose appropriate information." Attempts to make it an operational concept have taken the form of specific rules by authoritative groups designating information to be disclosed to users. In a sense, the disclosure method represents a broad umbrella guideline supplemented by an incomplete set of operational rules. The constitutive definition of the method exists, but the operational definition is far from complete.

Evidence of relevance

The type of evidence needed to assure accounting information users that the information provided is relevant to their needs has not been systematically developed. The assumption is that compliance with generally accepted accounting principles will indicate a certain level of evidence that the information is relevant. As yet, however, the task of developing evidence that the relevance requirement has been met is still unsolved. Illustrative of evidence indicating that relevant information is being disclosed are the following:

1. Present and prospective investors request accounting disclosures.
2. Analysts develop cost and revenue behavior functions for the company from accounting disclosures.
3. Economists consolidate the disclosed information with other entity information to develop national data.
4. Environmentalists determine pollution costs from the disclosed data.
5. Investors develop financial operating models of the company from the data.
6. The information is used by employees, investors, suppliers, and the general public.
7. Decisions are different when the information is not provided.

It has been proposed that accountants should indicate the standard or level of evidence used to support the view that accounting information is free from bias, fully disclosed by management, and relevant to user needs. Before continuing this analysis, it is necessary to define more precisely the notion of evidence.

EVIDENCE

Operationally, evidence is the means by which a belief can be established that, in turn, can be used as "proof" that an observation is valid. In this same context, relevant evidence would mean evidence reasonably appropriate to prove the existence of a characteristic of an activity. Proof, of course, would be all the evidence available to the accountant for confirming the existence or nonexistence of the characteristic under scrutiny.

It is singular that accountants do not systematically search for evidence before disclosing an activity. Thus Mautz, in 1954, could and did write in the following terms:

> Evidence in auditing is any document, procedure, or piece of information which assists an auditor in forming his professional opinion as to the accuracy of the financial information he examines. . . . Nine different types of evidence can be listed. These are:
>
> 1. Physical examination by the auditor of the existence of the thing represented by the accounts.

2. Authoritative documents prepared outside the enterprise under examination or within the enterprise.
3. Oral or written statements by independent third parties.
4. Calculations by the auditor.
5. Satisfactory internal control.
6. Complete subsidiary or detail records in good order.
7. Subsequent actions of the company under examination.
8. Formal statements by company's officers or employees.
9. Informal statements by company's officers or employees.[9]

Equally disturbing is the failure of the accounting profession to develop any systematic structure of the quality of different types of evidence. In fact, there is little weighing of evidence, so that it is not possible to build up various levels of proof of an activity. Stettler describes the auditing process as follows:

> The decision as to how much evidence the auditor should obtain in support of his opinion on a client's financial statements must be made in accordance with generally accepted auditing standards. In arriving at such a decision, the circumstances in each individual situation must be considered. These circumstances would include the amount of internal control associated with the accounting process, the materiality of each figure in relation to other figures in the statements, the relative risk that any given figure (or the statements as a whole) might be misstated, and the competence of the evidence available in support of the statement figures.[10]

Rather than the assignment of weights to different types of evidence, the burden of proof tends to be placed on a system of controls to provide the evidence to be used as proof in disclosing information. To a great extent, this approach has been assumed to be necessary, for any procedure calling for the collection of various types of evidence to support each detailed disclosure was assumed to cost far more than the worth of the disclosure. Efficiency in providing many detailed disclosures also appears to have necessitated a substantial restriction on the amount of evidence used to support accounting disclosures. Nevertheless, there seems to be a need for some method to designate different levels of proof as appropriate for different types of activities.

Knowledgeable accountants realize that accounting cannot now be a scientific investigation process directed to the disclosure of basic truth. Many aspects and methods of concern to the scientist must be omitted.

[9] R. K. Mautz, *Fundamentals of Auditing* (New York: John Wiley, 1954), pp. 33–34.

[10] H. F. Stettler, *Auditing Principles* (Englewood Cliffs, N.J.: Prentice-Hall, 1956), pp. 64–65.

Consequently, there must be recognition that for years to come, precisely accurate observations of business activity cannot be made. Accountants and users alike must learn to be content with rough approximations of the philosophical ideal.

A review of the legal requirements for evidence will provide a starting point for an examination of the evidential requirements of an accounting observation. According to the Uniform Business Records as Evidence Act (1936), referring to a business record, "A record of an act, condition or event, shall, insofar as relevant, be competent evidence if the custodian or other qualified witness testifies to its identity and the mode of its preparation, and if it was made in the regular course of business, at or near the time of the act, condition or event, and if, in the opinion of the court, the sources of information, method and time of preparation were such as to justify its admission." [11]

Although the purpose of this act was to admit business records as evidence without the need to call as witness the person originally making each record, the effect was to create a new type of evidence, more readily available than personal testimony of individuals. It should be noted that this adjustment in the concept of evidence in no way bears upon the underlying observation of activity. Examples of business records that have been accepted in court as evidence are such items as letters, receipts, time cards, and sales slips. Accounting needs to create new types of evidence, as the lawyers have.

Almost everyone would probably agree that the accounting concept of acceptable evidence is not precisely developed. Disturbing as this situation is, even more disquieting is the present lack of progress in solving the problem. Substantial work is being done on the development of rules to disclose observations, but the determination of the evidence needed to verify the existence of an activity has encountered many unsolved issues. This is unfortunate, for the unarticulated rules of accounting evidence are becoming more and more complicated.

As previously noted, accounting has developed no system of weights for different types of evidence. While admissibility of evidence is of primary concern, if no system for assigning weights can be developed, accountants could at least develop a relative ranking of classes of evidence when conflicting evidence of an activity exists. Whether a cancelled check or a purchase invoice is preferred evidence of an activity cannot now be settled by reference to a formal ranking of acceptable accounting evidence. At the macro level, current market values seem

---

[11] *Uniform Laws Annotated*, Vol. 9A (Brooklyn, N.Y.: Edward Thompson Company, 1965), p. 506.

to be preferred to acquisition-cost values as evidence only in such instances as readily marketable securities. But there is no ranking of types of evidence for different situations.

CHARACTERISTICS TO BE DISCLOSED

Underlying the various types of objectivity and the evidence aspects of an accounting disclosure is the problem of determining the characteristics of an activity that should be disclosed. As we have seen, the five characteristics of activities for which accountants have a responsibility are (1) the existence of the activity, (2) its value, (3) the time of its occurrence, (4) a description (classification) of resources involved, and (5) the independence of the parties associated with the activity.

The existence characteristic

The question of whether or not an activity exists apparently has different answers at different points in time. Not too long ago, long-term lease contracts were not recognized as an acquisition activity for accounting purposes. At present, many executory contracts are not recognized as an activity, but several accountants feel they should be.

Given some agreement on the types of activities to be recognized, the problem of the type of evidence needed to indicate that an event did in fact occur must be agreed upon. Broadly, the following types of evidence are available:

1. **Common knowledge** that the wear and tear of the elements of nature will ultimately destroy a piece of equipment is the objective evidence used to support the existence of the depreciation activity.
2. **Testimony** of both parties in an independent exchange transaction, to support the existence of most exchange transactions.
3. **Contractual agreement,** to support gradual performance of an activity as reflected in most accrual recognitions.
4. **Authoritative opinion,** to support the activity of creating goodwill, legal liability for damages, appraisals. This includes legal pronouncements. The assumption is that the authoritative opinion will be accepted.
5. **Accounting pronouncements,** to support such activities as the tracing and allocation of costs.
6. **Public recognition,** to support certain of the so-called public-cost activities of air, water, and land pollution. Illustrative of this activity is the 13-page insert, "Paper, People and Pollution," in the 1970 annual report of the Scott Paper Company.

Evidence of the existence of an activity is, of course, quite distinct from evidence of the time the activity occurred.

The time-of-occurrence characteristic

Evidence of the time an activity occurs is typically provided by a business document of some type. As to which business document is acceptable, it seems to be generally agreed that documents indicating mere receipt or issuance of an order do not provide acceptable evidence of the time an activity will occur. Normally, a business document that indicates the legal date of title transfer tends to be accepted as objective evidence of the time of an activity. But the call for relevance may require that a much more elaborate time schedule be developed for recognizing different types of activities.

In the case of certain activities, such as those in the form of losses in value, evidence of the time of occurrence is seldom available. As a result, managerial opinion is frequently sought and, subject to the judgment of a knowledgeable auditor, accepted as evidence that the activity has occurred. Even if managerial opinion is to be evidence in such situations—and it may be that better evidence can be created—there is a need for a specification of the level of management opinion required for different types of losses.

The description characteristic

Typically referred to as the problem of classification, this characteristic refers to the appropriate description of the activities to be disclosed. Normally, the objective evidence for the classification function is a set of rules or definitions of resources. These rules classify activities according to physical objects that can be confirmed by sense perception. For example, the distinction between the acquisition of "fixtures" and that of "furniture" is made on the basis of a rule indicating that physical resources permanently attached to a building are "fixtures," while a movable piece of equipment is "furniture." Since these characteristics of fixed and movable can be perceived in a physical sense, they are considered objective classifications, because the rule and the sensing were promulgated prior to the activity under examination.

As to the adequacy of this type of evidence, it may be noted that multiple-classification schemes could be developed to describe an activity. A survey of classifications for internal purposes indicates that functional, rather than object, classification of activities is growing. There is limited evidence to indicate that a similar shift is occurring in the classification rules used for public reporting.

There is, however, a considerable amount of public interest in the degree of refinement in the classifications used. Illustrative of this was the call by the SEC and others for more comprehensive disclosures of the activities of conglomerate companies.[12]

The value characteristic

Because of the accounting concern with quantitative measures, objective evidence of the value of an exchange is probably the most frequently discussed characteristic of an activity. The disclosure problem is not so much the objective evidence of a value, for objective evidence of both current market value and historical acquisition cost are frequently both available. Rather, the problem is the quality of the objective evidence. As previously noted, the two most acceptable types of objective evidence for valuation purposes are business documents of a historical transaction and the consistent use of certain formulas. There is, however, a growing belief that certain current market valuations or general price-level adjustment data meet the test of high-quality objective evidence for several valuation purposes.

The need for objective evidence of value before an activity is disclosed has resulted in a number of disclosures in the "president's letter" section of the annual report. For example, the "Report of the Chairman of the Board" in the 1970 annual report of the American Telephone and Telegraph Company disclosed information apparently supported by little precise objective evidence on future revenues and expenses, telephone rates, communication growth, service improvement, science and technology, telecommunications policy, and human affairs.

Although the desirability of a high-quality standard of objective evidence for accounting-valuation disclosures cannot be questioned, the extent of the disclosures in the "president's letter" suggests a need for an expansion of the accounting views of objective evidence for valuation purposes. Multiple valuations may be appropriate.

The independence characteristic

The evidence that exchange activities are between independent parties is taken for granted by the assumption that the profit motive will tend to motivate independent action by all parties concerned. Couple this with the well-publicized criticisms and penalties for non-independent activities, and the belief that activities are between independent parties is strengthened.

---

[12] See R. K. Mautz, *Financial Reporting by Diversified Companies* (New York: Financial Executives Research Foundation, 1968), for information on this aspect of the public-disclosure problem.

Nevertheless, any evidence to indicate that the activities are *not* between parties with independent interests in the activity is normally the basis for a call for additional evidence to verify that the normal objective evidence is not distorted.

SUMMARY

The conceptual problem of evidence to support accounting disclosures is second only to the conceptual problem of the scope of accounting disclosures. In general, the rule of common sense, supported by a variety of operational accounting rules, seems to provide the most dependable evidence of significant activities. Nevertheless, problems arise as social values and customs change, and as calls for greater relevance, to the neglect of stringent rules for objective evidence, prevail. One possible solution to the problem is multiple disclosures, particularly multiple valuation, which is one of the topics of the next chapter.

Overall, it seems that standards of evidence are needed to ensure to information users the extent to which accounting disclosuers are free from bias, fully disclosed by management, and relevant to user needs. Separate types of evidence are needed for each, and the quality or level of the evidence used needs to be specified. Clearly higher and broader standards of evidence are needed for effective accounting disclosures.

REFERENCES

BLANSHARD, B., *The Nature of Thought*. New York: Macmillan, 1940.

FRANK, P. G., ed., *The Validation of Scientific Theories*. New York: Collier Books, 1969.

LERNER, D., ed., *Evidence and Inference*. New York: Free Press, 1959.

MARGENAU, HENRY, *The Nature of Physical Reality*. New York: McGraw-Hill, 1950.

MORGENSTERN, OSKAR, *On the Accuracy of Economic Observations*, 2nd ed. Princeton, N.J.: Princeton University Press, 1963.

RITCHIE, A. D., *Scientific Method*. Paterson, N.J.: Littlefield, Adams & Co., 1960.

THOMAS, A. L., *The Allocation Problem*. Evanston, Ill.: American Accounting Association, 1969.

VATTER, W. J., "Limitation of Overhead and Allocation," *The Accounting Review,* April 1945.

WHITTAKER, E. T., and GEORGE ROBINSON, *The Calculus of Observations,* 4th ed. London: Blackie and Son, 1944.

CHAPTER SIX

The Feasibility
of
Multiple Disclosures

This chapter examines the practicability of a proposal for a comprehensive public report to which a number of special-interest subgroup reports could be tied in a coordinated manner, to ensure control of information flow throughout an entity. Distinguishing between innovation—as new ideas—and change—as the acceptability of the innovation—the requirements needed for change in disclosures to occur are examined. The conclusions reached are that conditions are such that change in accounting disclosures are now feasible. The proposed feasible comprehensive public report includes multiple measures, uses, communication media, disclosure formats, and classifications. In this way, accounting disclosures will contribute to a solution to the complexity of our society, for "handling complexity seems to be the major problem of the age, in the way that handling material substance offered the challenge to our forefathers." [1]

The third conceptual issue involved in an examination of accounting disclosures, once the scope of accounting (Chapter 4) and its standards or levels of evidence (Chapter 5) have been established, relates to feasibil-

---

[1] Stafford Beer, at the 11th meeting of the Panel on Science and Technology, Washington, D.C.: 1970.

ity. While conceptually it may be appropriate to expand the scope of accounting disclosure and to call for higher degrees of preciseness in accounting standards of evidence, the feasibility or general acceptability of it all must be considered before recommendations can be set forth.

But what is feasible, practical, or acceptable? What are the criteria or conditions that must prevail for a proposal to be considered feasible? The notion that something is feasible if it is capable of being dealt with successfully merely passes the question on to the meaning of *successful*. Likewise, the notion that a proposed accounting disclosure is feasible only if it is accepted as possible by everyone is too stringent a constraint. Actually, these polar views of the notion of the feasibility of proposed accounting disclosures may be somewhat ambiguous. In the sense of being capable of being carried out or dealt with successfully, a feasible accounting disclosure is one that technically can be quantified and one for which necessary controls are available to prevent misrepresentation under the guise of complying with the disclosure. This second aspect of a feasible proposal is particularly difficult, for in Morgenstern's harsh terms,

> There is overly often a deliberate attempt to hide information. In other words, economic and social statistics are frequently based on evasive answers and *deliberate lies* of various types. These lies arise, principally, from misunderstandings, from fear of tax authorities, from uncertainty about or dislike of government interference and plans, or from the desire to mislead competitors.[2]

If meaningful accounting disclosures are to be developed, both quantification and control must be included as a minimum before a proposal can be considered feasible. At the other extreme, a proposed disclosure of new types of information supported by new types of evidence is not feasible unless accountants as a group, companies as a group, and users as a group agree that the disclosure is appropriate. This psychological aspect of feasibility can be carried to an extreme by holding that a proposed disclosure is not feasible if any element in any one of the groups does not want to make the disclosure. But if the acceptability requirement is less than 100 percent, one still must decide the extent of acceptability required for the proposed disclosure to be considered feasible.

Gaining acceptance of a proposal for expanding the scope of accounting disclosures using new types of evidence is difficult. Confidence exists in customary disclosures. If one distinguishes between innovation

---

[2] Oskar Morgenstern, *On the Accuracy of Economic Observations*, 2nd ed. (Princeton, N.J.: Princeton University Press, 1963), p. 17.

(the development of new proposals) and change (gaining acceptance of the proposal), change is by far the more difficult. One may assume that a proposed disclosure that is technically reliable would be more likely to be accepted if it did not involve acts or procedures at variance from those customarily used in preparing present accounting disclosures. Thus, as a minimum, it appears an accounting proposal is feasible if the acts required to carry out the proposal have characteristics similar to those of acts customarily performed. More specifically, a minimum feasible proposal is one that does not materially change the methodology used to perform accounting. Greater emphasis on certain aspects of the known methodology may permit an expansion of the minimum feasible proposal, since it will appear not to violate substantially the minimum criterion of feasibility.

Dissatisfaction with existing disclosures may provide support for modifications of the prevailing methodology and thus expand further the concept of what is feasible. Illustrative of this possibility has been the use of price-level-adjusted measurements in other countries in times of rapid inflation. Modification of the prevailing accounting-disclosure methodology is normally systematic and gradual. Finally, change may be induced and the concept of a feasible proposal broadened by a systematic "educational" process, until everyone involved is familiar with the proposal and tends to view it as acceptable. The issuance of Statement No. 3 on the general price-level adjustment by the Accounting Principles Board, explaining the procedures to be followed in changing from historical cost to general price-level-adjusted financial statements, represents an educational step toward a possible future change that may make the use of general price-level adjustments in accounting a feasible proposal. It also provides a basis for adjusting to a changed accounting technique when one is considered appropriate by the business community.

As to whether or not current conditions are such that any significant departure from the conventional accounting and disclosure methodology is now possible, there seems to be no sound basis for judgment. Possibly a review of the demand for new disclosures may throw some light on the question.

Illustrative of the need for more detailed disclosures is the way economic activity goes out of control when information is lacking, as reflected in the report of the chairman of the Interstate Commerce Commission that railroad diversification posed a threat to "the economic vitality of the nation's railroads" that "cannot be underestimated," [3] and the ICC staff reports that there exist "detailed . . . instances of

---

[3] *Wall Street Journal,* July 6, 1971, p. 6.

railroad holding companies draining off carrier assets," [4] often with little benefit to the traveling public or to the efficiency of the transportation system. Marshall Armstrong's statement before the Economic Club of Detroit, while president of the American Institute of Accountants, indicates that general recognition of the need for greater disclosure prevails. He stated, "I want to discuss a matter of critical importance to the business and financial community, as well as to the accounting profession. It is the public demand for greater accountability on the part of business—specifically, a desire for more complete and useful information on corporate financial affairs. . . . The call for greater accountability is part of the general mood of our time. As society has become more complex the particular groups within it have become more dependent upon one another, but, at the same time, less able to know at first hand what the others are doing. From this circumstance stems a rising insistence for new standards of accountability." [5]

Whether or not situations such as the foreoing are sufficiently compelling to broaden the practicability or feasibility criterion adopted is another matter. They appear not to be sufficient to permit such a broadening to the extent that an attempt could be made to disclose all the information needed to provide for all contingencies. On balance, the criterion of feasibility might well be that proposals must be capable of being implemented with the accounting methodology, including in that term the application of proved methods in certain new areas, and not allocate information unfairly among parties.

Feasibility is an essential aspect of accounting disclosures. But it is not enough to designate which disclosures will be made, for there is constantly a changing demand on the part of the users of accounting disclosures and a supply cost facing the entity supplier of the information. In some instances, there may also be a supply push to supplement the demand pull, as would exist when firms want to provide more complete disclosure. Also, supply cost includes intangible factors, such as the benefit to competitors when disclosure is made, as well as the immediately recognized accounting costs. But beyond the balancing point between cost and benefit, given feasibility, disclosure occurs. The balancing point may be shifted either by reducing the cost of supplying the disclosure, which has been promised by the computer technologists, or by increasing the demand for the disclosure. Most calls for additional disclosures emphasize the increasing demand. Actually, the demand and supply curves for accounting disclosure are conceptual and as yet have no operational meaning. Broadly, however, the trend of technology,

---

4 *Ibid.*
5 *Ibid.*

coupled with social changes, suggests that gradually new disclosures will be made.

As new disclosures occur, the phenomenon of information overload occurs at times. In part because users are not familiar with the new information, but also because the additional information cannot be assimilated as a part of the decision maker's decision process, a reaction to new disclosures may result. It is certainly futile to propose disclosure of vast quantities of raw information based on new types of evidence if the effect is subsequently to increase the decision-making uncertainty of the user of the information. Such can indeed happen; and means must be found to prevent its occurrence, lest proposed advances in scope and quality of accounting disclosures initially accepted as feasible be subsequently rejected by users in a reaction to the resulting information-overload state.

Various proposals have been suggested to deal with the disclosure problem. The one uniform call from users is for greater relevance. Bevis relates the relevance issue to ethics by calling for "fair and full disclosure" in accounting reports, and suggests that supplementary disclosures are necessary to realize that objective. He states:

> No matter how extensively consensus on accounting practices is established and how closely they are followed, the principle of full and fair disclosure must remain the keystone of successful corporation–stockholder and corporation–society relations. No matter how clear and complete are the balance sheet and statement of income and retained earnings, nor how comparable among companies the practices used in preparing them, the information in these conventional financial statements invariably needs to be supplemented. The corporation is too complex to be compressed completely into such confines. Estimates, judgments, and contingencies cannot be reduced to penny-accurate amounts. It is hoped that enough specific subjects for supplementary disclosure have been mentioned to demonstrate this.[6]

COMPREHENSIVE DISCLOSURES

In compliance with the call for greater relevance in accounting disclosures, which necessarily requires different information for different purposes, the conclusion of this study is that only a single, compressed, comprehensive disclosure report, supported by subreports directed to specific user groups, can provide both the overall view necessary and the different disclosure needs of different users. This conclusion regard-

[6] Herman W. Bevis, *Corporate Financial Reporting in a Competitive Economy* (New York: Macmillan, 1965), p. 201.

ing a means for adjusting conceptually traditional accounting disclosures to meet the modern needs of society may be viewed as a compromise between the proposals of those advocating a series of unconnected accounting reports, each directed to a different user or purpose, and of those insisting that accounting reports "articulate" with each other.

The reasonableness of the conclusion is supported by the fact that detailed disclosures are now provided to internal management or external parties as special reports. That is, the information is now available. Although articulation of the various subreports with the overall report may require some modifications of the existing accounting procedures and methodology, it may be that no extreme modification will be necessary.

The proposal that it should be possible to articulate the multitude of internal reports for management and the special reports for special purposes with one broad general-purpose report is counter to a considerable amount of contemporary academic thought. The most realistic argument against the feasibility of articulation of the reports is that the present general-purpose public report cannot be adjusted sufficiently to permit the articulation. This argument reflects confusion regarding the fact that the present so-called general report is primarily a special-disclosure report for shareholders. If it is so recognized, the opportunity exists for a broader new general-purpose report, with the shareholders' report treated as a subreport.

It must be emphasized that this multiple type of disclosure need not and should not be viewed as a compromise of any type. It stands alone as a response to the needs of multiple users, for whoever contends that any specialized bit of information stands alone, without reference to the whole system to which it relates, runs the risk of serious misinterpretation. To exult because one department exceeded planned expectations by 10 percent is to err if the total entity exceeded planned expectations by 20 percent, or if the department gain of 10 percent caused poor performance elsewhere. The fact is that both overall and specific disclosures are relative. Only in terms of the total overall disclosure system can specific information be meaningful.

The fact that all disclosures must be interpreted in terms of an overall disclosure system may also be applicable to the report on a single entity, for it, too, is merely a part of the overall system of the total economic society. This was noted in a previous chapter, where it was proposed that four types of external data be included as a part of the overall accounting report of the entity.

Possibly the most compelling practical reaction to the proposal that external data be included in the comprehensive accounting disclosure is that this information is available from other sources. It may be contended that such public disclosures as *Barron's* "Pulse of Industry and Trade" or *Business Week*'s "Figures of the Week" provide appropriate information on general economic conditions; that developments in the industry are well publicized in trade and industry journals; that actions of competitors can be obtained directly from the reports of competitors; and that government activities are available in newspapers. The inclusion of this material in an accounting disclosure, it may be suggestion, is redundant, is not collected by the usual accounting process, and may not be as current as similar data from other sources. Also, the proposed report appears to fail the established criterion test of feasibility, in that the accounting methodology contains no formal method for sensing and recording such information. Only the somewhat informal methodology of supplementary footnote disclosure can be used to justify its inclusion. But supplementary footnote disclosures must relate or in some way explain the information in the formal accounting report. General external data do not meet this test. This apparently explains or accounts for the high degree of support for the nondisclosure of the external type of information in the past. It fails, however, to recognize the issue involved, for it is not just any external information that is appropriate. Only external information useful for interpreting the internal data in the accounting disclosure needs to be included. In this context, the selection process, by which decisions are made to indicate the appropriate external data to include, is crucial. Random external data could be quite confusing. An additional burden is placed on the accountant of selecting or developing the appropriate external data for supplementary disclosure. The feasibility of this undertaking has not been tested, because it does involve substantial broadening of the accounting methodology.

Tests by three larger department stores reveal that disclosure of the following external data is at least technically feasible, in the sense that it can be included as supplementary data in accounting disclosures.

1. General economic conditions
   a. General price-level changes during period—available in the various government publications
   b. Changes in national personal disposable income during the period—available in various public publications
   c. Interest rates—available in Federal Reserve Bank reports
   d. Unemployment rates—available in Department of Labor reports
   e. Gross national product—available in Department of Commerce reports
2. Developments in the industry
   a. New marketing trends—available in various trade surveys

    b. Standard cost for the industry—available in trade-association publications

    c. Total industry sales—available in trade publications

    d. Social problems of industry (pollution, etc.)—available in public media

    e. Trends in customers' wants—available in various surveys

3. Actions of competitors

    a. Products dropped and added to line of stock by competitors—available by surveillance of products offered for sale

    b. Sales and income of specific competitors—available from reports of competitors

    c. Advertising and sales policies of specific competitors—available by monitoring public announcements of competitors

    d. Social-problem contributions—available by monitoring newspapers

4. Government activities

    a. Treaties, embargoes, tariffs, and other international agreements—available from *Congressional Record.*

    b. Regulations as to quality of products—available from government agencies

    c. Regulations regarding financing, scope of activities, and other restraints on operations

    d. Government surveys, reports, and findings on consumer trends

The single comprehensive disclosure report proposed as a disclosure mechanism may follow the format of the conventional balance sheet (a status report), income statement (an activity report), statement of financial changes (a statement of change) and footnotes (supplementary) disclosure. The specialized reports believed appropriate would be directed to specific types of users.

Before the feasibility of a broad general-purpose disclosure statement can be examined further, various aspects of the many types of disclosures should probably be reviewed. Only in this way will it be possible to respond to the insight of the 1969–70 American Accounting Association's Committee on Foundations of Accounting Measurement:

> New guidelines are desperately needed for organizing two differently oriented areas of accounting into a harmonious system in terms of both theory and practice. In theory, a set of concepts and premises are needed at a higher level than those developed for traditional accounting only. In practice, ever-increasing demands for financial information, internally and externally, must somehow be regulated before the accounting or controller's department drowns under the flood of information requests.[7]

[7] Report of the Committee on Foundations of Accounting Measurement, *Supplement to Volume XLVI of The Accounting Review,* American Accounting Association, 1971, p. 48.

The point is that the comprehensive disclosure report involves multiple disclosures of activities. Thus the conceptual issue to be examined is the feasibility of multiple disclosures. Actually, multiple disclosures may refer to:

1. Multiple measures
2. Multiple uses
3. Multiple communication media
4. Multiple disclosure formats
5. Multiple classifications

Multiple measures

An accounting measurement is "an assignment of numerals to an entity's past, present or future economic phenomena, on the basis of observation and according to rules." [8] In accord with this definition, the quest becomes one of determining when it is feasible to assign numerals to phenomena. Clearly, the definition does not restrict the measurement process to one set of digits, as is implied by single-valuation methods. While single valuations may be preferred, the definition does include the following hierarchy of numeral assignments:

1. Single valuation
2. Single valuation (expected value) supported by a probability-of-error measure
3. An interval measure with extreme values single-valued
4. A ranking-order valuation process that would merely indicate the relative rank of an item or activity among a group of items or activities.

The third and fourth levels may be considered by some to be beyond the scope of the accounting methodology. Such is not intended, although the fact is that the bulk of accounting measurements are based on the first type of measurement. But such a restriction on accounting measurement may have hampered disclosure efforts in two respects:

1. It may not have fostered a structured itemization of measured elements composing the single valuation, such as would an itemization of the cost of an activity in such terms as its cash-outlay element, its variable element, its controllable element, and its fixed component.
2. It has not encouraged the use of level 2 measures, even though the "average" aspect of the single valuation is well recognized.

[8] *Ibid.*, p. 3.

The main difficulty with the use of level 2 measurement is general unfamiliarity with dispersion measures on the part of accounting-information users and with the tendency for dispersion disclosures to call attention to the uncertainty features of any measure.

There does seem to be emerging a general familiarity with the concept of standard deviation, although there is a considerable lack of understanding of the variability of the sample form from which the standard deviation is derived. For example, the computation of the average cost of items of inventory is based on the prices prevailing over a relatively short period of time. The standard deviation indicating the dispersion from the average would probably have to be based on a somewhat reliable sample composed of the whole universe of inventory on hand. On the other hand, the computation of the depreciation for a year, assuming straight-line depreciation, would require that both the average annual depreciation and the dispersion about the average be computed from experience with similar assets in the past or by other companies. Such experience would have to be derived from a relatively small sample and would be subject to the possibility that some of the experiences used in the sample are not comparable. The result may be that both average single-valued measures and standard-deviation measures will be based on different degrees of evidence. The seriousness of this variation has been mentioned in the accounting literature by noting the variation in the preciseness of measures of "depreciation expense" and "wages expense."

Apparently, readers of accounting disclosures have learned to use "average" single-valued measures of different quality in the same report. Seemingly, they could learn to use "standard-deviation" dispersion measures as well. The feature of which users cannot now be aware is the extent of the possible dispersion around the single-valued average. Thus, crude as some dispersion measures may have to be, they will at least call attention to situations where dispersion may be large or small.

The feasibility of providing an itemized disclosure of the elements of any one single-valued activity is technically satisfactory, but it must be recognized that it might be rejected by users because it would require each user to select the information relevant to his needs. This might require a careful analysis of the comprehensive disclosure report before the report could be used. Financial analysts apparently would be in great demand, and the information-overload state of the people to whom the report was directed could be increased. This does not mean that the detailed information should not be collected; but it does suggest that the detailed and specialized information be included in a subreport, a report for a special purpose.

In order to provide for effective articulation of the data in the various reports, the detailed elements of any valuation could be separated in a computer-based data base. When separate elements of any one valuation were extracted for a special report, an audit trail in the form of a classification scheme could be used to trace the element back to its basic source. This would prevent the use of unverified valuations in special reports. In this manner, articulation of all company information could be provided in the systematically developed data base. Implicit in this proposal, that articulation of the disclosures in the special and comprehensive report should be provided by the corporate data base, is the assumption that considerable details of all activities could be maintained and that procedures would be available to summarize these details for the comprehensive disclosure report.

Procedurally, the collection and maintenance of the detailed data base and the set of programs for summarizing the activities into information for a comprehensive disclosure report and various subreports that can all be related to each other in a corporate data base are technically feasible. This can be done, but probably should be implemented gradually over a period of time.

The proposal that articulation of accounting disclosures be provided for in the corporate data base is in accord with current efforts to develop computerized integrated data bases. The Western Electric Management Information System is being implemented along these lines. In a presentation at the Systems and Procedures Association's 1968 annual meeting, Warren A. Welsh explained the development:

> The predominant, if not exclusive, current approach to computer-based information system design is that of the project or subsystem. . . . Recognizing the shortcomings of these project-sized modules, Western Electric's Information Systems Engineering Organization has engineered the framework for a companywide information system which circumvents most of the shortcomings of the project approach. . . . The information system . . . is a companywide system with parts or elements at every company location having data-processing equipment. It can be considered as being composed of a headquarters system, various manufacturing location systems, various distribution house systems, and various regional systems existing as integral parts of the whole company system. Each of these location systems must be capable of serving the complete information needs of the organizations it serves and yet remain sufficiently flexible to accommodate changes imposed by growth and technical advances within the company and by hardware and software innovations throughout the data-processing industry.[9]

On balance, it appears that multiple-measure disclosures are feasible to a limited degree. Dispersion measures may have to be restricted to those situations where uncertainty of the single value is high. On the

---

[9] Warren A. Welsh, "Engineered Design of EDP Systems," unpublished paper.

other hand, it does appear feasible to construct a corporate data base or information system in sufficient detail that articulation of accounting disclosures on internal activities would be possible. That is, it should be possible to tie back any measured disclosure to broader classifications through a computer retrieval process. Articulation of internal data with external data may not be possible for some time in the future, although there are now proposals for national data bases of various types. The implication of such a degree of integration staggers the imagination and seems beyond the scope of feasibility, but note the following statement by the advisory committee to a Congress-supported study on *Measuring the Nation's Wealth:*

> Significant improvement and expansion of information relating to the wealth of the United States are both desirable and feasible. Firmly based wealth estimates, developed within a consistent framework and in reasonable detail, would enhance our ability to relate capital formation to economic growth, to project future production possibilities, and to analyze the demand for capital goods.[10]

Note also an advertisement by the First National City Bank of New York, in the July–August 1971 issue of the *Harvard Business Review,* calling attention to their computer system that makes available to subscribers on a rental basis a service that includes "a data base featuring a cast of hundreds of companies . . . to provide individual company financial comparisons or industry composites."

Multiple uses

The proposition that different accounting disclosures are appropriate for different uses is well recognized. Most of the reservations to the proposal for a comprehensive public report center around the concern that a report prepared for one purpose and so labeled would be put to another use. But control of dissemination of disclosures only to pertinent uses is not feasible.

Conceptually, the issue of disclosures directed to specified use, which necessarily involves multiple disclosures classified as to use, must be dealt with in terms of the different information needs of different users. Should users have a common demand for similar information, the case for multiple disclosure is weakened. But if the area of common information needs is small and the area of uncommon information needs is large, multiple disclosure would seem more relevant. Given a large area of common information needs and a large area of uncommon needs, it

---

[10] Joint Economic Committee, *Measuring the Nation's Wealth* (Washington, D.C.: U.S. Government Printing Office, 1964), p. ix.

would appear that one comprehensive report supported by more specialized reports for specific types of uses would be required. In this period of increasing specialization with greater universal interdependence, this last condition seems the most reasonable position.

If different disclosures are needed for different uses, the issue immediately arises of the degree of detail with which uses should be classified. The traditional classification of creditors, investors, management, and the general public is user-oriented rather than use-directed. The classification of planning, control, and stewardship is directed to uses but is a rather broad classification. A cross-classification of users and uses would provide a twelve-way breakdown and would recognize that different users have different planning, control, and stewardship information needs.

Ignoring for the moment problems of implementation, a broad general description of the information disclosures appropriate for each of the twelve classifications will provide conceptual goals for multiple disclosures.

1. *Creditor planning information.* According to Chamberlain, "Commercial banks have been one agency responsible for [the] extraordinary spread of annual budgets." [11] This agrees with the traditional short-term creditor's interest in the payback capability of the borrowing firm. Conceptually, one must infer that the information useful to a creditor in planning the allocation of his funds to borrowers would be the cash budgets of the borrowers.

2. *Creditor control information.* Ideally, the short-term creditor would want to be advised frequently of all significant variations from the cash budget experienced by the firm. Supplementing this basic information would be a number of tested safety-margin measures indicative of the probability that the loan will be repaid. Monthly reporting may be needed. Net realizable value of resources is significant.

3. *Creditor stewardship information.* Conceptually, the short-term creditor should have overall information on the general status of the borrowing firm in relation to other firms and according to tested standards such as ratio analysis.

4. *Investor planning information.* Since he is interested in the long-term future of the firms in which investment is being considered, conceptually the long-term investor (bondholder or equity owner) needs information on the long-range goals and the anticipated future of the companies. External information on developments in the industry and the actions of competitors is particularly useful. Because long-term planning for the future is fraught with uncertainties, the study of the company trends over the

---

11 Neil W. Chamberlain, *The Firm: Micro-Economic Planning and Action* (New York: McGraw-Hill, 1962), p. 25.

last five years becomes a reassuring type of information. The alternative uses of long-lived assets is also significant.

5. *Investor control information.* Control to the long-term investor is more in the nature of a replanning function. As expectations of a long-term nature change, the investor disinvests or holds present investments. Depending upon his goals, he may need portfolio analyses at frequent intervals.

6. *Investor stewardship information.* The information needed is a reassurance that the company is using resources as stated in long-range plans and that the present status of the firm has not placed it in a vulnerable position.

7. *Management planning information.* Whereas planning by creditors, investors, and outsiders is primarily a process of adjusting to factors beyond their control, planning to the manager includes as well the setting of company goals and devising of appropriate means for attaining these goals. Significantly, the most frequently requested type of information by managers just below the top level is for statements of company goals, objectives, and means. These requests refer to precise and detailed information on adopted objectives and means for attaining objectives, and have resulted in a significant increase in planning activities. Concurrent with the increased scope of the planning function, the information needs for planning explode in quantity and types. Conceptually, the need is for information on all possible future opportunities open to the firm, subject to policy restrictions. Information on past activities is relevant only to the extent that other information indicates the past will be repeated in the future.

8. *Management control information.* Management control aims to direct an entirely different set of variables from those of creditor, investor, or general-public control. Whereas the outside group seeks to control the actions of the top management of the company, management control is directed to all aspects of the internal operations of the firm. The information needed is that which will prevent activities from going out of control—which includes both psychological and physical motivation devices —and that which will enable rapid correction of variations from planned activities—which includes various analyses of variances.

9. *Management stewardship information.* Information needed here is of a reassuring nature that company activities have violated no covenants with outsiders nor any legal restrictions on activities. Also needed is reassurance that the fiduciary implications of management's actions are satisfactory.

10. *General-public planning information.* The public planning function is to the individual citizen, essentially one of giving directions to politicians regarding desirable goals and objectives of society. Of concern to the general public in the past has been the distribution of the firm's productivity among customers, employees, and owners. Indirect distributions have been of particular concern. More recently, public interest has centered on the process of production and distribution used by the com-

pany as reflected in pollution, conservation of energy, and its contribution to "society." Because the general public is such a heterogeneous group, essentially the only information that can be given them is general information on the past and proposed social and economic progress of the firm. While conceptually this is valid, operationally it is largely an undeveloped area of information disclosure.

11. *General-public control information.* The basic control exercised by the general public is to enjoin the firm from undertaking activities not considered desirable by society. Conceptually, the information needed for this purpose is on the firm's goals and objectives, operating methods, and prevailing practice in both social and economic terms.

12. *General-public stewardship information.* Essentially, the reassurance information here should reveal that past activities do not violate the social patterns of economic activity that support the American way of life. The information should reassure the general public that activities are honest and follow the accepted and designated code of conduct as to objectives and operating methods. This includes not only legal requirements but social-norm requirements as well.

The foregoing, rather far-ranging outline of the information needs that are relevant to accounting disclosures indicates that far more than accounting disclosures are needed. A great number of the information needs are not a feasible accounting undertaking, but as an idealistic framework the accounting effort should be to contribute to these information needs to the extent feasible. There is reason to believe that much more disclosure is feasible than commonly assumed. Ellsworth H. Morse, while president of the Federal Government Accountants Association, stated:

> The U.S. General Accounting Office . . . has obtained considerable experience in expanding the scope of its audits of federal agencies beyond the boundaries of conventional financial auditing.[12]

Multiple communication media

The "annual report" is the traditional communication means used for public disclosure of audited accounting information. Because it is audited, the reliability of this disclosure is high, but the time lag between the activities and the communication weakens the relevance of the report. More relevant but as yet unaudited public disclosures are the quarterly reports. Internally, monthly reporting of unaudited information is frequently completed before the tenth of the following month,

---

[12] Ellsworth H. Morse, Jr., "Performance and Operational Auditing," *Journal of Accountancy,* June 1971, p. 44.

thus increasing relevance. At lower levels of management, daily and weekly reports are used extensively. Partial reports, such as cash statements, are frequently prepared on a daily basis for higher management. For close control, particularly in the production area, hourly reports are not at all uncommon. In fact, under automatic-feedback systems, reports may be continuous. Thus, as far as time is concerned, accounting disclosures are already multiple. Seemingly, any delay between the completion of an activity date and the reporting date is due to the difficulty of gathering the information together. As progress in the use of the computer continues, this type of delay will be minimized. In any event, it should be.

The need for a communication medium to provide a quick means for correcting logical inferences from a past accounting disclosure is demonstrated by the activity whereby, in May 1971, Lockheed Aircraft Corporation and its lending banks agreed to let Lockheed reduce its net worth from $340 million to $225 million. The effect of this activity was to change the conditions under which prior reports on company status were issued, since the reports had implied a buffer of protection for other creditors that was apparently no longer available. Fair disclosure would require that this change, known to the lending banks, also be made known immediately to other creditors.

Other than for timeliness, multiple communication media have not been widely used for accounting disclosures. On the immediate horizon, however, is the prospect of a computerized television-display medium that not only will disclose information but will permit detailed disclosure of various aspects of initial accounting recordings. One must assume that before too long, television terminals in brokerage houses and public libraries, as well as those in management information rooms, will serve as a very effective communication medium. The management information system in its current state of development is more of an information-retrieval system than it is a formal information-reporting system. The possibility that there are limits to management information systems requires that further development be based on a careful examination of additional information needs, including determining when information is needed, where it is needed, and how and by whom it will be used. The information must be put in a form that will serve the users' needs. Microfilm may be an emerging communication medium to be used until the television-computer system is fully developed, especially if the film is so stored that "hard copy" of selected information can be produced.

As to multiple communication media now in existence, a number of financial newspapers and magazines are used to disclose accounting information. They are characterized by a high degree of simplicity, but there seems to be no doubt that they are very useful. They are also generally unsystematic and unstructured. It seems to be reasonable to propose that accountants should systematically arrange for these disclosures. The concept of "news" for accounting disclosures is not the same as the "news" concept of newspaper men, who emphasize the unusual. Thus, it seems that there is an excellent opportunity to introduce financial publications as an accounting-disclosure medium.

An extension of the annual-meeting concept into a series of monthly, regional information meetings represents yet another possible communication medium. Since financial analysts now arrange meetings similar to these to obtain views of officers of companies, and since increasingly these involve accounting disclosures, the insertion of the accountant as a personal communicator of accounting information should be fostered to the extent possible.

Overall, the need for multiple communication media for disclosing accounting information seems great, but all suggested alternatives, except for improvement in the timeliness of reports, involve a significant expansion of the accounting-communication methodology. Thus their feasibility must be questioned.

Multiple disclosure formats

A review of fifteen annual reports to stockholders in 1970, selected at random, revealed extensive use of pictures, graphs, trend lines, and block diagrams in their "president's letter" sections. Apparently, these disclosure formats are not accepted for the annual public accounting report. Interestingly, however, for internal accounting disclosure, trend-line charts are used frequently. Tests given students reveal that balance sheets blocked off by areas corresponding to the amount of the various assets, liabilities, and equities improved comprehension of different financial structures. Differences in current-assets and fixed-assets portions of total assets were sensed very precisely when the blocked area assigned to each was proportionate to its amount.

Terminology is always a problem and has been dealt with by accountants almost continuously for many years. Similarly, different valuation methods have been proposed for several years, even though few changes have been made. Other than a brief reference in *A Statement of Basic Accounting Theory*, however, a format of multiple disclosures has not been seriously considered. There are some who do advocate dual disclosure of price-level-adjusted statements and historical-cost statements, but widespread supports for multiple terminology or other valuation disclosures have little support. Conceptually, however, there is no reason why multiple disclosures could not be a standard accounting-disclosure format. Parenthetic disclosure is an inadequate means, for it results in only partial disclosure of alternatives. Based on existing methodology, however, multiple disclosures will have to be introduced gradually.

Multiple classifications

At present, accountants do, from time to time, classify expenses according to (1) the nature of the expense, (2) the function it performed, (3) the person responsible for it, (4) its fixed or variable features, and (5) many other schemes, such as by project and by source of funds. But the notion that multiple classification might provide greater disclosure has not been accepted, apparently on the assumption that excessive disclosures would be confusing. As a result of the adoption of the object-classification system for accounting disclosures, except for special purposes, Neil Chamberlain has been able to assert:

> The assets which a firm commits to the achievement of its objectives are not the same as those which appear on its balance sheet. . . .
>
> The real assets which it is up to management to manipulate, and on the strength of which the representational figures [cash, securities, etc.] emerge, are the firm's functional resources. . . .
>
> The real assets with which management must seek its objectives consist of a product line, a production organization, a marketing organization, and a financial structure.[13]

Because multiple classifications are included as part of the accounting methodology, they appear feasible. In fact, if data are stored in sufficiently minute bits in the data base, retrieval and disclosure of multiple classifications is technically easily done.

The demand for multiple classification is definite. Complaints from users that they cannot extract the information they want from accounting disclosures turned out, in thirteen of fifteen complaints investigated, to be related to an inability to recombine the disclosures in a manner to meet their needs.

Given the decreasing cost of multiple classification and significant demand, coupled with feasible methods, it seems that at least three classifications of company activities should be disclosed by accountants:

1. The nature of the resources involved.
2. The function or activity performed
3. The time aspects of the activity

[13] Neil W. Chamberlain, *Private and Public Planning* (New York: McGraw-Hill, 1965), p. 23.

OVERALL FEASIBILITY OF MULTIPLE DISCLOSURES

The essential question under examination in this chapter is the conceptual feasibility of providing for the disclosure of more relevant accounting information by using one broad, generalized disclosure report to which would be attached appropriate subreports directed to different users. In previous chapters, it was established conceptually that the scope of accounting disclosures needs to be expanded and that evidence, equal in objectivity and in proof to that now used, to support such an expansion is available. In this chapter, the feasibility of the proposal is under examination. Examination of the various characteristics of the proposed multiple disclosure indicates that, except for communication media, it is feasible to develop the type of information needed to support the comprehensive and directed disclosure proposal.

But feasibility of the overall proposal must be examined in terms of its acceptability. Clearly, the proposal is so much at variance with customary thinking that immediate implementation is not feasible. Neither accountants nor users could produce or use the statements proposed in an effective manner at this time. On the other hand, so noted is the credibility gap of accounting disclosures that something really should be undertaken as soon as possible. Patching up the now-divorced systems of public accounting disclosures and management accounting disclosures is something like patching up worn-out trousers. They never look nice, and new holes appear in unexpected places. Maybe we do indeed need a new accounting disclosure framework to reunite the accounting profession and meet the needs of society more effectively. Maslow is not unrepresentative of the views of social scientists when he states:

> I am impressed again with the necessity, however difficult the job may be, of working out some kind of moral or ethical accounting scheme. Under such a scheme, tax credits would be given to the company that helps to improve the whole society, that helps to improve the local population, and helps to improve the democracy by helping to create more democratic individuals. Some sort of tax penalty should be assessed against enterprises that undo the effects of a political democracy, of good schools, etc., etc., and that make their people more paranoid, more hostile, more nasty, more malevolent, more destructive, etc. This is like sabotage against the whole society. And they should be made to pay for it.
>
> Partly it must be put up to the accountants to try to figure out some way of turning into balance-sheet terms the intangible personnel values that come from improving the personality level of the workers, making them more cooperative, better workers, less destructive, etc. It does cost

money to hire this kind of personnel; it costs money to train and teach them and to build them into a good team, and there are all sorts of other costs involved in making the enterprise attractive to this kind of worker and this kind of engineer, etc. All these real expenditures of money and effort ought somehow to be translated into accounting terms, so that the greater value of the enterprise that contributes to the improvement of the whole society can somehow be put on the balance sheets. We all know that such a company, for instance, is a better credit risk, and lending banks will take this into account. So will investors. The only ones who don't take these things into account are the accountants.[14]

The demand is such and the methodology is such that innovative disclosures need to be considered by the accounting profession. An examination of such a possibility is the purpose of this study.

For discussion purposes, the following disclosure framework will be used: [15]

I. The comprehensive accounting disclosure report
   A. External data
      1. General economic conditions
      2. Actions of governmental bodies
      3. Developments in the industry
      4. Activities of competitors
   B. Internal data
      1. Statement of plans (budget)
         a. Economic aspects
         b. Social aspects
      2. Statement of status (balance sheet)
         a. Economic aspects
         b. Social aspects
      3. Statement of activities (income statement and statement of financial change)
         a. Economic aspects
         b. Social aspects

II. The specific disclosure reports
   A. Legally required reports (income tax, SEC 10K, etc.)
   B. Planning reports
      1. Cash budgets, for *short-term creditors*
      2. Long-range plans, for *investors*
      3. Detail project analyses, for *management*
      4. Proposed policies and plans on role of the firm in society, for the *general public*

[14] Abraham H. Maslow, *Eupsychian Management* (Homewood, Ill.: Richard D. Irwin, 1965), pp. 59–60.

[15] For an alternative proposal for a change in the accounting-disclosure framework, see John H. Myers, "A Set of New Financial Statements," *Journal of Accountancy*, February 1971, pp. 50–57.

C. Control reports
1. Actual and budgeted cash-flow comparisons, supported by statement of realized values of other assets for *short-term creditors*
2. Five-year trend comparisons of actual with long-range plans for *investors*
3. Statistical analyses of variances from budgets, past results, and industry norms, for *management*
4. Contribution of the firm to social goals and objectives (employment practices, economic production, pollution, way of life), for *general public*

D. Stewardship disclosures
1. Status reports on utilization and sources of liquid resources and current resources, for *short-term creditors*
2. Sources and uses of long-lived resources and status reports, for *investors*
3. Comparison of all legal reporting requirements with actual reports filed, with areas of contingent assets and liabilities, for *management*
4. Status and activity reports on both economic and social goal attainments, for *general public*

It is believed that the foregoing broad disclosure-format framework meets the minimum test of feasibility in terms of the existing methodology of accounting; complies with the increasing demand for greater disclosure; will permit an articulation of a comprehensive accounting-information system with multiple reports; and should be capable of implementation in an economical manner, using a computer-based information system.

ACCEPTABILITY OF THE FRAMEWORK

Excluded from the framework was reference to special unarticulated reports for employees, customers, and suppliers. This may appear to be an error, for companies now do prepare special reports for employees, and to some degree for customers. Suppliers are, of course, interested as short-term creditors. Actually, there are reasons for and against special reports for each of these three groups. But the interests of the groups are not particularly at variance from the interests of other segments of the general public. To the extent that management issues special reports that do not articulate with other reports to employees and to customers to motivate support for the firm, such reports represent managerial reports. In any event, once the effectiveness of the comprehensive framework, including the subreports, is established, it would be relatively simple to add special disclosures for employees, customers, and suppliers that would articulate with the total disclosure framework if the demand for such particularized disclosures increases at a later time.

Details to fill in the foregoing framework are needed. A good deal of research on information needs of various groups is required, involving a mass survey of society and business firms throughout the United States. Technical research on computer storage and retrieval systems should be undertaken in a systematic manner to deal with the need for cost reduction in disclosures. Furthermore, too rapid a crystallization on one standard disclosure format might prove undesirable, in that a rigidity may develop that would preclude improvements in the disclosures. Variations in the details of the framework are now desirable, but adherence to the general framework should be a requirement for all accounting-disclosure efforts.

During a period of transition, when a change from one generation of reporting to a new generation is under way, the great danger is confusion. The threat of complete failure of disclosure efforts must be considered. During the transition, it is obviously imperative that traditional disclosure methods continue and that efforts to improve them continue unabated. This must be recognized as nothing more than a transitional process, which may well span a ten-year period, for the scope of the disclosure changes now demanded precludes any expectation that the existing methods can be patched up.

Consideration of the feasibility of the transition to multiple disclosures, in terms of the possibility that it destroys entirely the credibility of all accounting disclosures, must proceed in terms of the alternative. When one considers the credibility of prevailing public disclosures and the usefulness of traditional internal cost-accounting disclosures for planning, control, and reassurance, the alternative available is most unattractive; and the conclusion must be that substantial changes must be made in accounting disclosures.

On the positive side of the feasibility case for multiple disclosure are the amazing growth in size of corporations, the increasing specialization throughout all phases of life, and the increasing complexity of society generally. Illustrative of the new type of thinking about the activities of large corporations in society is a speech by George W. Ball to the American Bar Association at its London meeting in the summer of 1971, in which he anticipated the emergence of large multinational companies having responsibilities to people of all nations. For these multinationals, he proposed some form of world-companies laws to overcome nation–state restrictions. If all countries would agree to an international law for multinational companies, these companies would become "citizens of the world." With them would come enormous accounting-disclosure responsibilities. Clearly social change is unrelenting, and accounting disclosures must change with them.

Accountants were justifiably proud of their accomplishment in the early 1920's, when the general-purpose public accounting report was established. The consolidation of reporting practices provided for a unification of the scope of accounting disclosures. But to rest on that 50-year-old accomplishment without an adjustment to change could be to destroy the accounting profession. Specialized needs now dominate society. Doctors refer patients to specialists. Students learn from specialized professors. Accounting firms have a number of specialists in various areas. It has long been recognized that managerial information needs differ from those of investors. Surely the evidence must be that multiple disclosures are now the need of the land.

Public accountants must now label the present public accounting report the Report to Shareholders, and they must assume a means for making that report more meaningful to shareholders by relating it to the *Comprehensive Public Report* of the company to society at large.

COMPANY VS. ACCOUNTING DISCLOSURE

It may be contended that the *Comprehensive Public Report* is the responsibility of the company and not that of the accountant. This is also true of the present annual report to shareholders. But someone must systematically study the type of information to observe, collect, store, analyze, and disclose to various users. Furthermore, the need for reasonably broad uniformity throughout society in disclosures requires the support of an organized profession. On a feasibility basis, accountants should assume the responsibility both at the educational level and at the practice level for the Comprehensive Public Report.

Actually, there is much evidence to indicate that both educators and practicing accountants are interested in providing for the additional disclosure. The lagging element is not accounting. Rather, it seems to be business managers and government officials who apparently have not yet become aware of the need for multiple disclosures as a systematic disclosure process supported by independent audits and having great reliability. It seems that the accounting profession needs a comprehensive research undertaking, which can be used as a basis for presenting information to management and to governments—information that will cause them to adopt multiple disclosures.

For the development of a feasible means for implementing this recommendation, it appears likely that the issue of responsibility for disclosures will have to be reexamined and conclusions widely publicized.

Is management or the accountant to be responsible for the disclosure? The argument will be made that only management can know company plans for the future and that familiarity with such intentions is essential for a comprehensive disclosure report. Thus, if management intends to dispose of certain fixed properties in the near future, net realizable value may be a more appropriate disclosure valuation than any going-concern valuation. Militating against this tendency to turn over completely to management the responsibility for the comprehensive public disclosure report is the ever-present tendency for any unethical managements to aver an intention contrary to their plans. Again, a balance must be developed before the question of responsibility can be assigned.

Although management is undoubtedly in a better position to make the comprehensive disclosures proposed, a quick review of newspaper reports suggests that too frequently management does not do so. Even supported by SEC disclosure requirements and APB pronouncements, a few certified public accountants have been unable to control completely inappropriate accounting disclosures, as "unfavorable" court decisions testify. The implication is that the development of an adequate comprehensive disclosure report is a joint responsibility of management and accountants. The report requires knowledge of management's intent and understanding of the company, coupled with the independence and public responsibility of the certified public accountant. The balance between the two appears to be closer to the independent accountant than to management. The comprehensive report must be management's, and yet the need for the independent accountant to lend credence to the disclosures will always serve as a strong restriction on the types of disclosures that can be made.

SUMMARY

When research was started on the conceptual issues of accounting disclosure, the notion of a Comprehensive Public Report supported by specialized subreports was not included as a possibility. As the research revealed the great credibility gap of both public and internal accounting reports, it became apparent that a broad information-disclosure process was needed.

The resulting investigation of the nature of accounting disclosures, derived from interviews with educators, managers, and accountants, revealed that a wider scope for accounting disclosures was appropriate. A limited investigation of the standard of evidence suggested that by developing new types of evidence, disclosure standards need not decline when the scope of disclosures is expanded.

Proposals for implementing the proposed expansion abounded, but it soon became clear that immediate replacement or expansion of the current public report was not possible. Furthermore, the collected evidence showed that abandonment of present disclosure reports was not an acceptable solution. Also, the evidence revealed a growing belief over the past five years that management accounting and public accounting are two distinct areas. An examination of the consequences of such a separation indicated that the overlap was substantial and that common knowledge was required in each area. Congressional reports and mass public opinion indicated a growing interest in the social aspects of corporate activity. The conclusion was reached that the concept of a Comprehensive Public Report was appropriate. Its feasibility was tested and, while the results were not conclusive, the indications were that this proposal should be submitted for consideration.

In no sense is the framework proposed considered complete or even adequate. It is more in the nature of a hypothesis than a conclusion, but it has sufficient empirical support to suggest that companies should attempt to implement it. The current trends in accounting disclosures are toward a broader scope for accounting, improved methods for developing evidence, and a decided shift toward more complete disclosure.

REFERENCES

ARMSTRONG, MARSHALL S., *Corporate Accountability: A Challenge to Business.* Detroit: Economic Club of Detroit, April 12, 1971.

BEVIS, H. W., *Corporate Financial Reporting in a Competitive Economy.* New York: Macmillan, 1965.

Joint Economic Committee of the Congress of the United States, *Measuring the Nation's Wealth.* Washington, D.C.: U.S. Government Printing Office, 1964.

MASLOW, A. H., *Eupsychian Management.* Homewood, Ill.: Richard D. Irwin, 1965.

ORKLAND, D. S., et al., *Feasibility Analysis of a Public Investment Data System.* Springfield, Va.: Clearinghouse, U.S. Department of Commerce, 1967.

"Report of the Committee on Foundations of Accounting Measurement," *The Accounting Review,* Supplement to Volume XLVI 1971.

PART THREE

THE CURRENT TRENDS

CHAPTER SEVEN

The Thrust of Theoretical Expansion

Creative theoretical work in accounting has been questioned at the theory level. The reaction has been to develop systematic research activities that span both creative efforts and implementation, with the result that there has been an expansion of theoretical efforts on accounting disclosure into an overall system framework that includes a creative function, a verification function, and a measurement and communication function. Specifically, theoretical expansions in accounting disclosures include an examination of the theory of the public and ownership "right to know," the theory of information overload, the theory of retrieval systems, a theory of relevance, and a theory of "preciseness" that refers to an expansion of accounting methods. The expansion of the scope of accounting-disclosure theory, it is hoped, will provide a needed broader base for expanding accounting disclosures, because "a society whose maturing consists simply of acquiring more firmly established ways of doing things is headed for the graveyard—even if it learns to do these things with greater and greater skill. In the ever-renewing society, what matures is a system or framework within which continuous innovation, renewal, and rebirth can occur." [1]

In an earlier chapter, we noted the distinction between conceptual views and operational procedures in accounting thought. It was recog-

---

[1] John Gardner, *Self-Renewal* (New York: Harper & Row, 1964), p. 5.

135

nized that concepts must be operational before they can serve as a basis of recommendations for accounting action. In response to this need, a considerable amount of theoretical interest now centers on efforts to develop means to make conceptual views operational and to test the validity of assumptions used in the past to operationalize concepts.

The more promising efforts appear to rest on a process of clarifying the precise meaning of concepts, or of restricting concept-formulation efforts to a specific format. That is, it seems to be accepted by most accounting theorists that an object or activity has multiple characteristics and that it is impossible to deal with all these features, characteristics, properties, attributes, and other aspects of the subjects of accounting study. While a few writers cling to the notion that an enormous data base could be established in which all features of entity activities could be recorded, most consider this an impossible undertaking. Instead, most theorists think it is necessary to select and specify in advance certain of the properties or attributes of the activities of an entity, and then develop concepts relating to the specified properties. The selection of the properties of the activities is, when expansion of accounting is under consideration, a problem of major proportions. It requires a description of the attributes or properties in conceptual terms, supported by relational concepts among properties. For preciseness, these conceptual notions must also be made operational. An explanation must be made of the operations to be undertaken to implement the concept.

If operations cannot be developed to implement a concept, most theorists now tend to discard the concept as not particularly meaningful; thus they have discarded such abstracts as happiness, satisfaction, and the like, as not being accounting concepts. The result has been to confine the scope of accounting creativity, and to offset this, theorists are now very much interested in developing ways to make all concepts operational.

Broadly, the process by which concepts are conceived and are made operational involves the following steps:

1. A creative function flowing from theoretical inquiries, imaginative thought, and innovative perceptions, which leads to crude constructions of concepts. They are sometimes referred to as *constructs*.

2. An analysis and verification of the construct by breaking it down into its parts. This clarifies and specifies the concept in detail. To illustrate, the construct of "success" might be broken down into many parts. Some of these parts might be dropped and others might be added before the construct is modified into the concept of "income." This distinction between construct and concept explains a considerable amount of "clarification" literature in accounting.

3. The third step is the determination of indicators that reveal the existence of the conceptual activity. Transactions, for example, may be indicators that an income activity is taking place. Normally, many surrogate indicators, with varying degrees of objectivity, can be proposed that will serve to reveal to an observer that the conceptualized object or activity exists or has taken place. For example, the changes in published price lists of resources held might also be used to indicate income. These indicators (transactions, price lists, etc.) are then arrayed in terms of objectivity, relevance, and other characteristics.

4. At this point, the various parts of the construct will be known and various operational indicators for each part will have been developed. The final step is the selection or amalgamation of the parts and indicators to be used to measure the object or activity. For example, the selection of the December 31 price list of producer X to indicate the cost of product A might be the final step in making a cost concept operational.[2]

The process of making concepts operational, it is hoped, will ultimately lead to great improvement in accounting concepts. Not only will it facilitate the development of meaningful new concepts, but it may also be used to improve and clarify existing concepts. As yet the process is still in an early stage of development, and skill in its systematic use has yet to be developed.

The foregoing framework for the development, expansion, or construction of accounting disclosures assumes that the creative development of constructs will occur at a pace equal to or greater than the demand created for them by changes in society and the desires of accountants to advance the role of their profession in society. Actually, there is no way of knowing even the amount of effort being applied to the creative activity. The effectiveness with which the process is performed is even more indeterminate. Until the last decade, creative thought in accounting was the primary interest of theoretical accountants. Prestige accrued to the academic with innovative perceptions of accounting alternatives. Some disillusionment set in when many proposed constructs were not adopted by the profession. As a consequence, it appears that the current thrust of theoretical expansions in accounting disclosures gives relatively less emphasis to the really creative function. New creative concepts are not widely discussed unless their operational aspects are also proposed.

The implications of the restriction in creative work may be likened to the impact on technology by a drop in fundamental scientific research. No immediate consequence is evident because of the lag between

2 For a basic discussion of this process, see Paul F. Lazarsfeld, "Evidence and Inference in Social Research," Publication No. A-276 of the Bureau of Applied Social Research, Columbia University, New York, 1958.

the fundamental research and its utilization in practical affairs. This withdrawal from speculative creative activity, in the sense of what "accounting disclosures might be," has in part been replaced by various normative models of what "accounting disclosures should be." Nevertheless, the withdrawal from speculative accounting theory is, to some extent, a new development. Accounting theoretical proposals have for ages had a "might-be" underpinning. Consider the following creative efforts of the past:

1. In 1872, the Italian Giuseppe Cerboni introduced a new system of book-keeping, which he called *logismography.* It divided the ledger into three parts and in some instances required triple and quadruple, as well as double, entry accounting systems to disclose the information Cerboni thought significant.

2. The *statmography* accounting systems, invented by Professor Emanuele Pisani of Bari, Italy, around the turn of the century, sought to meet the needs of "all industries managed by representatives of the people for the good of the people."

Neither of the "might-be" systems survived, although Pisani's proposals seem to be reflected in some of modern-day government encumbrance accounting.

The case for nonempirical, nonoperational theoretical work was well illustrated by Esquerré in 1914, in the following terms:

> Just before the dawn of the French Revolution, there was, at the Military College of Brienne, a young student whom his classmates called the "Visionary." Never mixing in their noisy pastimes, he would spend hour after hour in his room, drilling tin soldiers on a large table. . . .
>
> A few years later, when the English fleet blockaded the port of Toulon, and threatened the existence of the Revolutionary Government, the visionary youth, now an officer in the army of France, pitted his "theoretical" knowledge against the "practical" knowledge of men . . . and to their astonishment and to the dismay of the invader . . . compelled the immediate retirement of the enemy's fleet.[3]

Actually, the case for speculative theory rests on the realization that it is part of the creative process of developing operational concepts. Just as construct formation normally precedes its operational development, so does speculative theory precede normative theory and construct formation. Construct formation is essentially an innovative process, and innovation does not spring full-blown out of nothing. Innovation has its

[3] P. J. Esquerré, *The Applied Theory of Accounts* (New York: Ronald Press, 1914), p. iii.

antecedents in the form of ideas drawn from a complex commingling of perception and recall. In fact, innovation is essentially a fusion of various ideas into a new distinct whole, totally different from its parental ideas even though it necessarily resembles each of them in some respects. In accounting innovative theory, the perceptions and ideas recalled may be traced back to old speculative theories on what "might have been." In a sense, the development of accounting thought seems to proceed from speculative theory to normative theory to empirical confirmation of theory, with improvements taking place in each stage. As a consequence, concern must attach to any diminution of speculative accounting theory.

The cause of the slackening of interest in speculative innovative theoretical work in accounting is due not solely to the reluctance of the profession to change, although a comparison of Esquerré's 1914 textbook with modern ones indicates that few fundamental changes have occurred. In addition, the extremes of a great deal of so-called speculative activities of the immediate past created a disillusion concerning the importance of such efforts. Illustrative of these questionable creative efforts is the proposal that accountants ought to observe everything, advance the theory of mathematics, and generally assume responsibility for all of society. Editors and publishers seem to have neglected their responsibility to make the careful distinction between creativity and idle speculations.

Whatever the cause of the shift of emphasis from the creation of concepts to the verification of proposed concepts and the reverification of established concepts, there is a tendency to believe the pendulum may have swung too far. Few, if any, things can be verified completely, and the constant retesting of the appropriateness of concepts must be accounted for either as an inability of accounting researchers to verify concepts or as support for the notion that meaningful concepts in the human area change so rapidly and extensively that verification is not possible. Accounting theory may have to remain as it has been—an art.

Theoretical efforts are now extremely sensitive to developments in other areas of society. The impact of the following two statements may well result in a series of theoretical articles on means for verifying methods of accounting for equity and for social progress. The first statement, from the SEC, calls attention to the disclosure problem when conflicting objectives exist.

> A basic purpose of the Act and the Securities Exchange Act of 1934 is to require dissemination of adequate and accurate information concerning issuers and their securities in connection with the offer or sale of securities to the public, and the publication periodically of material business and financial facts, knowledge of which is essential to an informed trading market in such securities. It has been asserted that the increasing

obligations and incentives of corporations to make timely disclosures concerning their affairs creates a possible conflict with statutory restrictions on publication of information concerning a company which has securities in registration. As the Commission has stated in previously issued releases, this conflict may be more apparent than real. Disclosure of factual information in response to inquiries or resulting from a duty to make prompt disclosure under the antifraud provisions of the securities acts or the timely disclosure policies of self-regulatory organizations, at a time when a registered offering of securities is contemplated or in process, can and should be effected in a manner which will not unduly influence the proposed offering.[4]

The second statement calls attention to the need to disclose social as well as economic progress, as follows:

The mounting public demands for better social performance necessitate corporate goal setting and performance measurements—just as demands are being made for an improved process for formulating objectives and measuring performance in government. There is little in the present accounting and reporting systems of corporations that enables anyone to determine whether corporations have well-formulated sets of goals for social performance, or to measure the extent of progress toward realization of these goals.

The first step is to formulate corporate goals, not just for the stockholder constituency in financial terms but also for all constituents in as definitive terms as possible, and for the relevent scope of corporate social activity. For example, it should be possible to establish reasonably tangible goals with respect to pollution abatement on the basis of air and water quality standards and criteria projected three to five years ahead. Similarly, goals with respect to employment and advancement of minorities can be projected without great difficulty.

The second step is to utilize the advance methodologies which are beginning to emerge to develop means for measuring corporate performance in meeting its various goals. Some of this may not be as difficult as it seems. The biological oxygen demand (BOD) load of effluent on receiving waters is now being measured precisely, as are an increasing number of other pollutants, and these measurements can be related to goals previously determined.

The third step is to report to the corporate constituencies and the interested public the definitive measurements of performance toward established goals. These clear objective evaluations of actual corporate performance will be more credible to the public than general rhetoric about how well the company is living up to its social responsibilities; they will also be much more meaningful than expenditure data alone.

By operating in a goldfish bowl of reporting progress toward goals, a management veering too far in pursuit of one constituency to satisfy its interest at the expense of another is likely to be brought into check by those whose interests are slighted. In the *laissez-faire* system, it was the

---

[4] *Release No. 5180,* Securities Act of 1933, Securities and Exchange Commission, Washington, D.C., August 16, 1971.

unseen hand that was counted on to lead the pursuit of selfish private interests into realization of the public good. In the alternative system suggested here, it is the visible hand that is expected to achieve the same result.[5]

There are a number of opportunities for theoretical accounting work aimed at operationalizing the foregoing concepts. Equally interesting will be theoretical efforts to verify various aspects of these concepts and their operational derivatives. With such opportunities, it is not surprising that accounting theoretical studies have turned increasingly toward the development of means to make conceptual views operational.

OVERVIEW OF THEORETICAL EXPANSION
OF DISCLOSURES

The essential thrust of theoretical expansions in accounting has been toward the development of an overall (total) system for framework in which "continuous innovation, renewal, and rebirth can occur." The emerging framework previously involved (1) a creative function, (2) an analysis and verification function, (3) an operationalizing function, and (4) a measurement and communication function. Efforts to improve this framework are under way. Illustrative of this effort is the report of the Committee on Auditing Concepts of the American Accounting Association, which broadens the concept of auditing by holding that:

> Auditing is a systematic process of objectively obtaining and evaluating evidence regarding assertions about economic actions and events to ascertain the degree of correspondence between those assertions and established criteria and communicating the results to interested users.[6]

Based on this definition of auditing, the committee then related the audit function to the communication framework of the accounting process. In the process, the committee necessarily added a significant feature to the communication framework as a total system view of the accounting-disclosure function, as indicated on the diagram in Figure 7–1.

Other examples of the thrust toward an overall systems view of accounting are available, although aberrations are evident and the rate of progress is unsteady. The implications are that the scope of accounting theories may well expand into an interdisciplinary structure of thought,

5 Committee for Economic Development, *Social Responsibilities of Business Corporations* (New York: CED, June 1971), pp. 46–49.

6 Report of Auditing Concepts Committee, American Accounting Association, 1971, Chapter 2.

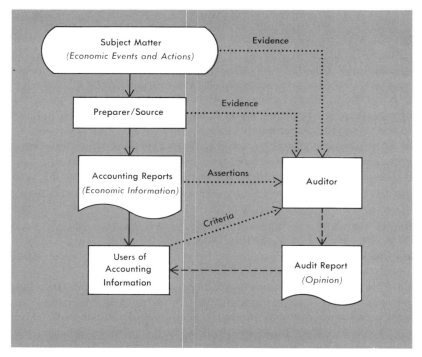

FIGURE 7–1

*The communication of accounting information
and role of audit function*

Conditions: Conflict of interest between preparer and users
Consequence of information to users
Complexity of subject matter and audit process
Remoteness of users from subject matter and preparer

with parts borrowed from both the behavioral and creative fields. Traditional restraints on theoretical efforts, such as the transaction requirement, are giving way to the notion of quantitative information as the scope of accounting-disclosure responsibilities. The computer will be an essential tool of the accountant of the future, and this tool will enable the development of a substantial amount of additional information of improved quality. Leo Herbert has diagrammatically provided an intuitively meaningful representation of the growth of accounting knowledge in the 1775–1975 period. The main point of emphasis of the chart, Figure 7–2, is that the growth of accounting knowledge is increasing at an increasing rate. This condition suggests a need for an expansion in the scope and amount of accounting theoretical studies to guide the growth of the discipline and the profession.

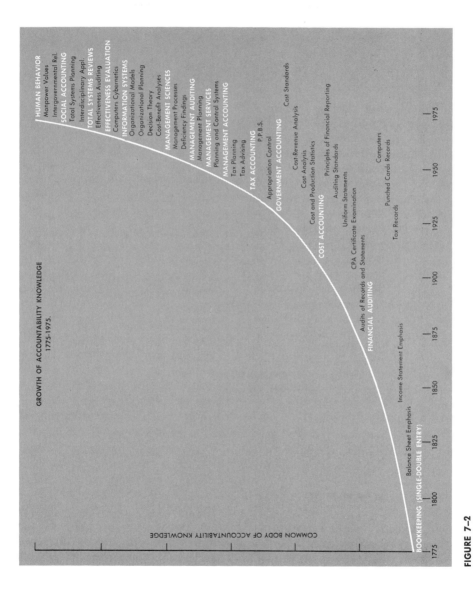

FIGURE 7-2

Source: Leo Herbert, Washington, D.C., August 1971.

143

Implicit in the theoretical assault on the problem of developing an overall system or structure is the notion that constant change in the information needs of all parts of society is to be the common expectation of accountants in the future. Arising from this broad view of the structure of accounting thought are a series of attitudes of "theorists" influencing accounting-theory development, of which the following are representative:

1. Theory of "Right to Know"
    a. Public right
    b. Owner right
2. Theory of "Information Overload"
    a. Contraction
    b. Compression
3. Theory of "Retrieval Systems"
    a. Self-retrieval
    b. Project retrieval
4. Theory of "Relevance"
    a. Human asset
    b. Market value
    c. Nonfinancial measures
5. Theory of "Preciseness"
    a. Rigor of analysis
        (1) System analysis
        (2) Consistency doctrine
    b. Unambiguous concepts
        (1) History of physical science
        (2) Symbolic representation

An examination of each of these "theories" will indicate the general direction in which advanced accounting theory is pushing the expansion of accounting disclosures.

THEORY OF "RIGHT TO KNOW"

Effective communication and exchange of views is necessary for the effective operation of a society. Interferences with this flow tend to impede the coordinated operation and development of society. From this generally-accepted proposition has emerged the notion that certain people need to be informed so they can function in society: they have a "right" to information. But who has the right to what information at what time and costs? Answers to this question compose the bulk of the theory of the "right to know." Accountants are concerned with the rights of people to know in order to perform their disclosure function. Two groups with which they are particularly concerned are the general public and owners.

Public "right to know"

The constitutional provision for "freedom of the press" has been undergoing a substantial change in the courts of the land in recent years. While freedom of the press was originally defined as the right of a publisher to publish, within the last 30 or 40 years the courts have tended to interpret this "right" as the right of the public to know. This change in the meaning of the concept dealing with restraints on the flow of information throughout society, possibly fostered by the press in order to gain public support for the right of mass communicators to have access to all sources of information, is of considerable significance to the accounting-disclosure issue. Of the three rights—the right to publish, the right to have access to information, and the right of the public to know —the last seems to be absorbed as an assumption underlying accounting theory or theories of disclosure. The notion is that the public has the right to know information on activities in which it is involved. Under this doctrine, the emerging theoretical assumption is that the public accounting report is a report to all citizens of the land. Under an extreme interpretation of this doctrine, the theory of accounting disclosures would no longer be confined to a disclosure of information useful only to creditors, shareholders, employees, and management. Rather, an accounting disclosure would be an accountability report of a company to society at large, on its contribution to that society.

The point is that almost without recognizing the growing social theory of the "right to know," accounting theory seems to have increasingly assumed that the public does have a right to know much more than had previously seemed appropriate. There appears to be a close relationship between the increasing social and legal emphasis on the public right to know and the increasing emphasis of theoretical proposals for the expansion of accounting disclosures. As the social right to know becomes increasingly taken for granted, accounting-theory proposals seem to emphasize expanded disclosures even though the effect may not be in the immediate best interest of the company. Thus the rights of the public appear to be viewed as more important than the rights of the company in several theoretical accounting-disclosure proposals.

The development of the notion of the right of the public communicator to have access to information tends to strengthen the role of the mass communicator in society. In keeping with or responding to this development, accounting-theory proposals increasingly call for the gathering of additional information by accountants and for the right of accountants to decide what is significant. Implicitly, as a result of the "right to access to information," accountants have been held liable for failing to exercise this right. Coupling this liability with the natural tendency for a profession to develop its status in society, accounting theorists have tended to support expansion such as divisional reporting, budget disclosure, multiple measures, and a host of others at the same level. Furthermore, the theorists tend to support the view that these disclosure decisions are a responsibility of the accounting profession and not a managerial decision of the disclosing company. Theorists imply that the disclosure problem is a public responsibility forced on the accounting profession by the social support for the public "right to know" and the auditor's "right to access to information." An unrestricted right to access to such information, and increased social support for the philosophy of a public right to know, portend significant expansion of accounting disclosures. The disclosure implications are beyond comprehension.

The fact is that these "rights" notions have been inserted into accounting theoretical thought and will have to be dealt with at some time. In general, their effect will be to open the door for more complete disclosures of all types. Whether they gain strength or are abandoned may well be determined by the type of society into which our nation emerges. Should the trend toward greater participation of all citizens in the policy-making activities of the country continue, the public "right to know" doctrine seems destined to foster significant expansions in certified disclosures. On the other hand, should the complexities of society become so great that further expansion of public participation in public policy making is not possible, one may expect the doctrine of public "right to know" not to have much of an impact.

Owner's "right to know"

The "right to know" doctrine includes not only the public right to know but also an owner's right to know. The concept of private property is well established in our society, and the rights of ownership are well supported in the courts of the land. The nature of ownership rights has been set forth variously. Including such rights as the "right to dispose," the "right to use," the "right to restrict access," the "right to profits," and similar rights, ownership rights represent the essence of the concept of private property on which American society rests. Singularly, however, no list of the legal rights of ownership specifically includes the "right to information" about the property, even though the very existence of public annual reports implies that some ownership right to information exists. The court interpretations of the right to know, and government legislation over the past 30 or 40 years, appear to have strengthened this ownership right to information. The implication of the "right to know" doctrine is that the corporate shareholder, as a co-owner of the corporation, has a right to know anything he desires about the corporation. If it is indeed true that shareholders are the owners of the company, it would appear that the owner's right to know should be relative to the extent of his ownership equity. While some theorists seem to distinguish between an "owner" and an "investor" and treat a shareholder as an investor with indeterminate "rights," stock certificates refer to ownership shares, and most theorists consider "investor" a broader term including both ownership and creditor investments. The concept of private property implies that a shareholder is part owner of the company.

The ownership rights in property are not necessarily all-inclusive. "Mineral rights" in real property are frequently sold separately from other rights in it. In line with this notion, the concept of "co-owner" implies either that all owners own all the rights in the property, or that in some way some rights belong to one co-owner and some to another. In general, the courts of the land imply that ownership rights are proportional to the extent of the ownership equity. The right to vote for the governing management of a corporation is proportionate to the number of shares held. Rights to dividends are also proportionate to the extent of the ownership equity. Accordingly, it would appear that a shareholder with a greater ownership equity would, as a greater owner, have a right to more information than would an owner with a smaller ownership equity. At the present time, this ownership right to information is not well conceptualized, and most theorists have done little more than develop it as a construct.

The construct does imply that the ownership right to information would open wide the disclosure requirements of a corporation. It is at times contrary to most of the desires of the top management of a company, who fear disclosure of information to competitors. Some court decisions appear to support the right of management to withhold information in preference to the right of owners to know, but most accounting theorists seem to view these decisions as special situations and believe the trend toward an increasing ownership right to know is much more the dominant consideration. Nevertheless, the theoretical construct apparently does balance the two rights (management rights and shareholder rights) by providing that the owner with a large equity shall have a greater amount of information than that available to the small investor, on the assumption that it would not be in the interest of the large-equity owner to disclose confidential information to competitors. The small-equity holder would, as an owner, be entitled to less-complete information but apparently would have access to all company information not considered to be of possible benefit to competitors.

The ownership "right to know" seems to underlie a number of accounting studies that indicate that the owner, present and prospective, needs additional information in order to improve his personal decision-making process. This call for more disclosure to owners implies that the rights of users of financial disclosures, rather than the rights of the issuers of the disclosures, should govern accounting disclosures.

The implications of the growing theoretical support for the notion of a owner's "right to know" include the following:

1. Different types of disclosure reports are appropriate for different types of owners.
2. There is a need for a systematic independent determination of the rights of management to withhold disclosures and the rights of owners to have information. These two interests do conflict and a settlement is needed.
3. The ownership right to know deserves more emphasis than the creditor's or employee's right to know, under our present form of government. The creditors right to know, the employee's right to know, and others' right to know are normally determined by bargaining between management and creditors, employees, or other outside parties. Theoretical studies on the type of information creditors need represent ideals toward which creditors should aim in negotiating with management for information disclosures. Labor unions now call for information disclosures as a bargaining point in their negotiations with management. Governments, by legislative decree, tend to provide for the public's right to know.

Overall, the emerging "right to know" doctrine, as a theoretical consideration in accounting thought, presages much controversy and a significant expansion of accounting disclosures for the future. Horngren reflects the situation in the following terms:

> Accounting principles will continue to develop in an evolutionary manner, and the rule-making bodies, in whatever form, will continue to be sensitive to the views of both the producers and consumers of financial statements. Because accounting is a practical art, the thought of having a cohesive overall framework shorn of inconsistencies is an impossible dream. But that does not mean that the search for an overall framework should be abandoned. Without some framework, however imperfect, chaos would result. Even though the framework will always be faulty, we must make it stronger than it is today. To make it stronger requires continuing vigilance and a focus on the decision needs of the users of financial information.[7]

[7] C. T. Horngren, "In Defense of the APB," *Financial Executive*, February 1971, p. 4.

THEORY OF "INFORMATION OVERLOAD"

Psychological studies suggest that the human brain has a limited capacity to store and utilize information effectively. There seems to be a point where additional data so confuses the thinking process that additional disclosures hinder rather than help the decision-making task. Without a debate on the studies, for intuitively it seems reasonable that a condition of "data overload" could occur, it does seem appropriate to note that there now exists so much misinformation in the minds of decision makers that a replacement of misinformation with information in the human brain should permit a significant expansion of accounting disclosures. The theoretical thrust toward improving accounting has recognized these two aspects of disclosures, as follows:

1. Disclosures that remove misinformation in the form of beliefs, assumptions, and relationships, which are derived from rumor, authoritative pronouncements, and the like that are inaccurate.
2. Disclosures providing information that not only helps remove the decision maker's initial uncertainty as to the appropriate decision, but that in fact also motivates decisions that tend to realize the decision maker's objectives. This means that two types of information may be disclosed:
   a. Information that reduces decision-making uncertainty prior to the decision point
   b. Information that reassures the decision maker, after the decision point, that the decision is appropriate

Most accounting disclosures in the past have been of the form in 2b. Income statements, ex post, have informed managers and others that decisions producing an income were or were not correct. Interperiod-cost comparative reports have provided similar assurances to decision makers. In part, this emphasis on reassuring disclosures is due to the relative ease with which such information can be provided, or so some theorists contend. There exists the utopian hope, which probably should never be realized if the world is to remain an interesting habitat, that such a degree of stability will ultimately prevail that reassuring information will not be called for by decision makers.

Theorists for the past two decades have been insistent in their call for greater disclosure of type 2a information. Although it is frequently more difficult to develop because it relates to the future, decision makers have increasingly been calling for this type of information to aid in the initial decision-making activity. Budget projections and analyses of various types have been developed in response to this demand for information.

At the leading edge of theoretical work on accounting disclosure is type *1* information. Only in recent years has it become evident that misinformation is a major problem in decision making. It is a particularly difficult problem because it is difficult to determine the way in which a decision maker is misinformed. So deeply ingrained in the mind of decision makers is some misinformation that it manifest itself in emotional reactions by them. It may prevent a decision maker from accepting reliable information. Frequently referred to as the behavioral aspects of decision making, or as the problem of determining the decision model in the mind of the decision maker, the misinformation problem represents an opportunity for a substantial expansion of accounting disclosures.

Even an intuitive sensing of the scope of accounting disclosures, as implied by the foregoing classification of quantitative decision-making information, suggests that a mammoth expansion in accounting disclosures in the future is anticipated by the theoretical studies.

Even now, the amount of data provided decision makers is so large that one may wonder if business is already in a state of information overload. But whether or not accounting disclosures are now beyond the point of maximum information is unknown. Consideration of the twenty-fold increase in paperwork in organizations since World War II suggests that the construct of information overload may already be pertinent to a discussion of the expansion of accounting disclosures.

Accounting theorists are sensitive to the growing complexity in socioeconomic society and recognize information as the only means for combating the detrimental impact of complexity on decision making. Intuitively, they tend to support the expansion of accounting disclosures; but they are caught between the problem of sensing a need for more information in society to combate the growing complexity and, seemingly, an awareness of the inability of the human brain to absorb too much information. Actually, the latter awareness is an implied or inferred awareness, but by their proposals one must assume that accounting theorists either consciously or subsconsciously assume the limitations of the human brain as a critical factor. While the notion is sometimes expressed as the fundamental tendency toward efficiency in communications, exemplified by the growing use of acronyms, the underlying implication is that more involved terms or reports are inefficient in that they are not handled well by the human brain.

After becoming familiar with the issue in one way or another, accounting theorists have begun to suggest that proposals for accounting disclosures should give consideration to means for contracting the amount of information disclosed and to means for compressing the disclosed information itself.

Information contraction

Contraction of information is viewed as a reduction in the quantity of information transmitted. Presumably, it implies that the least-useful information should be eliminated. This view of contraction encounters a problem, however, in that no one knows what information is significant to each user. Apparently, this construct needs to be broken down into its parts so that various categories of information could be verified as more or less useful than others as accounting disclosures. Alternatively, it might be possible to specify the types of information useful for different purposes, and by issuing different reports for different purposes, contract the amount of information in any one report. But eventually, the theoretical implications are, some means must be devised to determine the value of different bits of information so that the least valuable bits can be dropped to contract the quantity of data presented.

Clarke has called attention to uncertified information in the annual report of corporations and suggests that some of it should be certified by extending the attest function.[8] This distinction between attested and unattested information disclosure suggests that contraction of accounting disclosures could be accomplished by presenting several grades of information in the one report. Information users could then use as much of the disclosure as they wished, and still be assured that they had received the most relevant information first.

Information compression

Compression of information in accounting disclosures, in contrast to contraction, refers to the process of categorizing information in broader groupings. If this process were carried to an extreme, an accounting disclosure could be compressed to a certified recommendation statement, such as a statement that a shareholder should buy or sell shares of a company's stock at some designated price. This would greatly compress the information disclosed but it would pass back to the certified public accountant the responsibility for making the decision normally considered to be the province of an owner-shareholder. Furthermore, such a degree of information compression would undoubtedly place a liability responsibility on the CPA disclosing the information for its accuracy. Because of the large element of uncertainty in society, not only would

---

[8] R. W. Clarke, "Extension of the CPA's Attest Function in Corporate Annual Reports," *Accounting Review*, October 1968, pp. 769–76.

the liability aspects of such a compression be so great that no CPA would attempt such a disclosure, but also, even if such a disclosure were made, little confidence in it could be expected from users. Although the idea of merely telling a decision maker what to do might be the ultimate aim of compression—and it must be assumed that accounting research will keep in mind this ultimate objective of developing information to such an extent that accountants in fact become the decision makers of society—a lesser responsibility is appropriate for the foreseeable future.

It is clear that telling a decision maker what to do and providing data that guides or aids him in deciding what to do are both parts of the same spectrum. The more informational aid that is given the decision maker, the closer the role of the accounting discloser approaches that of the decision maker. If it is true that decision making is necessarily all based on some type of information, the possibility does exist that the accounting role could be placed anywhere in the spectrum between minimum data disclosure and decision making.

Alternative to a decision-making role, accounting disclosures might assume a lesser role in the spectrum between "no action" and "action," and seek a direct compression of data disclosure without causing a significant loss of information. For example, a less-comprehensive compression of data might be to restrict the bits of information included in any accounting disclosure to fifteen or twenty pieces.

The rule of restricting accounting classifications to fifteen or twenty categories as the scope of accounting-disclosure statements is now reflected in most balance sheets and income statements. Seldom will more than twenty items be listed in a financial statement and, typically, when less than ten are included, criticisms arise pointing out that the disclosure is inadequate. Given a requirement to disclose more information, an even broader classification system must be devised to disclose the traditional information revealed. Cash and receivables, now treated as separate items, might be compressed into one account, for example. Merchandise and supplies might well be afforded the same compression into one account. Expenses and revenues could be grouped into broader categories. Using such a compression of traditional disclosures, there might be inserted into the accounting-disclosure medium additional information of a new type. The only requirement would be that the value of the new type of information to users must be greater than the value of the information lost by compression. There are a few theoretical studies supporting the view that compression of traditional disclosures into a smaller number of accounts might result in no great loss of information to users. Empirical support for these theories is now under way.

There are other studies indicating that the information-overload problem, now present or expected in the future, may be dealt with by using a new format for accounting disclosures. Moving-picture presentations, charts, graphs, and trend lines have been suggested. This method of compression has not been widely adopted, even though it has existed for some time in accounting literature. Certain modern management-reporting systems at larger companies now appear to rely more heavily on the use of these multimedia disclosure devices than they have in the past. But there is a need for empirical verification of their effectiveness in dealing with the problem of information overload.

Overall, the implication of the theory of information overload to accounting disclosures is that new disclosure methods will have to be developed and that research is needed to determine the validity of the theory.

THEORY OF "RETRIEVAL SYSTEMS"

Psychological studies indicate that the thinking processes of decision makers vary widely, and this is undoubtedly one reason for the wide variation in their information needs. The process by which an artistically inclined manager makes a decision may be markedly different from that of his logically oriented competitor, even through both may perform very effectively in identical situations. This phenomenon has attracted the attention of accounting theorists and inclined some to the view that accounting disclosures must be "tailor-made" for each decision maker Management-information-system authorities have long insisted that management information systems must be tailor-made for each company; now the notion that each decision maker needs different information has emerged.

The theory suggests that general-purpose accounting disclosures have limited usefulness. Specific information disclosures are needed for different decision makers and for the same decision in different situations. To these theorists, proposals for the expansion of accounting disclosures should be directed toward multiple disclosures in separate media. According to this theory, decision makers themselves would have to indicate the information disclosures most appropriate to their needs. If one couples this theory with the growing complexity of the business environment, the task of accounting-information disclosures becomes particularly difficult. As Salton indicates, reliance on the computer becomes a possible solution:

> That there are substantial problems in the information field, everyone is agreed upon: More and more information is generated and put into circulation; the existing tools, classification schedules, and storage arrangements are often inadequate, particularly in the newer fields; and it gen-

erally becomes more difficult and more expensive to get to know what one needs to know.

This situation is reflected in the variety of pressures on the administrations of information-handling organizations: Budgeting problems become more severe every year; staff positions are increasingly more difficult to fill, particularly in areas requiring specialized skills and know-how; and many of the intellectual problems appear intractable in the present environment. . . .

This general climate has helped to foster the notion that new techniques and modern computing equipment may be capable of alleviating and solving to some extent the so-called "information problem." Specifically, many people now believe that there exists the required capacity to store many data or document collections of interest, that procedures are available for analyzing and organizing the information in storage, and that real-time software and hardware can be used to ensure that the stored information is retrieved in response to requests from a given user population in a convenient form and at little cost in time and effort.[9]

In general, this notion of different information for different people has not received extensive support in either the accounting literature or accounting practice. Proposals in the past for picture and graph disclosures to some executives and numerical disclosures to others have tended not to survive. There seems to be a belief on the part of accountants that a standardized decision model exists in the mind of all decision makers and that this standardized decision model will require uniform information for each decision problem. Different uniform information for different problems, on the other hand, is widely recognized. Also, it must be noted that the growth of schools of business administration in which somewhat standardized decision models are presented to future administrators suggests that if standardized models did not exist in the past, they are rapidly being standardized by the educational process. Nevertheless, the notion of different decision models for different decision makers cannot be easily dismissed. Far too frequently, different decision makers facing similar problems and provided with identical information make different decisions. The implication is that different decision models do exist in the minds of different decision makers.

Information self-retrieval

Out of this theory has emerged the notion that accountants ought not to make disclosures; rather, the accounting function should be restricted to one of collecting data to be stored in data bases. Disclosure would be an information-retrieval process to be performed by the decision maker. To be effective, this procedure would require massive data

9 G. Salton, *Automatic Information Organization and Retrieval* (New York: McGraw-Hill, 1968), pp. 1–2.

banks, from which different decision makers having need for different types of information could retrieve only the information needed. This retrieval-system approach to the information problem would be a means for dealing with the information-overload phenomenon and would also provide for the possibility that different executives do need different information even when they are performing identical tasks. There are two broad problems involved: It would require a great expansion in the type of information collected and stored by the accounting process, and it would require that accountants develop a greater capacity to sense the information needs of various types of decision makers. Sensing future information needs for different types of decision models of an unknown nature for future unknowable problems is an impossible task, but it would represent the ideal objective of the accounting collection and storage process under the self-retrieval system theory.

The theory also assumes that elaborate retrieval systems can be developed and, by means of computer consoles, that information can be obtained immediately as needed. Actually, there is a need for a great deal of intellectual work on retrieval algorithms before it would be possible to implement such a retrieval system. The general thrust of a significant number of theoretical proposals clearly tends to support the notion that ultimately the retrieval-system approach will dominate accounting disclosures. This will not lessen the role of the accountant, for the development of a reliable data base to support data management systems will require a significant expansion in opportunities for additional accounting disclosures.

The concept of information-retrieval systems implies that executives or "outsiders" with rights to information will have the capacity to use these systems. The existence of such a capacity is not present now, and it may be some time before it is a common qualification of decision makers.

Information project retrieval

Some students of management, although they support the view that formal accounting-disclosure media are inadequate, doubt the effectiveness of a retrieval disclosure system because they think managers will never accept responsibility for accurate information retrieval. As a practical alternative, they propose development of project-retrieval systems wherein decision makers are provided information by certified information retrievers after the decision makers have specified in detail the decision-making problem or project under review. Project-retrieval systems assume that each decision maker will have continuous access to certified project-retrieval reports, and that the decision maker can describe a project in sufficient detail that the project-information retriever will be able to determine the proper information to extract from the computerized data base. In its ultimate extreme, this theory assumes nationwide data bases, including both internal and external information on company activities, with appropriate restricted access to information.

Since the theoretical implications of the retrieval-system concept are that ultimately, formal routine accounting-disclosure methods will no longer be needed, and that the accounting task will be one of maintaining an appropriate data base, accountants may have to assume new responsibilities in the information-disclosure area. Whether accountants can or will assume responsibility for the organization of the basic data bank into a meaningful information source, retrievable by various algorithms and procedures, has not been considered extensively. Some theorists believe that the accountant should become a certified information retriever and assume responsibility not only for collecting and storing data appropriately, but also for the retrieval and appropriate disclosure of information to decision makers as needed. Implementing this proposal would require a complete reorientation and reeducation of many members of the accounting profession. But such is the thrust of this theoretical view of the future role of accounting disclosures. The development of a well-organized data base, however, is something into which the present accounting profession should be able to move quite easily. It would require merely an expansion and rearrangement of the conventional accounting ledgers. On balance, it seems that the theory of retrieval systems suggests an expansion of accounting educational programs to provide for the expanded disclosure requirements.

THEORY OF "RELEVANCE"

Accounting theory varies widely in level. Sometimes it is mere speculation. At other times it is supported by scientific verification of the explanations. At times, accounting theory is so detailed that it is difficult to distinguish it from accounting-procedure requirements. At another level, it is sometimes difficult to distinguish accounting theory from microeconomic theory and certain behavioral-science theory. Underlying all levels of theory is the notion that theory is an explanation of why certain information disclosures are appropriate for different purposes. Theory may explain why a given accounting procedure is appropriate or why a given concept is appropriate for any of a variety of objectives. Clearly the "right theory" depends upon the purpose for which the accounting disclosure is to be used. Criteria are needed to determine the "right theory." Broadly, these criteria would be used to select the theory relevant to the problem under review. The relevant theory may then be used to determine the relevant cost measures, the relevant disclosure requirements, or the relevant communication medium.

Possibly reflecting belatedly the relativity aspects of all things, or possibly reflecting a dissatisfaction with the low level of uncertainty reduction (information) provided by conventional disclosures, efforts and proposals to improve accounting disclosures abound. The construct of relevance is a notion that seems to expand the number of levels of accounting theories. Essentially, the theory of relevance, to which a considerable amount of academic loyalty attaches, means that information disclosed should be appropriate to the problem and the needs of the decision maker. Although some theorists view it as including a determination of the decision model in the mind of the decision maker in order to know what is relevant, the more conventional view of the relevance concept relates it to a standard decision model. This standard decision model is seldom specialized, but the microeconomic decision model of economic man tends to be assumed. Given that the decision maker's mind functions like that of a microeconomic man, the theory of relevance suggests that accounting disclosures be made of all types of information appropriate for that decision model and the problem situation. The types of disclosure proposals abound, ranging from the cash cost of attaining an objective to a measure of a possible risk to be incurred at some future date.

At a lower conceptual level, the theory of relevant disclosures has been used to call for the development of five to ten special accounting reports to cover the scope of accounting disclosures.

One of the more interesting theoretical developments arising from the relevance concept is the proposal that all acounting disclosures be given a rating of the degree of relevance of the information to various types of decision situations, a rating of the degree of objectivity (intersubjectivity) of the information, and a rating of appropriateness for different types of decision models. Scaling from 1 to 7 for each of the three characteristics of each information piece appear to be adequate. Thus, the expansionary thrust of the theory of relevance is to provide for an evaluative disclosure of the relative value and appropriateness of various pieces of information in accounting disclosures.

The theory of relevance has been used not only to support an evaluation of conventional disclosures but also to support the disclosure of additional information having a high relevance evaluation, even though the objectivity evaluation might be low initially. The three most frequently cited types of additional information proposed as appropriate for disclosure are:

1. Human assets
2. Market values
3. Nonfinancial measures

The case for the relevancy of all three is based on the assumption that information must be immediately useful for various decision problems and that it must provide the greatest possible degree of decision-making flexibility. According to this assumption, the theory of relevance would require that human-asset accounting include not only disclosure of the cost or value of human resources, but also a measure of their loyalty to the company, and their possible utilization in the future. Disclosure of the market values of physical resources would include not only current replacement cost, but immediate sales value and estimated alternative values if put to various uses. Nonfinancial measures might include statistical data on the physical flow of resources and services in, throughout, and out of the company.

Overall, the theory of relevance suggests an expansion in the scope of accounting disclosures and an evaluation of the disclosures presented. It supports specialized reports for different purposes, where the purpose of each report is designated on its face. Of all theoretical considerations now current, the relevance theory seems to be the one must likely to have the greatest near-term effect on the expansion of accounting disclosures in practice.

THEORY OF "PRECISENESS"

It has been recognized for some time by accounting theorists that most accounting disclosures have the characteristic of an average or the expected value of a probability distribution. Depreciation is typically valued at its "average" (expected value), and so are most other measures. The main theoretical objection to the use of expected value as the accounting disclosure is the sin of omitting a measure of the dispersion around the expected value disclosed. In a sense, the theoretical objection is that accounting disclosures have been determined according to precise laws, when statistical laws are the relevant ones.

Most accounting theorists, however, believe the dispersion disclosures would add a degree of preciseness to the accounting measure not now available from expected value alone. Whether the statistical reality of accounting disclosures causes it all or not, throughout the accounting literature the constant effort is to improve the preciseness of the accounting measurement. Actually, information needs of a more complex society probably better account for the phenomenon, but the clear evidence is that there is a consistent pressure for improvement in the preciseness of accounting disclosures. An increase is clearly evident in the rigor of analysis used to determine precisely information needs of different types. System analyses are used extensively to determine appropriate information disclosures. The doctrine of consistency is applied much more rigorously and is extended in scope. Many articles and textbooks now use mathematical symbols to provide the degree of preciseness believed necessary.

The problem with words as disclosure symbols is that they (1) have vague meanings, (2) have alternative definitions and mean too much, and (3) arouse emotions. All three are contrary to the concept of preciseness. Mathematical symbols avoid these problems and are susceptible to more rigorous analysis.

The emergence of this theoretical thrust toward preciseness in accounting disclosure seems to be following the same pattern as that of the physical sciences. The history of the development of sciences indicates that as each develops, it becomes more mathematical. Three hundred years ago, physicists used words rather than mathematics in their work. Now mathematics is becoming the common tool of social scientists, and the thrust of the accounting effort for preciseness is clearly toward mathematical analysis in developing accounting disclosures. But the use of mathematics expands opportunities for the improvement of accounting theories. As Kemeny has pointed out:

> Mathematics is invaluable for science because, by showing us an endless number of statements which are contained in our theories, it gives us an infinity of ways of testing our theories.[10]

SUMMARY

Information disclosure on business activity is very much under discussion at the present time. Newspaper articles abound with disclosures of all types. Even projections of the future are not uncommon. Illustrative of disclosures on future developments is the following early July, 1971, statement. "Indiana National Corp. expects to show a gain of about 10% of earning before securities transactions for all 1971, J. Fred Risk, president, said in an interview." [11] The implication of such projections to accounting disclosures is that information is now one of the most important products of American society. The theoretical accounting stu-

[10] J. G. Kemeny, *A Philosopher Looks at Science* (New York: Van Nostrand Reinhold, 1959), p. 29.

[11] *Wall Street Journal*, July 6, 1971, p. 23.

dies suggest that accountants have an opportunity to expand substantially their disclosures to all types of potential users. Both intellectual work and practical applications of an expanded scope and quality will be needed.

REFERENCES

Accounting Review, Supplement to Vol. XLVI (1971).

BARNETT, H. G., *Innovation: The Basis of Cultural Change.* New York: McGraw-Hill, 1953.

CHAMBERS, R. J., *Accounting, Evaluation and Economic Behavior.* Englewood Cliffs, N.J.: Prentice-Hall, 1966.

CHURCHMAN, C. W., *Prediction and Optimal Decision.* Englewood Cliffs, N.J.: Prentice-Hall, 1961.

COOPER, W. W., N. DOPUCH, and T. F. KELLER, "Budgetary Disclosure and Other Suggestions for Improving Accounting Reports," *The Accounting Review,* October 1968, pp. 640–48.

MUELLER, G. G., ed., *A New Introduction to Accounting.* New York: Price Waterhouse Foundation, 1971.

ROSENBLATT, D., E. GLAZER, and M. K. WOOD, "Principles of Design and Appraisal of Statistical Information Systems," *The American Statistician,* October 1970, pp. 10–15.

SALTON, G., *Automatic Information Organization and Retrieval.* New York: McGraw-Hill, 1968.

STERLING, R. R., ed., *Asset Valuation and Income Determination.* Lawrence, Kans.: Scholars Books Co., 1971.

STONE, W. E., ed., *Foundations of Accounting Theory.* Gainesville, Fla.: University of Florida Press, 1971.

CHAPTER EIGHT

The Expansion
of
Accounting Methods

Essential for any expansion of accounting disclosure is the availability of a set of accounting methods to enable new disclosures to be made. The historical record indicates that accounting has had the ability to develop new methods to provide expanded accounting disclosures. A study of more recent changes in certain accounting methods—research, measurement, recording techniques, and new methods for new services—tends to support the proposition that there is a continuous gradual change in accounting methods over time. Limited evidence indicates that the expansion of accounting methods is increasing at an increasing rate. From this the inference is drawn that the opportunity exists, in a technical sense, for a significant expansion of accounting disclosure. The admonition of the poet seems appropriate:

> *"Build thee more stately mansions, O my soul,*
> *As the swift seasons roll!*
> *Leave thy low-vaulted past!*
> *Let each new temple, nobler than the last,*
> *Shut thee from heaven with a dome more vast,*
> *Till thou at length art free,*
> *Leaving thine outgrown shell by life's unresting sea!"*

The Chambered Nautilus
OLIVER WENDELL HOLMES

161

There is a process of gradualism in accounting methods, subtle and all-pervasive in its ultimate impact but also imperceptible in its growth. An accurate awareness of this gradualism, to the extent it is recognized at all, is particularly important at the present time, for it seems to be sensed as following a linear line of expansion, whereas an exponential path may be more appropriate. Furthermore, an understanding of this phenomenon in accounting practice will provide a basis for estimating the possibility that accounting methods can be adapted quickly enough to adjust to technological, social, and economic change.

HISTORICAL PERSPECTIVE

As background for an examination of current evidences of gradual change in accounting, consider the following long-range historical perspective of accounting in relation to social developments by a social scientist.

Records and summary reports have accompanied the distribution or exchange of goods and services from the earliest times. Systems of recording—writing and numerical notation—as by-products of permanent human settlement and the emergence of towns and cities, can be traced back to Mesapotamia, the Indus Valley, Egypt, and Central America. The emergence of paper and pen in Egypt in the fifth century B.C., the development of government records in ancient Rome, and the preparation of tax and expenditure statements, including perhaps the preparation of the first budget (attributed to Emperor Augustus in the year A.D. 5), represent important milestones in the development of accounting procedures and practices. The church and government both contributed to advances in accounting during the medieval period.

The utilization of accounting methods for private business is associated with the rise of Italian commerce during the thirteenth century. Double-entry records and summary reports characterized the activities of business ventures and provided both creditors and investors, and merchants and customers, with information about their positions. Public accounting became a recognized profession performing auditing functions for business enterprises. Public accountants were at first part-time and itinerant functionaries whose activities included the practice of law or teaching, but, by the second half of the seventeenth century, full-time public accountants were practicing their profession in England.

The continued development of systems of writing and of numerical notation—and their use in the keeping of records, the writing of summary reports in "accounting" and auditing—are associated, of course, with the increased size and density of population. Urban living produced increased division of labor, specialization, interdependence, and vulnerability. These necessitated the development of mechanisms of coordination, integration, and control, which generated and stimulated the development of records and accounting procedures.[1]

The process by which the accounting information system changes is not entirely clear. Apparently, new data or information is first collected outside the accounting system. In certain cases, somewhat elaborate, uncoordinated, and unorganized nonaccounting data collecting has been undertaken. Ultimately the separate unorganized statistics are organized into a systematic reporting plan. The sequence of development has proceeded from a centering of interest on the more reliable sources for the data to, finally, the development of regular systematic collection devices. At that point there appears, according to the historical evidence, a tendency to merge the statistical disclosures into accounting. Leo Herbert describes the phenomenon:

> Those who have studied the history of accounting know that prior to, during, and immediately after World War I, cost accounting was not considered a function of accounting but a statistical function, a means for measuring production costs. Many accountants with a record-keeping background did not want to be a part of this production-measuring capacity any more than many accountants today want to be a part of a managerial-measuring capability. Because accountants had to provide this service, cost accounting became a legitimate extension of traditional accounting.
>
> All of this development took place within the context of finance, commerce, and business—the profit-making sector. Accounting had started out as an asset-recording tool, had become an income-measuring tool under investor conditions, then had moved into production measurement with the evolvement of cost accounting.[2]

· When accounting shifted to the operational point of view, using the matching concept to measure income, it added a very powerful concept to the technology of accounting. Although the matching of costs against revenues to measure income did not change substantially the amount of income reported from that of the previous income-measurement process—determining "gross income" and "expense" as separate elements, with income being the difference between them—the conceptual change was substantial. The cause-and-effect relationship between effort and accomplishment was recognized, and the resulting income figure was more a measure of income-creation effectiveness than a measure of an increase in economic wealth. The usefulness of the matching concept of

---

[1] Philip M. Hauser, "Social Accounting," Exhibit I of the appendix to *Hearings Before the Subcommittee on Government Research of the Committee on Government Operations on S. 843,* part 3 (Washington, D.C.: U.S. Government Printing Office, July 28, 1967), pp. 423–24.

[2] Leo Herbert, "A Perspective of Accounting," *The Accounting Review,* July 1971, p. 435.

income was quickly recognized by accountants and by society generally, even though reactionary claims, that accounting income measures the increase in the wealth of a company over a time period, are still frequently encountered. Once the usefulness of the effort-and-accomplishment measure of income was recognized, attempts were made to expand its use. Because no revenue measure of government accomplishment was available, it was at first assumed that the matching concept could not be applied in areas where no revenue measure was available. Soon, however, the concept of "benefit" was substituted for the term "revenue," and the matching of costs and benefits, as an extension of cost–revenue matching, emerged. Herbert explains the expansion in the following terms:

> This new tool, instead of being that of cost–revenue, was determined to be that of cost–benefits. Benefits—the results intended—for many programs, were more difficult to determine than revenue for a selling organization. But they could be ascertained. The cost–revenue tool had been used in only one sector of the total economic system—the profit-making sector. The cost–benefits tool could be applied not only to that one sector of the system, but also to each other sector or all sectors.[3]

Although the introduction of the operational point of view into the accounting discipline, as reflected in the matching of costs and benefits, has enabled accounting to provide more useful information to society, it may be necessary for accountants to invent equally revolutionary concepts in the future if accounting is to continue to contribute meaningfully to a more complex society in time to come. There are many conflicting views regarding the future of accounting, but it is interesting to observe that the most pessimistic appear to be held by those who have never really accepted the matching concept. Accountants entertaining a more optimistic outlook seem to be those who have accepted and use the cost–benefit concept as a powerful tool of accounting. Accountants most enthusiastic about the future of accounting appear to be those engaged in efforts to develop new improved tools for the accounting discipline. Interest in the computer is another characteristic of the most optimistic group. Reflecting the optimistic view of the future of accounting is the statement that ". . . not only will the accounting profession—particularly the leaders and teachers—accept the challenges we know current conditions are creating, but also must take part in directing future conditions. Think of the challenges—either the environment's influencing the profession or the profession's influencing the environment—that can readily be identified." [4]

[3] *Ibid.*, p. 437.
[4] *Ibid.*, p. 439.

There are many pressures on the accounting profession to expand. The pressure to which accountants appear to be most sensitive is the threat of loss of professional status, together with the possibility that an opportunity for even higher professional status may be missed. Illustrative of this pressure is the statement that ". . . to retain its present commanding role in society and to play a more significant one in the future, the accounting profession must legitimately extend its boundaries and capabilities. It then will not only have to accept what changes the environment forces upon it but will be able to direct needed changes in social, economic, governmental, and other environmental conditions." [5]

The record of history, however, is not sufficiently documented to enable one to sense precisely the rate or direction of the gradual-expansion trend of accounting methods. But discrete bits of the historical records suggest that such a trend does exist; they reveal that progressively over time, accounting methods have expanded, and this fact may be used to justify an examination of current developments in accounting methods, and to relate them to "gradualism" and the future expansion path of the discipline and the disclosures. A selection of the methods undergoing current developments that are representative of the total gradual changes in process was derived from the accounting literature of the last five years, public literature on the accounting profession, and personal interviews. Broadly, the following current developments in accounting methods are believed to be representative of gradual changes occurring in accounting methods that will influence future accounting disclosures:

1. Changes in academic research methods
2. Changes in measurement methods:
   a. Discounting methods
   b. Sampling methods
3. Changes in recording methods—computerized accounting
4. Changes in types of accounting methods—impact of management advisory-services activities

The examination of these changes will, it is hoped, support the proposition that gradual continuous change is a characteristic of accounting methods. Once the notion of gradualism in accounting methods is established, an attempt will be made to establish its trend. Finally, the implication of gradualism in accounting methods to accounting disclosures will be investigated.

---

[5] *Ibid.,* p. 440.

CHANGES IN RESEARCH METHODS

Traditional research methods in accounting have been something of a creative endeavor, with the researcher searching for new ideas or new concepts that could either provide a rationale or justification for existing practice, thus validating practices currently in use, or provide a possible alternative practice that could be subject to a trial-and-error process in practice. More frequently labeled *theoretical studies* than *research studies*, these findings were not conclusive. The decision as to which theory to adopt was left to an authoritative group of some type, such as the Committee on Accounting Procedures, the Accounting Principles Board, the Securities and Exchange Commission, or merely the reputation of some well-known accountant. Skepticism in regard to such authoritative determination of accounting methods has resulted in an extreme reaction on the part of several academic researchers, who take the rigid counterposition that no right to establish accounting methods shall be granted anyone prior to a research investigation. Empirical research, such as the studies underlying a number of the pronouncements of the Accounting Principles Board, has become, to many young academic accountants, the only type of acceptable accounting research. The creative type of research effort of the past is considered no more than hypothesis development, and not research in itself. Overall there is, however, still great interest in efforts to avoid the restrictions of "narrow empiricism." Thus, the changes in accounting-research methods represent a development of rigorousness and preciseness not previously required in accounting research. What are the causes and consequences of this, and how rapidly is it developing? Schlesinger implies that changes in research methods may be based on "tendencies within modern society." He states, regarding changes in history-research methods:

> After a marked recession in the nineteenth century, "eyewitness history"—history written by persons who themselves took part in the events they record—has undergone a revival in the later twentieth century. This revival has met with a certain skepticism and resistance from professional historians. Yet it may well be related to deeper tendencies within modern society; and, since these tendencies will only intensify in the foreseeable future, we may expect eyewitness history to continue to spread among us for some time to come.[6]

Whether or not the accounting-research interest in empirical studies is related to a tendency in modern society to emphasize eyewitness re-

6 Arthur Schlesinger, Jr., "The Historian as Participant," *Daedalus*, Spring 1971, p. 339.

search, it is possible to trace something of a cause-and-effect relationship that might explain the accounting interest in empirical research in more intuitively satisfying terms. That is, the origin of the orientation toward empirical research and field studies appears intuitively to rest in the emergence of a gradual awareness of inconsistencies in authoritative pronouncements and accepted accounting practices. The concept of consistency, rightly or wrongly, was traditionally accepted as the criterion for evaluating accounting proposals, practices, and theories. The enthusiasm with which both the academic community and leading practitioners applied the consistency criterion in the analysis of accounting thought revealed a number of inconsistencies to be corrected, but it also created an unrest and a critical attitude toward all accounting assumptions and methods.

The cynical frame of mind that resulted soon extended to accounting reasoning. So many diverse procedures were justified by lines of intuitive reasoning that the decision as to which was "right" could not in many cases be made unequivocally. Analyses of these different reasonings ultimately revealed variations in assumptions as to objectives, facts, and business values. Thus the need to know the validity of the assumptions and reasoning led to a realization that all "facts" should be verified. Empirical research seemed to be the logical approach.

The shift to empirical research was further stimulated by developments in the social sciences. Human behavior, individual and group, became a topic of social-science interest. Awakened by anthropological studies, sociologists and psychologists sought to determine human motivation and to understand human actions. As students of accounting became aware of these developments and called them to the attention of other accountants, young academic professors, having access to the social-science research findings at universities, realized that empirical research might reveal interesting features of the behavioral aspects of accounting disclosures.[7]

The emphasis on empirical research is not confined to academic research, as the following report on research activities of the National Association of Accountants reveals:

> Two new studies in NAA's Research Series for Management Planning and Control will be published this month. . . .
> The initial study in the series, *Computer-Based Information Systems for Management: A Survey*, was published in March 1969. . . .
> The second study, *Management Control of Information Systems Development*, focuses on the area of corporate systems management. The

[7] See John L. Carey, *The CPA Plans for the Future* (New York: AICPA, 1965), pp. 3–27, for a general revelation to accountants of the social aspects of accounting.

study's field research was conducted in 18 large and diverse U.S. corporations. . . .

The third study, *Information for Marketing Management,* is oriented toward marketing and sales operations. . . . As part of this study, 35 top marketing and systems executives in a mix of 25 industrial and consumer-product manufacturers throughout the U.S. were interviewed.[8]

The problem with empirical research as an accounting-research method is the inability to conduct studies of sufficient scope to encompass all relevant variables. Although various limited empirical studies have attempted to provide evidence on the behavioral reactions of selected users to alternative accounting valuations, few if any broad generalizations have been established as yet. Also, conflicting results of similar studies suggest that essential variables have not been recognized and isolated. Broader systems seem to be needed.

Over the long run, the gradual changes in academic accounting-research efforts appear to be somewhat cyclical in nature. They appear as a series of repetitive attempts to develop new solutions to accounting problems, each followed by disillusionment. Again and again the sequence seems to repeat itself, although the pace seems to be quickening in recent years. Further, there is a general feeling that each iteration of the process moves accounting theory to a higher level.

The changes in research methods, from (1) validating generally accepted accounting practices, to (2) criticism of such practices, to (3) creative theoretical hypothesis, to (4) empirical research, to (5) normative theory of what should be and on to some disillusionment, until (6) the possibility that resort to pragmatic authoritarianism may again be necessary, but at a higher level of knowledge, imply that research does foster the expansion of accounting methods. Although uneven in their impact, the constant changes in research methods appear to be reflected in somewhat cyclical changes, around an upward secular trend of improved preciseness and broader scope, in accounting methods.

CHANGES IN MEASUREMENT METHODS: DISCOUNTING

Possibly the most rapidly expanded accounting methods in practice in the last ten to twenty years have been discounting methods. Owing largely to the growing stability of modern government and economic society, the concept of predictable growth rates, as exemplified by long-term interest rates, has become more and more imbedded as a part of

---

8 "NAA Research Studies Digest," *Management Accounting,* July 1971, p. 63.

the accounting methodology. Whereas the present-value concept has long been used in valuing interest-bearing bonds and other contractual relationships, the expansion of present-value methods into such areas as capital budgeting, pension-fund liabilities, asset valuation under liquidation and merger proceedings, depreciation, and a host of others represents an expansion of accounting methods.

Some theorists have suggested that the current expansion of present-value methods is due to the higher interest rates over those prevailing in the past. Others, more academically hopeful, have accounted for the expansion in terms of the growth of accounting education and developments in statistical methods. Still others have suggested that increased competition has increased the need for improved preciseness in valuations. As an adjunct to this suggestion that a need for preciseness has caused the expansion, some imaginative thinkers have attributed the increased use of present-value methods to the increased size of business firms. The thought is that in an absolute sense, interest is a large amount of company income for a large firm and must be measured precisely.

Although the present-value methods originated as means of adjusting for the difference between the present and future value of money, it has since undergone a conceptual change. That is, some now view present value as an adjustment for any risk situation. Thus, a high risk that a future sum of money will not be received would be discounted at a much higher rate than would a less risky future sum. In this context, it has been proposed that present value be expanded to include both objective and subjective probability-of-risk estimates. In such an ultimate form, the present-value method might be viewed as the probability that one alternative is more or less probable than another. For example, two identical houses might have different valuations placed on them if the probability were greater that one could be more readily sold than the other. Most theorists, however, draw a distinction between present value and probability and compute dispersion measures to disclose the latter and reveal its sensitivity.

In terms of the time sequence within which the increased use of present-value methods occurred, the bulk of the uses have taken place since 1950. The implication of this expansion of accounting methods is that methods that improve the preciseness of accounting information tend to be adopted. But it also implies an acceptance of probabilistic thinking. For example, underlying the computation of pension-fund charges are statistics on the probable life expectancy of employees and statistics on the probability that an employee will remain with the company.[9]

[9] For a description of probabilistic thinking in accounting, see Appendix A of APB Opinion No. 8, on *Accounting for the Cost of Pension Plans*.

The increased use of present-value methods reflects a greater willingness on the part of accountants and users of accounting information to anticipate the future and provide for it at the present time in accounting disclosures. The stage of development of this phenomenon in accounting thinking is changing constantly. A number of theorists in more recent years have proposed current market valuation of assets and some have suggested net realizable value for this purpose. Both these proposals, particularly the latter, assume that an anticipation of future developments should be considered in valuing assets. Reliance on past acquisition cost tends to decrease as the present-value notion grows almost subconsciously in accounting thought.

A second implication of the increasing use of present-value methods, unrelated to the tendency of accountants to "think present value" in all situations, relates to the accrual process. As present value is recorded, based on an expected future sequence of events, the tendency prevails to accrue these expected future activities. The accrual of interest on bonds is well accepted; but the accrual of vacation pay, pension liability, deferred income taxes, and similar developments represent more recent expansion of accrual methods. These are directly related to a willingness to anticipate future developments and thus are fostered by present-value methods.

CHANGES IN MEASUREMENT METHODS: SAMPLING

Closely related to the development of present-value methods are probability measures. The development of probability measures from sampling procedures is a consequence of reliance on statistical sampling methods.

The first authoritative recognition that accounting methods should be expanded into the area of statistical sampling was in the 1962 special report of the AICPA's Committee on Statistical Sampling. That report stated, "A broader education in and knowledge of statistical sampling and further research as to its applicability on the part of the profession is desirable." [10]

This report was followed in December 1963 by the *Statement on Auditing Procedure No. 33,* issued by the AICPA's Committee on Auditing Procedure. This statement supported statistical sampling in auditing in the following terms:

[10] Report of Committee on Statistical Sampling, *Journal of Accountancy,* February 1962, p. 62.

In determining the extent of a particular audit test and the method of selecting items to be examined, the auditor might consider using statistical sampling techniques which have been found to be advantageous in certain instances. The use of statistical sampling does not reduce the use of judgment by the auditor but provides certain statistical measurements as to the results of audit tests, which measurement may not otherwise be available." [11]

By 1967, statistical sampling had become so much a part of the auditor's kit of tools that the American Institute of Certified Public Accountants issued a programmed-learning textbook, *An Introduction to Statistical Concept and Estimation of Dollar Values.* This booklet has been widely used, both by individuals and in various professional development courses.

Not only statistical sampling methods, but other probabilistic methods as well, have been used to expand accounting methods in recent years. Increasingly, articles in the *Accounting Review* and other leading accounting journals contain reports on the use of probability measures for depreciation and other allocation procedures. In the area of management accounting, probability models are frequently developed by accountants.

The impact of probability concepts on business thinking is just beginning to emerge, but once the probability nature of almost every accounting measurement is appreciated, it seems reasonable to expect an explosion in the use of probability measures. Illustrative of future opportunities for the use of probability measures in accounting methods is the following description of a new sampling technique:

> Refusal to respond and the deliberate giving of false information are known to be two principal sources of non-sampling error that can bias sample estimates in surveys involving human populations. Recognizing that such evasive answers are more frequent when respondents are queried about sensitive or embarrassing matters, [Stanley L.] Warner developed an interviewing procedure designed to reduce or eliminate this bias. He called the technique "randomized response." . . .[12]

The implication of including probability measures among accounting methods is that a more rigorous professional education at the university level may be needed. The rapidity with which the auditing profession has adjusted through self-study and professional courses re-

[11] Committee on Auditing Procedure, *Auditing Standards and Procedures* (New York: AICPA, 1963), p. 37.

[12] B. G. Greenberg, R. R. Kuebler, Jr., R. Abernathy, and D. G. Horvitz, "Application of the Randomized Response Technique in Obtaining Quantitative Data," *Journal of the American Statistical Association*, June 1971, p. 243.

veals the ability of the profession to adjust to the technological and social changes now abounding. It must be emphasized, however, that as yet the accounting use of probability encompasses a rather small part of mathematical probability theory. Whether the profession has the capability for rapid and continuous expansion, utilizing more sophisticated aspects of probability theory, is doubtful without greater mathematical education at the university level.

Possibly the most significant advantage of the use of statistical sampling in accounting methods is that it provides a means for accountants to collect new data not previously available under traditional methods. This in turn opens up an opportunity to include measures of social cost and benefit for various entity activities. In the long run, statistical sampling may be the means used to bring social statistics into the scope of accounting. In any event, this expansion of accounting methods affords a means of expanding disclosures in a significant manner.

COMPUTERIZED ACCOUNTING

The observation has been made that almost every company of any size now maintains its accounting records in a computerized data base and uses computer programs to analyze and prepare accounting reports. Auditors continue to advance their auditing methods to deal with computerized accounting, as is illustrated by the the following report:

> The auditor can bring the power of the computer under his direct control and apply it to the fulfillment of certain audit responsibilities through the use of recently developed, general-purpose software packages. This conclusion is based on experience. . . . Since then, the audit staff has written computer audit procedures and applied computers to the auditing process without either intervention by or technical support from programmers or other data-processing personnel.[13]

The immediate implication of this well-recognized development in accounting methods is to change the character of lower-level accounting personnel from bookkeeping to computer data-processing operators. As a result of this expansion of accounting methods, payrolls, accounts-receivable subsidiary ledgers, inventory subsidiary records, detailed payable ledgers, and all types of detailed recording are performed more economically.

[13] G. F. Reid and J. A. Demcak, "EDP Audit Implementation with General Purpose Software," *Journal of Accountancy*, July 1971, p. 35.

But the full opportunities for computerized accounting span three distinct levels or areas:

1. Routine detailed record keeping for operating reporting
2. Control and variance analysis reporting for control decisions
3. Planning and modeling for top-management decision making

Justification for computerized accounting in area 1, routine reporting, rests on the more economical performance of the function. The payoff is entirely a record-keeping and reporting-cost saving.

The payoff for level 2 of computerized accounting is a cost saving by reducing the variance costs. While this may or may not result in a record-keeping and reporting-cost saving, the basic justification for this level of computerization is that total operating costs will be lower than they would have been without the aid of the computer-developed control information. Whereas level 1 computerization aims to reduce accounting costs, level 2 aims to reduce total company costs by eliminating inefficiencies.

At level 3, computerization is justified on the grounds of greater net income. Thus it may result in either reduced or increased costs, but it must result in such additional revenue that these computerized disclosures result in a higher net income for the company than would otherwise obtain.

In fact, most present applications of computerized accounting are in the first area, although there are increasing applications at level 2. It is generally agreed that area 3 is the promised land. That is, there is a general belief that the greatest benefits from computerized accounting will result when applied at level 3; but as yet, these higher-level applications have not been well developed. Rather, they appear to represent an opportunity for the future expansion of accounting methods.

Overall, computerized accounting represents a significant expansion in accounting methods. This new method promises to be a means for a significant expansion of accounting disclosures. In addition, it opens the door for matrix bookkeeping, more refined methods for analyzing variances, and more systematic budgeting and planning procedures. Furthermore, it implies more timely and more directed disclosure methods. Conceptually, at least, the expansion of accounting methods resulting from computerized accounting suggests that accounting may eventually expand into a comprehensive management information system.

MANAGEMENT-SERVICES ACTIVITIES

Any attempt to list the management-services activities of either external certified public accountants or the internal accounting department of a company is not particularly revealing, because the list will depend more on the extent of the research than on the actual number of services provided. That is, so extensive are the management-services activities of accounting that it is almost impossible to develop a comprehensive list of them.

It is possible, however, to note certain expansion types of management services and to use these to indicate that management-services activities appear to be expanding. According to reports from large CPA firms, the following broad classification represents areas of expansion:

1. Organization structuring for coordination and control
2. Development of systematic internal-control procedures
3. Personnel management, including salary planning
4. Project review, analysis, and system design
5. Feasibility studies on expansions, mergers, computer equipment and software, and operation surveys
6. Communication systems
7. Manpower-utilization studies
8. Marketing analyses
9. Executive recruiting
10. Applications of management-science methods to a variety of business problems

Expansion of activities in almost any of these areas will involve an enlargement of accounting methods, if the foregoing are to be labeled accounting. The educational implications are great. Illustrative of the expansion of educational material into management services is a description of a new accounting course directed to "Accounting Services to Management," which deals with the role of the CPA as a consultant to management.[14] The breadth of knowledge, in the form of expanded accounting methods, needed to carry out the expansion in the management-services area implies specialization within and by accounting firms.

One is reluctant to project an ultimate end to the expansion in accounting methods that might result from management-services activ-

[14] Robert F. Hartman, Jr., "A New Course: Accounting Services to Management," *The Accounting Review*, January 1967, pp. 141–43.

ities. Certainly the availability of various management-science methods to accountants indicates that expansion of accounting disclosures into the area of management audits and management evaluation reports, including evaluation of and reporting on project performance, is a realistic expectation.

THE RATE OF THE GRADUALISM TREND

The foregoing recitation of the gradual expansion of accounting methods in various areas is more illustrative than comprehensive, but it will serve to provide a projection of future accounting activities. As background for that projection, it may be well to keep in mind John L. Carey's conclusions to his study of the CPA profession in the 1937–1969 period. He states:

> This summary of the Institute's planning efforts seems an appropriate conclusion to the story of the rise of the accounting profession in the United States. The character and temper of the certified public accountants are accurately reflected in the 13 years of intensive work so briefly outlined in this final chapter. The results show clearly that large numbers of thoughtful, intelligent, high-minded, energetic, and able men were deeply concerned about their role in society and their opportunities for service. Their goals were inspiring. The organization and procedures adopted to achieve the goals were superior to those of the vast majority of similar organizations. The time, energy, and money which thousands of certified public accountants freely contributed to the development of their profession was impressive evidence of their dedication.
> The accounting profession, when viewed in the perspective of the 80-odd years since its beginnings in this country, appears as a body of men possessed of amazing vitality, an extraordinary capacity for self-criticism, an ability to act effectively on many broad fronts, and a determination to render constructive service to the society of which they are a part.[15]

The development of a quantitative base to reflect the rate at which accounting methods are expanding may be approached by examining the rate of changes in accounting methods as these are reflected in textbooks, activities of CPA firms, activities of internal accounting departments, the CPA examination, and accounting literature. It is difficult to develop an acceptable cardinal measurement of the extent of these changes, but for purposes of this examination, a weighted average of

---

[15] John L. Carey, *The Rise of the Accounting Profession* (New York: American Institute of Certified Public Accountants, 1970), pp. 503–4.

estimation by various knowledgeable educators of the number of changes in each area in each activity by three five-year periods may give some general indication of the rate at which accounting methods are changing. The following results were obtained:

	Percentage of previous 5-year date		
	1960	*1965*	*1970*
I. New accounting methods included in widely used textbooks (all courses)			
(1) Research methods	100%	100%	105%
(2) Discounting methods	100%	115%	100%
(3) Statistical sampling	105%	120%	135%
(4) Computerized accounting	not available	200%	500%
(5) Management services	no change	110%	120%
Average	102%	129%	192%
II. Activities of CPA firms			
(1) Research methods	+%	++%	+++%
(2) Discounting methods	100%	100%	+%
(3) Statistical sampling	+%	++++%	++++%
(4) Computerized accounting	?	++++%	++++%
(5) Management services	+%	++%	++%
Average	+%	++%	+++%
III. Activities of internal accountants			
(1) Research methods	+%	+%	+%
(2) Discounting methods	+%	++%	+++%
(3) Statistical sampling	+%	+++%	++%
(4) Computerized accounting	+%	++%	++++%
(5) Management services	+%	++%	+%
Average	+%	++%	++%
IV. The CPA examination			
(1) Research methods	100%	100%	100%
(2) Discounting methods	100%	105%	115%
(3) Statistical sampling	105%	115%	115%
(4) Computerized accounting	100%	110%	120%
(5) Management services	110%	115%	125%
Average	103%	109%	115%
V. Accounting literature			
(1) Research methods	110%	140%	160%
(2) Discounting methods	110%	105%	105%
(3) Statistical sampling	110%	120%	125%
(4) Computerized accounting	110%	150%	200%
(5) Management services	115%	130%	120%
Average	111%	129%	142%

Note: The +'s refer to above 100% measures.

The foregoing tables may be interpreted to indicate that new accounting methods included in textbooks were about 2 percent greater in 1960 than 1955, 29 percent greater in 1965 than in 1960, and 92 percent greater in 1970 than in 1965. That is, the percentage change in excess of 100 percent represents the change since the previous five-year date. In general, the tables indicate that new methods are expanding at an *increasing* rate.

The foregoing percentage changes are not and should not be used as absolute measures. But because the criteria used in making the valuations were uniform and objectively applied over the fifteen-year period, the trend may indicate that relatively the rate of change in accounting methods is increasing at an increasing rate.

A comparative list of accounting methods developed and applied in different periods of time is difficult to develop for short periods. The following illustrative list of new accounting disclosures may serve to provide intuitive support to the belief that accounting methods are changing:

1. Divisional disclosures by conglomerates
2. Computer accounting reports
3. Management-science reports
4. Quarterly public reporting
5. Use of statistical sampling in auditing disclosures

Furthermore, there are widespread professional educational programs under way to provide for the dissemination of information on these methods throughout the profession. In addition to university curriculum adjustments, professional organizations support legislation to require professional development, as is illustrated by the support of the American Institute of Certified Public Accountants for state legislation making continuous education a prerequisite for the continuing right to practice as a CPA. More directly, the American Institute of CPA's itself offers a continuing educational program. For example, twenty-two courses, including the following, were available in 1971 to disseminate knowledge on new accounting methods:

1. Developing and using standard costs
2. Flexible budgeting and performance reporting
3. Direct costing and contribution accounting
4. Costs for decision making
5. Effective cash management
6. Economic evaluation of capital expenditures
7. Basic data-processing concepts and techniques
8. Management information systems design

9. Inventory management and control

10. Management accounting for hospitals

11. Accounting for foreign operations

12. Concepts and uses of accounting for executives and managers

13. Behavioral-science implications for management accounting

14. Communications and report writing

15. Linear programming: accounting applications

16. Statistical sampling for accountants and auditors

17. Computers and internal control

18. Accounting information for pricing

19. Management science for budgeting and profit planning

Supplementing these courses were fifteen seminars on other accounting methods.

These intense and widespread educational endeavors are mute evidence that new types of accounting methods have been developed in recent years. The fact that several National Association of Accountants courses are offered several times during the year, as are courses by other professional accounting organizations, suggests that knowledge of the developing accounting methods is being widely disseminated.

It is not sufficient, however, that accounting develop and disseminate information on new methods if the environmental need for new accounting methods grows more rapidly than the rate at which they are developed. There are some indications to suggest that the environment in which accounting operates is indeed changing rapidly. For example, studies of technological changes indicate that they are increasing at an exponential rate.[16] Assuming that the increased complexity induced by increased technology will require new accounting methods, one may infer that accounting methods will have to increase at an increasing rate just to keep up with technological changes.

The implication of an acceleration of the "gradualism" in accounting methods is that the profession must develop an atmosphere that encourages adaptation to changed methods. An expectation of "improved" methods must be created. Furthermore, this attitude must prevail throughout the profession to enable the adjustment—educational and in sensitivity to the information problem of society—to the apparently increasing needs, and the opportunity to expand accounting methods in the future. There are studies to indicate that unified groups

[16] For a description of the rate of technological change, see James R. Bright, ed., *Technological Forecasting for Industry and Government* (Englewood Cliffs, N.J.: Prentice-Hall, 1968), pp. 57–94.

reinforce members and foster an ability to change, given the development of an expectation of change.[17]

IMPLICATIONS FOR THE FUTURE

The current trend of changes in accounting methods appears to be one of an exponential nature. Whatever the cause of this, apparently the changes have been or are being accepted by accountants and users of accounting disclosures. Assuming merely a continuation of this acceptability, the past suggests that a further, more rapid expansion of accounting disclosures may be expected in the future. In turn, this implies a need for creative work and the development of innovative accounting disclosures in the future.

The fundamental issue of concern is whether accounting methods can be expanded rapidly enough to adjust to the technological, social, and economic changes. In terms of the previously cited authorities and statistics, both accounting methods and the accounting environment appear to be changing at an increasing rate. Without means for determining which is increasing more rapidly, one can only reflect the enthusiasm of students of accounting and intuitively state that accounting methods will expand even more rapidly than the environmental changes. The consequence will be an educational and professional capacity for an enlarged scope of activities and a larger role for accountants in society.

Further support for the view that accounting methods can and probably will expand more rapidly than the environmental changes can be found in an extensive study of the causes and consequences of industrial innovation by Jewkes, Sawers, and Stillerman. They found that:

> Despite occasional wild talk, there is still no solid evidence that technical advance is now going on more rapidly than before or that the inventions of the present century are any more significant for mankind than those of the nineteenth.[18]
>
> * * *
>
> There are three rival doctrines about the future scale of invention. The first is that there will be an exponential growth in inventions, since each one opens up the way to several others. The second is that the flow of inventions is carried forward by major advances around which a large

[17] See K. L. Dion, R. S. Baron, and N. Miller, "Why Do Groups Make Riskier Decisions than Individuals?" in *Advances in Experimental Social Psychology*, ed. L. Berkowitz (New York: Academic Press, 1970), pp. 305–77.

[18] J. Jewkes, D. Sawers, and R. Stillerman, *The Sources of Invention*, 2nd ed. (New York: W. W. Norton, 1969), p. 195.

number of smaller inventions appear, so that the flow over the long period will depend critically upon the frequency of major inventions. The third is that since all easy inventions have been made, the future flow may well decline. In the absence of reliable measurement, all three continue to command their supporters.[19]

If it is possible that technological changes are the cause of social changes and that the future scale of invention is an unsettled question, it would seem that the increasing rate at which accounting methods are changing should assure us that accounting will at least retain a role relatively equal to that of the past, and might well grow in relative importance to society if the rate of technological change does not continue to increase.

Before accepting this conclusion, it is necessary to question the assumption that technological change is the cause of social change. Reason to doubt the assumption arises from various expressions of policy-making scientists that recognize no direct relationship between economic growth and scientific discoveries. Furthermore, there are neither short-term nor long-term data to indicate that a direct cause-and-effect relationship exists between the amount of research expenditures and economic growth. In fact, Jewkes, Sawers, and Stillerman point out:

> In the United States and the United Kingdom, the two countries which relatively spend most on research, the rate of economic growth in the past two decades has not been higher than in earlier periods. Moreover, American and British growth in recent years has often been exceeded in other countries where the scale of expenditure on research has been much lower.[20]

In the examination thus far of the question of whether accounting methods can be expanded rapidly enough to adjust accounting to environmental changes, the assumption has been implicit that different accounting methods will be needed for the changed environment. But what is the evidence that there is a direct relationship between changes in accounting methods and environmental changes? The fact is that there is precious little. Nevertheless, if one must assume that such a relationship exists, one then asks if the relationship is between accounting methods and technology, between accounting methods and social change, or between accounting methods and economic change. As the foregoing discussion of the relationship between technological change and economic change implies, there may be no direct relationships among technology,

---

[19] *Ibid.*, p. 196.
[20] *Ibid.*, p. 199.

social changes, and economic activity. To examine the adequacy of the rate at which accounting methods are being expanded, one must first decide whether changes in · accounting methods are needed most to adjust to technological changes, to social changes, or to economic changes.

As yet no satisfactory measure of the rate of social change is available to use. Furthermore, there is a long-established assumption that accounting is closely related to economic activity. The inclination is to accept the assumption and make the comparison between the rate of economic change and the rate of changes in accounting methods. A survey of business activities, however, suggests that both social and economic changes need to be related to the rate of changes in accounting methods.

A list of the business responsibilities of large business firms, which indicates that accounting must be concerned with both social and economic changes, could well include the following:

1. Providing and distributing in an equitable manner the economic goods and services needed by society
2. Providing individual status, prestige, and a social life for individuals who are unable to develop their own
3. Providing for the improvement of the esthetic features of man's life and for the improvement of the physical features of man's environment
4. Providing for the adjustment of social norms and cultural values of society to cope with technolgical changes and for the improvement in man himself through advances in the quality of education

It takes very little imagination to realize that if business moves into these areas, there will be calls for accounting measures of human prestige and success, for measures of ecological damage, and for measures of human satisfaction. Although there are reasons to question the extent to which business will be engaged in these activities, it appears that governments will and can call on accounting for measures that cannot now be made with current accounting methods.

Overall, whatever the nature of the change to which accounting must adjust, it appears that accounting methods may be expanding rapidly, and could be expanded even more rapidly if this were demanded by the changes to which they are related. The conclusion is that, *technically,* accounting methods can be adjusted rapidly enough. The tools with which to change accounting disclosures will apparently be available. *Using* the new methods may be another issue. It may be that while technical accounting methods will be available, there may be behavioral aspects to their use that will impede the needed expansion of accounting disclosures. One way to examine this possibility is to analyze current expansions in accounting practice where the new methods are applied. If the implications of this analysis are that practice, too, is changing rapidly, one may conclude that both intellectually (methods) and behaviorally (practices), accounting is advancing adequately to meet the needs of society and that relevant proposed expansions for accounting disclosures will ultimately be accepted.

REFERENCES

Accountants' Handbook, 4th and 5th ed. New York: Ronald Press, 1956 and 1970.

The Accounting Review, Supplement to Vol. XLIV (1969), pp. 43–123.

BERKOWITZ, LEONARD, ed., *Advances in Experimental Social Psychology.* New York: Academic Press, 1970.

CAREY, JOHN L., *The CPA Plans for the Future.* New York: American Institute of Certified Public Accountants, 1965.

———, *The Rise of the Accounting Profession.* New York: American Institute of Certified Public Accountants, 1970.

JAEDICKE, R. K., Y. IJIRI, and O. NIELSEN, *Research in Accounting Measurement.* Evanston, Ill., American Accounting Association, 1966.

CHAPTER NINE

The Implications of Expansions in Current Practice

There are a multitude of changes in accounting disclosures now developing in current accounting practice. Many represent significant changes that will influence developments in future disclosures. An analysis of a selected number of these current developments suggests that quite a few changes in accounting disclosures may be expected in the future. It is reassuring to find support, for proposals to expand accounting disclosures, in current practice rather than merely in books. Long ago Marcus Aurelius observed the need to move to the world of action: "Do not wander from your path any longer, for you are not likely to read your notebooks or your deeds of ancient Rome and Greece or your extracts from their writings, which you have laid up against old age. Hasten then to the goal, lay idle hopes aside, and come to your own help, if you care at all for yourself, while still you may." [1]

The preceding chapter called attention to the current trend toward an expansion of accounting methods. Equally significant to the issue of expanding accounting disclosures is the question of the subject matter to which the expanded accounting methods may be applied. An under-

---

[1] Marcus Aurelius, *Meditations,* Book III, No. 14, trans. A. S. Farquharson (London: J. M. Dent & Sons, 1961), p. 15.

standing of both the expanded methods and the expanded applications should provide support for proposals to expand accounting disclosures. In this chapter, an attempt will be made to portray and generalize to some degree the multitude of expanded applications now taking place in accounting practice and provide something of a projection of future opportunities.

Before undertaking this analysis, it is necessary to keep in mind the great difficulty of making changes in accounting disclosures. Illustrative of this difficulty is the problem encountered by the Accounting Principles Board when it attempted to gain acceptance for uniform valuation disclosures of marketable equity securities. As reported by the *Wall Street Journal:*

> Last March, when the principles board invited public comment, it said it was considering four possibilities for dealing with changes in market values: including realized and unrealized gains and losses in income as they occur; including them in income, but averaged with prior years' experience; including realized gains and losses in income, but accounting for unrealized gains and losses in a special balance sheet account, and accounting for both realized and unrealized gains and losses in such an account.
>
> Ironically, according to statements already submitted, the principles board committee can expect to hear almost as many different "solutions" to its current problem as their are parties set to testify.
>
> Not least among the "solutions" is that offered by the Securities and Exchange Commission. The commission said it "isn't yet persuaded" that, as an across-the-board rule, marketable securities should be carried at their current value.
>
> Two financial-analyst groups endorsed the inclusion of both realized and unrealized gains and losses in income as they occur. An AICPA committee on insurance accounting reported a majority in favor of counting such gains and losses in income, provided they were averaged with prior years' experience.
>
> Two financial-analyst groups endorsed the inclusion of both realized and unrealized gains and losses in income as they occur. (One group limited its comments to insurance accounting.) An AICPA committee on insurance accounting reported a majority in favor of counting such gains and losses in insurance-company earnings, provided there was averaging with prior years' experience.
>
> Otherwise, almost all the companies and organizations that submitted statements oppose the inclusion of unrealized gains or losses in income. Insurance companies generally expressed dismay over the possibility, in part, they say, because short-term stock market fluctuations are too erratic a measure of investment performance. In addition, if unrealized gains were considered income, the companies fear that stockholders would expect dividends on the "income," tax authorities might tax it, and rate-making authorities might consider it in setting rates.[2]

2 *Wall Street Journal*, May 25, 1971, p. 14.

With the foregoing in mind and in order to provide some boundaries for a discussion of the multitude of changes in process, the implications of the following expansions in current accounting practice will be examined.

1. Penson-fund accounting
2. Earnings-per-share disclosure
3. Accounting for leases
4. Technological-change and depreciation accounting
5. The management audit

Efforts to develop meaningful implications from established and changing practices are normally not particularly successful, because of the subjective tendency for each investigator to make different inferences. The tendency prevails to infer what one wants to infer. But the point under consideration is whether or not reasonable inferences can be made to support a proposal for the expansion of accounting disclosures. In this context, the foregoing list of expansions are significant in that they represent advanced or early breakthroughs in accounting disclosures that have a "carry-through" effect. They set a precedence for similar types of disclosures. That is, they create a new accounting-disclosure concept or, more often, provide authoritative support for an accounting disclosure previously not widely used in practice. They have ' implications" for future accounting disclosures.

Subsequent to an individual examination of the selected expansions, a search for a common thread may reveal in a broad sense the implications of these expansions in accounting practice to future accounting disclosures.

PENSION-FUND ACCOUNTING

When the Accounting Principles Board issued Opinion No. 8 on "Accounting for the Cost of Pension Plans," it took an unnoticed and unheralded herculean step having significant implications for future accounting disclosures. These implications have not been examined, and there is a very real danger that exposure may vitiate their development as readers become aware of them. This could occur if readers, being emotionally unprepared and unable to adjust to them, take such actions that the implied changes in accounting disclosures are not realized.

On the other hand, an awareness of the implications may abet the expansion of accounting disclosures once the similarity of possible new disclosures to the generally accepted disclosure requirements of Opinion No. 8 is revealed.

The disclosure paragraph of Opinion No. 8 reads as follows:

> **46.** The Board believes that pension plans are of sufficient importance to an understanding of financial position and results of operations that the following disclosures should be made in financial statements or their notes:
>
> 1. A statement that such plans exist, identifying or describing the employee group covered.
> 2. A statement of the company's accounting and funding policies.
> 3. The provision for pension cost for the period.
> 4. The excess, if any, of the actuarially computed value of vested benefits over the total of the pension fund and any balance-sheet pension accruals, less any pension prepayments or deferred charges.
> 5. Nature and effect of significant matters affecting comparability for all periods presented, such as changes in accounting methods (actuarial cost method, amortization of past and prior service cost, treatment of actuarial gains and losses, etc.), changes in circumstances (actuarial assumptions, etc.), or adoption or amendment of a plan.[3]

Since a pension plan is merely an arrangement according to which a company provides a benefit, estimatible in advance, to retired employees, it may be viewed as a type of executory contrast that binds employee and employer to a future action. It is a special type of executory contract, varying from executory contracts like lease agreements in that the only requirement of the "arrangement" is that the benefits be determinable or estimatible in advance "from the provisions of a document or documents or from the company's practices." It would be too much to contend that the requirement to disclose the existence of such a pension plan could imply that disclosure of all executory contracts is to be given accounting recognition. In fact, if the arrangement is merely "company practice," there might be an implication that disclosure of those future events that might be inferred from company practice—such as company support of a community project for a number of years—may well be appropriate. Public disclosure of such commitments is appropriate, will reveal company concern for social issues, and could be supported on somewhat the same grounds as the pension-fund disclosure requirement. Both pensions and business contributions to the community are now established customs, and in a sense the obligation is "earned" by employees and the community over the years.

Seemingly, the requirement that the existence of an arrangement

---

3 *Opinions of the Accounting Principles Board,* No. 8, "Accounting for the Cost of Pension Plans," (New York: AICPA, November 1966), p. 84.

for future cash payments to employees be disclosed could be followed by similar requirements for other arrangements where the future payments can be estimated in advance from the provision of documents or company practice. This might be considered particularly appropriate if a social interest arose in having the disclosure made. One thinks of the cost of replacing natural resources used and generally restoring the environment to the condition it would have been in had the company operations not been carried out, or even the cost of improving the environment. Various pollution costs to which the company is committed represent the most probable area where disclosure expansion might next be proposed because of their similarity to pension-fund accounting. Disclosure that plans exist to restore polluted areas, whether because of legal requirement, contractual arrangements, or company practices, would be in keeping with disclosure requirements suggested by the Accounting Principles Board in paragraph 46. Such an implication is warranted by the expanding role of business in society. The June 1971 statement of national policy by the Research and Policy Committee of the Committee for Economic Development points out:

> We have . . . attempted to open up a vista of business pioneering in new fields of activities, new societal responsibilities, and new cultural achievements that will be a new frontier for business over the next several decades. And we have suggested that responsible management must have the vision and exert the leadership to develop a broader social role for the corporation if business is to continue to receive public confidence and support.[4]

In regard to the future, if the disclosure requirement of Opinion No. 8 is interpreted to imply that arrangements for future cash payments should be disclosed, it seems to support an incipient trend toward more complete disclosure of future company plans to pay cash. Future interest charges have been disclosed for some time by indicating the maturity dates of notes and bonds and the interest rates to be paid. Pension-plan cost disclosure represents an immediate step between legal contract requirements and company plans. In a sense, the pension-fund disclosure requirement may be introducing a new concept for the equity side of the balance sheet; a concept of a nonliability obligation. Somewhat similar to encumbrance accounting, the nonliability obligation would provide a means for disclosing company intent on objectives to which it is committed. Although it is inappropriate to imply that the Opinion has established the concept of a nonliability obligation, it is

[4] Committee for Economic Development, *Social Responsibilities of Business Corporations* (New York, 1971), p. 61.

evident that it does take a step further than merely disclosing interest rates on bonds to indicate future cash-payment commitments.

The second disclosure requirement of Opinion No. 8 apparently exists because companies follow different accounting and funding policies for pension plans. Recognizing that accounting for pension cost is in a transitional stage, the Accounting Principles Board permitted alternative practices, even though it established minimum and maximum limits to these alternatives and then called for disclosure of the accounting practices followed. This is a somewhat new disclosure concept, for the implication of this second requirement is to support the view that a practical means for expanding accounting disclosures exists when measurements are difficult to obtain: Alternative measurements are to be permitted and the method used is to be disclosed. Giving overt recognition to this means for expanding accounting disclosures implies that in the future, opposition to proposed disclosure expansions cannot irrefutably be based on an inability to measure precisely what is to be disclosed.

By far the most significant of the five disclosure requirements is the third, for it formally supports the use of actuarial and discounting techniques as an accounting measurement method for valuing liabilities. Because actuarial and discounting assumptions are based on expected future events that may not materialize exactly as anticipated, provision for adjusting the assumptions was provided for in the Opinion, and the possibility of a fluctuating liability amount exists.

There are other implications, too. Seemingly, other estimated liabilities of various types of risks could be quantified on a discounting basis and the cost factor could be accrued as a cost of business operations. If one hesitates to accept this proposed expansion of accounting disclosures because it might involve measurement of liabilities of uncertain amounts, consider the possibility that the assumptions underlying pension costs and liabilities may mean that such a measurement will be undertaken. The first step in making a valuation of a pension plan is to determine the present value on the valuation date of the future payment to be made to employees after retirement. An actuarial cost method is then applied to the computed present value to determine the employer's pension-cost liability. The uncertainties underlying the foregoing measurement include:

1. Uncertainty as to the interest rate that would be earned on the funded or unfunded pension reserve.
2. Uncertainty as to the future administrative costs of the pension plan. This includes every cost from record keeping to actuary fees involved in administering the pension plan.

3. Uncertainty as to the payments that will have to be made, owing to changes in (a) employee wage rates, (b) mortality rates, (c) future retirement age, (d) employee turnover, and (e) other, similar factors.

The net effect of the acceptance of such measurement methods for the development of accounting disclosures is to open up opportunities for a number of proposals for similar applications. Specifically, the following proposals, among others, may be anticipated:

1. Accounting for self-insurance programs covering various types of risks
2. Accounting for human resources as an entity asset
3. Accounting for pollution costs on an accrual basis

The fourth disclosure requirement involves acceptance of a group-liability concept based on mathematical and statistical measurement methods. The excess of the actuarially computed value of vested benefits of all employees over provisions represents an expected-value measure of the liability to be paid to the group as a whole. This is indicated when actuarially computed value of vested benefits is defined as "the present value . . . of the sum of (a) the benefits *expected* to become payable at future dates to present employees, taking into account the probable time that employees will retire. . . ." [italics added].

To the extent that the present value of a "group" of probable liabilities becomes accepted as the basis for valuing entity liabilities, the accounting liabilities-valuation concept will not only clarify the distinction between the present and future value of money—now a blurred concept because the time value of monetary amounts due for payment at different future dates is not provided for under current concepts of a liability—but also tend to establish the notion of a group liability where the amount of the liability is not the amount owed to individuals but the amount expected to be paid to the entire group or class.

The implications of complete acceptance of the present value of a liability concept are indistinct. Bonds payable, for example, would be valued at the present value of the sum of the future interest payments and the maturity amount, rather than merely the maturity amount plus or minus any bond discount or premium. The effect would be to include as a liability the contractual future interest payments as well as the principal sum. Adjustments for changes in the market interest rates presumably would be treated like a change in the measurement assumption and be afforded similar accounting treatment. To the extent that market value reflects present values, some support for the net-realizable-value concept for asset valuation may be inferred from this disclosure requirement.

Clearly, the fourth disclosure requirement implies acceptance of group statistical measures of liabilities. The expected or probable benefits of a group of employees would apparently be based on life-expectancy statistics and the retirement-time statistics of the company, and would represent the most probable facts of the situation. It also seems to suggest that intuitive judgments of liabilities are no longer adequate. Thus, support is given to more precise or formal methods for valuing somewhat broad contingent liabilities.

The fifth disclosure requirement emphasizes the importance of the consistency doctrine in valuing liabilities. It implies further support for the growing emphasis on disclosure of variations from consistency in accounting practice. Although the reference is to consistency over time for the same firm, implicit in the Opinion is the asumption that accounting policies and procedures should be disclosed to facilitate some intercompany comparison. It seems possible to suggest that the effect of the fifth disclosure requirement will be to implant in the minds of accountants and users alike a receptivity to subsequent requirements for disclosure of the accounting methods used.

EARNINGS-PER-SHARE DISCLOSURE

A significant feature of any disclosure is the degree of definiteness with which the disclosure is made. Disclosure of uncertified information is normally neither as precise nor as widely accepted as certified data. As a consequence, when the Accounting Principles Board, in Opinion No. 15, "concluded that earnings per share or net loss per share data should be shown on the face of the income statement," it not only broadened the scope of accounting disclosures; but the supporting procedures established to provide preciseness to the measurement improved the quality of the data. In one sense, the implication of requiring disclosure of "earnings per share" is that accounting disclosures would be contracted rather than expanded. If the one figure of earnings per share became the only disclosure to which users referred, the effect would be to weaken efforts to disclose in more detail the activities of the company. The fact that earnings-per-share disclosure was proposed by user groups rather than by accountants suggests a general lack of understanding of accounting disclosures on the part of users; and implies that future accounting-disclosure requirements should be unequivocal.

In another sense, however, Opinion 15 opened the door significantly, for it expanded practiced accounting disclosures significantly when it provided for both multiple measurements and pro forma disclosures. The Opinion, in paragraph 15, indicates that the reporting entity "should present two types of earnings per share data (dual presentation) with equal prominence on the face of the income statement. The first presentation is based on the outstanding common shares and those securities that are in substance equivalent to common shares and have a dilutive effect. The second is a pro-forma presentation which reflects the dilution of earnings per share that would have occurred if all contingent issuances of common stock that would individually reduce earnings per share had taken place at the beginning of the period." [5]

The implication of the earnings-per-share disclosure requirement for future accounting is that multiple measurements may be needed to disclose complex situations. The Opinion supports disclosure of descriptive explanatory information in financial statements, for paragraph 19 includes the following statement:

> The Board has concluded that financial statements should include a description, in summary form, sufficient to explain the pertinent rights and privileges of the various securities outstanding. Examples of information which should be disclosed are dividend and liquidation preferences, participation rights, call prices and dates, conversion or exercise price or rates and pertinent dates, sinking fund requirements, unusual voting rights, etc. [6]

Supporters of general price-level-adjusted disclosures may feel that the dual disclosure of earnings per share will introduce the notion of dual disclosure to accountants and thus gain support for a dual disclosure of both historical cost and general price-level-adjusted data. The basis for this implication is that once any dual disclosure is provided for as a generally accepted accounting principle, a considerable amount of emotional support for single disclosure tends to give way. Subsequent proposals for other dual disclosures may tend to be accepted.

More fundamental, perhaps, is the implication of Opinion 15 that in a complex society, the accounting disclosures must eliminate confusing interpretation of the data presented. To this end, an interpretation of the data, as illustrated by the requirement to disclose the potential dilution of earnings by conversion of securities to common stock, is necessary. The distinction between data and interpretation of data is somewhat indefinite, but assumption of a responsibility to disclose results that might prevail if changes occur in the future is certainly interpretative information. Broadly, so-called interpretation is merely more complete disclosure not only of certain data but also

[5] *Opinions of the Accounting Principles Board*, No. 15, "Earnings per Share" (New York: AICPA, May 1969), p. 221.

[6] *Ibid.*, p. 223.

of the relationship of the data to external events or to other data. If the interpretative role implied by the requirement to disclose fully diluted earnings per share is indeed a precedent, one may expect disclosure of the following interpretative data on the face of financial statements:

1. Certified ratios (current ratio, return on capital, etc.)
2. Certified comparisons with industry trends
3. Certified long-term (10-year) comparative statements

The trend toward interpretative disclosure is revealed clearly in APB Opinion 19:

> The Board concludes that information concerning the financing and investing activities of a business enterprise and the changes in its financial position for a period is essential for financial statement users, particularly owners and creditors, in making economic decisions. When financial statements purporting to present both financial position (balance sheet) and results of operations (statement of income and retained earnings) are issued, a statement summarizing changes in financial position should also be presented as a basic financial statement for each period for which an income statement is presented.[7]

This trend toward inclusion of interpretative information, information that might also be developed by an analysis of conventional disclosures, is aimed primarily at the communication aspects of financial disclosures.

ACCOUNTING FOR LEASES

A third expansion of accounting disclosures adopted by the Accounting Principles Board that has implication for future disclosures is contained in Opinions No. 5 and 7. Opinion 5, dealing with the reporting of leases in the financial statements of a lessee, calls for capitalization of "leases which are clearly in substance installment purchase of property" and for disclosure of other leases involving "the right to use property and a related obligation to pay specific rents over a definite future period." The disclosure statements indicate that rather complete disclosure of noncapitalized leases is appropriate.[8]

Opinion 7, dealing with the accounting for leases by lessors, dis-

---

[7] *Opinions of the Accounting Principles Board,* No. 19, "Reporting Changes in Financial Position" (New York: AICPA, March 1971), p. 373.

[8] *Opinions of the Accounting Principles Board,* No. 5 (New York: AICPA, 1964, Paragraphs 16, 17, 18, pp. 32–33.

tinguishes between "leasing activities of entities engaged in, perhaps among other things, lending money at interest—e.g., lease-finance companies, banks, insurance companies or pension funds" and leasing activities where companies "retain the usual risks or rewards of ownership" or where "the leasing activity is an integral part of manufacturing, marketing or other operations of a business." For the former, it is proposed that "the aggregate rentals called for in the lease should be classified with or near receivables." For the latter, "The investment should be classified with or near property, plant and equipment." The disclosure paragraph also calls for a description of the principal accounting methods used in accounting for leases, for disclosure of "sufficient information to enable readers to assess the significance of leasing activities to the company," and for the conventional disclosure requirements such as pledged leased properties.[9]

By tracing the trend of accounting for leases from Chapter 14 of *Accounting Research Bulletin No. 43* through Opinion 7, it is possible to discern a consistent trend toward a clarification and improvement in preciseness of accounting measurements. It is apparent that a narrowing of alternative practices is in process.

Conceptually, as the board noted in paragraph 7 of Opinion No. 5:

> The question of whether assets and liabilities should be recorded in connection with leases of this type is, therefore, part of the larger issue of whether the rights and obligations that exist under executory contracts in general (e.g., purchase commitments and employment contracts) give rise to assets and liabilities which should be recorded.[10]

The opinion of the board, as previously noted, in providing for the recognition of certain types of leases, seemingly indicates further support for the recognition of executory contract requirements and rights as liabilities and assets.

Opinion 7 reflects a trend in practical disclosure problems to expansion of accounting classifications of assets and liabilities. A distinction is drawn between leases directed to accomplish alternative objectives, and this distinction is used to classify leases as receivables or as property, according to the objective in making the lease. Although this classification is logically derived, its implication is that the functional classification of assets may be more useful than the natural classification. To the extent that functional use of a resource is a managerial determination, the implication is that asset classification should reflect

[9] *Opinions of the Accounting Principles Board,* No. 7 (New York: AICPA, 1964), p. 29.
[10] Opinion No. 5, p. 29.

managerial intent. This has been customary: For example, real estate may be classified as inventory or property, depending upon its "normal" use. But Opinion 7 extended the concept by including, among others, "the specific objectives of [the] leasing activities" as a factor in choosing the appropriate selection of an accounting method. In Opinion 10, the board reasserted the functional aspects of classification by suggesting in paragraph 4 that "the accounts of all subsidiaries whose principal business activity is leasing property or facilities to their parents or other affiliates should be consolidated." The result of this Opinion is to remove "leases" as an asset on the parent company's statement by inserting the underlying assets, classified as to the functional nature, for the leases.

In concluding this analysis indicating further impetus is given to the functional classification of assets, note that four distinct objectives of leasing by a lessor are presented: (1) investing funds, (2) facilitating the sale or use of lessor's manufactured product, (3) retaining control of locations when property operation by others is desired, and (4) making available to others property operated by the lessor for profit. One is hesitant to speculate on the ramifications of this classification. Multiple-use resources are clearly being replaced by special-use resources as a consequence of the genral trend toward specialization in society. Further, companies are redirecting efforts constantly to adjust to change. It seems quite evident that Opinion 7 may be opening the door for greater functional disclosure of resource uses than now exists.

Assuming that the disclosure requirements of Opinions 5 and 7 are extended as has been implied, the following changes in accounting for assets and liabilities may be expected:

1. Executory contracts having a high degree of completion expectation will be recorded as assets and liabilities and be measured at their present value.

2. Expectations of management will be given greater consideration in the classification of assets and liabilities. Whether or not expectations relating to future operations, as reflected in company budgets, will be disclosed is not entirely unrelated to this issue, but no inference seems to be appropriate.

3. Functional classification of assets may be expected to increase in the future.

TECHNOLOGICAL-CHANGE AND DEPRECIATION ACCOUNTING

The traditional accounting view of depreciation is reflected in paragraph 55 of *Accounting Terminology Bulletin No. 1,* in the statement:

. . . the term *depreciation* as here contemplated has a meaning different from that given it in the engineering field. The broad distinction between the senses in which the word is used in the two professions is that the accounting concept is one of systematic amortization of cost (or other appropriate basis) over the period of useful life, while the engineering approach is one of evaluating present usefulness.[11]

The accounting and engineering uses of the term also differ from its everyday use, and from the original source of the term as a decline in value. One might speculate on the possibility that there exists in nature a systematic process by which assets decline in value, price, usefulness, or any other characteristic. Then one could endeavor to determine this systematic process through research, develop it into a functional relationship of some type, and so allocate depreciation charges that the accounting, engineering, economic, and social concepts of depreciation coincided. Aside from the doubtfulness of the existence of such a systematic process in nature that would be generally applicable, the research task of determining the process and developing the apparently quite involved function to permit its use in the periodic determination of depreciation makes it unworthy of consideration.

The depreciation of an asset is highly dependent upon the concept and amount of maintenance applied. That is, a concept of maintenance and maintenance policy must be established before depreciation can be allocated in a systematic manner. There is a great deal of interdependency between the cost of maintenance and the cost of an asset. Both represent the cost, value, usefulness, and price of service resources. Asset life can be shortened or lengthened by decreasing or increasing maintenance charges if the technology does not change. If technology does change rapidly, maintenance costs become less needed. Replacement substitutes for maintenance as a source of service capacity. Replacement of existing assets with identical new assets also becomes less of a significant consideration in periods of rapid technological changes. Furthermore, technological changes tend to induce more rapid changes in price, value, and usefulness than might otherwise occur. It has been suggested that because of the influence of technology on depreciation, it may be that variations among accounting, engineering, economic, and other concepts of depreciation may be narrowing somewhat.

It is now generally recognized that technological changes have a carry-through impact on social and individual values and beliefs. Current technological developments may be changing the accounting concept of depreciation as new accounting treatments of depreciation are adopted. That is, in order to ensure modernization of equipment and

---

[11] *Accounting Research and Terminology Bulletins,* final edition (New York: AICPA, 1961), p. 25.

investments in new equipment, tax-incentive depreciation is allowed. Companies aware of the technological changes and sensitive to the tax advantages of a rapid write-off of depreciable assets tend to adopt accelerated depreciation methods and shorten estimates of the economic life of resources. Where the impact of technological change on assets is not significant, even though the uncertainty of change is quite evident, maintenance is increased to maintain existing service capacity, secure tax deductions, and improve flexibility for adjustment to change if it occurs. The result is a shift from depreciation to maintenance as an operating cost.

Not only does technological change influence production equipment and depreciation accounting, but it also seems to have an impact on consumer demands. That is, technology permits consumer consideration of alternative opportunities previously not available.

> By adding new options in this way, technology can lead to changes in values in the same way that the appearance of new dishes on the heretofore standard menu of one's favorite restaurant can lead to changes in one's taste and choice of food.[12]

Since the technological impacts on production and consumer demand are additive, the combined impact of technology on the products produced and consumed in society may be quite significant. As to the implication of these changes in depreciation-related costs on the expansion of accounting disclosures, one might infer that the tendency to write off assets more rapidly will increase. Studies of technological change indicate that changes are increasing at an exponential rate. Human assets and created goodwill, both unrecorded as accounting assets, may well have, now or in the future, greater constancy than many fixed assets. To the extent that human assets and goodwill are amortized immediately in most cases, the case for immediate full depreciation of technical assets with a more unstable future may be appropriate.

Although the foregoing practical developments are more in the business area than in accounting, as practical developments they seem to call for a more complete disclosure of depreciation methods and to place more emphasis on cash-flow than on income-flow disclosure. The implication is that funds-management decisions need to be more fully disclosed than in the past.

Assuming that the trend of technological change continues to increase as it has in the past and that business entities adjust to these

---

12 E. G. Mesthene, *Technological Change: Its Impact on Man and Society* (New York: New American Library, 1970).

changes in one way or another, the following changes in accounting for the utilization of assets may be anticipated:

1. The probability nature of depreciation charges will be recognized by disclosing both expected depreciation and a statistical dispersion measure of possible variation up to a 95 percent confidence level. This development is implied by the growing uncertainty of the economic life of an asset.

2. Assets subject to technological change will depreciate very rapidly; possibly many will be charged to expense at the time purchased, in the way created goodwill is now charged to advertising or some other expense at the time created. Other assets, not so sensitive to technological change, may also be depreciated more rapidly than they have in the past because of the all-pervasive impact of technological change. Such is the implication of investment credits for income tax purposes and the growing need to expense rather than capitalize research and development costs.

3. The tendency for technological change to induce rapid depreciation of physical assets, coupled with the increasing importance of the education and reliability of human capital, implies that disclosure of the nature, capability, and loyalty of the human resources will be more important in the future. One may therefore expect, as this trend continues, that accounting disclosure of human resources and goodwill will be required in the future.

THE MANAGEMENT AUDIT

For several years, accounting literature has examined the feasibility and desirability of an audit of management operations. Gradually, this notion is being clarified. The trend seems to be toward the view that it is not necessarily immediate management success or failure in a financial sense that is to be audited. Rather, the thing to be audited is the effectiveness with which various management operations are performed. This amounts to a disclosure that management did or did not utilize effective procedures in performing operations. Apparently, the implication is that financial success or failure will be disclosed by the subsequent audited financial statements. In the public area, where financial success on a cost-plus contract depends in part on the bargaining ability of the contracting parties, there is a tendency to attach greater importance to the disclosures resulting from the management audit. This seems to account for the substantial interest of the Federal Government Accounting Office in the management audit.

The success of management-audit methods in government seems to be leading to the use of the management (or operations) audit as an internal-control method by top management of large companies. The operations-audit function of the internal-audit division is an evaluation and disclosure of management operating procedures in various parts of the country.

For a company subject to the pressures of the market price, the use of the management audit as a public disclosure means has not been widely used. There are several reasons for this, including the realization that management procedures are not standardized to such a degree that they can be subject to audit. Only the test of financial success in the marketplace can reveal management success.

The concept of a management audit is becoming rather well established. From a public-disclosure point of view, an audit of the management of an entire company represents something of a preview of a subsequent financial audit. In this sense, a public management-audit disclosure would represent an expansion of accounting disclosures, in that information would be provided earlier on probable company success. This view is not well verified.

Variations in the marketplace may provide unexpected gains or losses in volume, price, and income that would not be accounted for by management audit. There is a growing belief on the part of the public, however, that managerial success ought not to be judged merely in terms of financial success. Other criteria may be more relevant. In this environment, a reliable technique for performing a management audit would seem to provide the setting in which the management-audit disclosure would be more widely used in the future. A condition for the development of such a reliable technique seems to be the existence of standardized ways of administration. Authorities on administration indicate that many management operations can indeed be standardized to some degree. Inventory management is a typical case where standardized procedures may exist. All in all, there still remain many operations of management that have not been standardized, and in fact the tendency is toward constant improvement in management methods. As a consequence, a management-audit disclosure may never be able to keep up with both the improvements and the diversity of management operations.

The inferences of the developments in management-audit disclosure over the past two decades indicates that the following accounting disclosures may be expected in the future:

1. Disclosure of management methods used—without evaluation of the appropriateness of the methods
2. Disclosure of managerial decisions having long-run effect on future company activities
3. Disclosure of managerial objectives as set forth in the annual operating budget, compared with actual results

4. Disclosure of qualifications, ages, financial interests, and responsibilities of management personnel

SUMMARY

Singular as it may be, the collected evidence of expansions in accounting disclosures now taking place in practice implies an expansion greater than that suggested by many authoritative announcements. Extrapolation of trends in practice is far from conclusive evidence of the future disclosures that will be made, but intuitively and logically, any analysis of developments in practice in the last ten years suggests that the following representative expansions in accounting may be anticipated:

1. The profession will develop more effective means for effecting change throughout the profession. Expansion in education programs, seminars, and the centralization of authority for the development of these expansions will result.

2. Research activities of the organized profession will be expanded substantially. Only in this way will the profession be able to maintain its current rate of expansion in the development of accounting disclosures.

3. There will be greater acceptance of recommendations for expansion in accounting disclosures by the organized profession if the current trend continues. Sociologically, there appears to be corroborating support for this tendency in the experience of other professions.

4. The concept of a liability will be extended further into the general area of an obligation of almost any type. This trend in practice is supported by studies of the increasing risk produced by technical change.

5. The concept of assets will be expanded to include all services reasonably expected to flow in to the organization. Assets arising from executory contracts may well be the first to be so recognized.

6. Acceptance of statistical-sampling results will prevail generally in business society. This will permit an expansion of accounting measurement methods used in practice and provide for a more complete and accurate disclosure of the socioeconomic efforts with which a company is concerned.

7. If the present trend continues, the development of quantitative methods will result in the inclusion of more precise information in accounting disclosures than is now included.

8. Although the trend in accounting disclosures has been toward an expansion in the use of explanatory notes, it may be that this means of disclosure is at a maximum. Accordingly, one may expect future accounting disclosures to expand in the use of quantitative information as a communication method.

9. The current trend in practice indicates that there will be increased consistency in both methods and scope of accounting disclosures in all parts of the society. This may or may not result in greater uniformity, depending upon the way accounting principles are developed.

10. The increasing complexity in our society suggests that accounting principles in the future may be broadened and less procedural than is evident in the current trend of accounting practice. The role of interpretation of principles will expand significantly as a function of the organized profession.

11. Disclosure of the social costs as well as the private costs of company operations may be expected, possibly within the next ten years if the present trend continues.

12. Disclosure of both human assets and goodwill elements in some fashion will become more widespread in the future than it has been in the past.

13. Disclosure of management plans and expectations on an annual and possibly on a five-year basis may be anticipated, as the present trend toward full disclosure gains strength.

14. The role of judgment in accounting disclosures will be supported by quantitative methods to the extent possible. The implication of current trends is that greater public confidence is created by quantitative measures than by judgmental opinions in a dynamic society.

15. Disclosure of different information for different uses is implied by the criticisms of present disclosures and by the trend toward multiple disclosures. Apparently the specific disclosures will be supplemental to the general disclosure. This may require different measurements, classification methods, terminology, and disclosure formats for different purposes.

16. If the current trend in price levels, both general and specific, continues as it has in the past, the suggestions in the current practical literature that accounting disclose their effect will be realized in practice.

17. If the current trend continues, the role of certified disclosures to increase reliability will be expanded. Quarterly public reports will be audited, and the notion of continuously audited reporting will gain strength.

18. The trend toward functional classification of resources according to expected uses will represent expansion in the amount of information disclosed in accounting reports.

19. The distinction between maintenance and acquisition cost will be merged into a concept of service costs, embodying both the outlaid costs and the anticipated cost of having the full bundle of services available for use over the entire life of the asset.

20. Disclosure of risks related to business operations will be more fully disclosed, possibly by sensitivity-analysis methods or by judgmental opinion.

21. If the present trend in expansion of accounting practice continues, the role of the certified public accountant in society will become much more important.

So staggering are the implications of the current trend of accounting practice for the future, and so inadequate any extrapolation of past trends, that it is proposed that substantial research funds and effort are necessary to examine in detail the future expansion of accounting disclosures and to develop a program to realize the expansion opportunities.

REFERENCES

BERNSTEIN, L. A., "Materiality—The Need for Guidelines," *The New York Certified Public Accountant,* July 1969, pp. 501–10.

CLARKE, R. W., "Extension of the CPA's Attest Function in Corporate Annual Reports," *The Accounting Review,* October 1968, pp. 769–76.

GARDNER, J. W., *Self-Renewal.* New York: Harper & Row, 1964.

MESTHENE, E. G., *Technological Change: Its Impact on Man and Society.* New York: New American Library, 1970.

Opinions of the Accounting Principles Board. New York: American Institute of Certified Public Accountants, 1961 to present.

SECOY, T. G., "A CPA's Opinion on Management Performance," *The Journal of Accountancy,* July 1971, pp. 53–59.

PRENTICE-HALL
CONTEMPORARY TOPICS IN ACCOUNTING SERIES

Alfred Rappaport, Series Editor

The Prentice-Hall Contemporary Topics in Accounting Series discusses significant recent developments in accounting through brief self-contained studies. These independent studies provide the reader with up-to-date coverage of key topics that deal with changing business methods. The series offers a succinct overview of developments in research and practice in areas of special interest and its authoritative analyses of controversial problems will stimulate independent and creative thinking.

The books that form this series:

PRENTICE-HALL, INC., Englewood Cliffs, New Jersey

0-13-298083-

Index

DATE DUE
